I
Arab

An open letter to the world's leader

Slim Zeghal

"If everyone is thinking alike, then no one is thinking."

Benjamin Franklin

*One of the founding fathers of the USA**

** For those who might ignore it, or doubt that it could be cited by an Arab and a Muslim*

I Arab

CONTENTS

I Arab

INTRODUCTION

Let me first introduce myself. If you are going to read this book, you had better know who is behind it! I am a Tunisian fellow, 55 years old, called Slim, just like your old fifties favorite nick name! Wait a minute, Tunisian, does that ring a bell? I am not sure George W himself knows what or where that is… When I was in the US as a student, I often got: "Indonesia, well, how come you do not have stretched eyes?". To be honest, Tunisia might share with Indonesia the fact that it is a Muslim country, but it is really different! We are talking about a small 10 million people country in North Africa versus a 200 million one in South East Asia. And again, just because North Africa is, yes, north of South Africa, don't you think that we speak Afrikaans.

Most Tunisians are not black either. However, as I said earlier, most of them are Muslim and, something I have not mentioned yet, are also Arabs. This does not necessarily make us terrorists, but it is definitely making our life in this modern world, carved by mass media, closer to hell! Today, being a Muslim & an Arab makes you a very potential terrorist in the minds of a big chunk of the world's population, definitely in the minds of those who have most power and money, and certainly in the circles close to our friend Donald… I am not even talking about my poor fellows who happen to be Arab, Muslim, and Black. Life is very very tough for them.

Now that you know a little bit more about me, you do not necessarily want to go further. You probably feel that we are very different and that you do not want to be listening to me. You might be tolerant, but tolerance has its limits… In fact, I wanted to address you, the American citizen, just to let you know a different story, a different perception. I certainly feel closer to you than you feel for me, and that is just OK. You have not studied at the University of Tatooine (that is in Tunisia, not the planet in Star Wars) just like I have studied in Davis (that is in the US, in California, close to Sacramento); you do not speak Arabic (at least statistically this is a true assumption) while I am quite proud to be fluent in English; and you have probably never heard of Couscous or Tajine, while I have had tons of burgers, frozen yoghourt, and so on. I am certainly not alone to have such a feeling for you, we are billions in "the rest of the world", that feel certainly very close to you, to your country and to your culture, because we have made some effort for that and because, that is true, the world is not equal. Just like a society, any society, that of nations has made the US the prominent nation in the world. A little digression about this "rest of the world", it was something I heard when I was working for a French multinational group. The very funny thing is that for US managers, there were the US & "the rest of the World", and for the European ones, that were the US, Europe and "the rest of the rest of the World". I will not tell you about Tunisia, my home country, of which I am very proud… it would be in some "rest of rest of…"!

In a way, I have a chance of coming from a much smaller country. This gives me the privilege to know more about other countries and cultures. It is not just a choice; it is a matter of survival. We have to be open to the big world outside. Remember, we stand in only one small corner of the rest of the rest of the World. We have to be tolerant, to be humble. May be this is not exactly the first image you would have of an Arab Muslim: tolerant? Open-minded? This leads me to why I am writing this book as you might wonder… Well, I wanted to restore my image, I wanted you to look at me as I really am, not as the potential terrorist that you have been told I could be, just being an Arab and a Muslim, and I will come back later even to my perception of being an Arab or a Muslim, which will probably surprise you in some ways. I want for my children and grandchildren some freedom in this world in the future, and some respect too.

I live away from the US now, I still travel there sometimes, as I travel to other parts of the world. However, I can tell you that I felt humiliated when I heard that several students that I know have been "investigated" after the 11th of September and put on file at the FBI, just because they were Arabs & Muslims. I have friends who have French passports, who can enter the US on a Visa Exemption Program and who were held for a few hours before being freed to enter the country, just because they had Arab names, and as history repeats itself, that is what we have experienced once again at the beginning of the Trump Presidency, and his tentative bans of nationals from various Arab countries.

As a famous French journalist has pointed out after the German Wings Airbus crash in France in March 2015, having an Arab or Muslim name could provide the motive for a terror act! M. Elkabbach (that's his name, does not sound very French does it?) has asked an official after the crash if they had on the passengers list any names that could sound susceptible of being involved in the crash! Poor Andreas Lubitz, his name is too German. He cannot be classified as a terrorist despite the 150 people he has killed! A mere foolish insane guy who has consulted some 41 doctors in the last 5 years of his life as so many newspapers have told us… To be seen as a terrorist, you have to be called Mohamed or Osama, and there, even the smallest mistake you will make can earn you the title! No one will investigate if you have consulted any doctors or if you were suffering from a depression or any other psychological disturbances…

TOLERANCE

Tolerance is a virtue that seems to be disappearing... What does it mean really? It is commonly accepted that Tolerance, from the Latin word "Tolerare" means the capacity to allow and respect something one does not approve. It is not acceptance nor submission or indifference. It is in a way linked to the notions of absolute good and bad.

If you decided to keep your religion for yourself (see chapter on religion!), chances are that you are on a good path for being a real tolerant person! You will tolerate the others as they are, no matter how different they can be from you or how far they can be from your ideals. They might even be or think completely opposite to you, and still, you will not be looking to convert them, or change their minds or prosecute them or attack them verbally or physically.

Unfortunately, tolerance is becoming harder to find, either at the personal level or the community level or the nation's level. It is however the necessary ingredient to democracy; it is the necessary basement for peace; it is the necessary terrain for diversity...

Many people are not tolerant because they are convinced they know the absolute truth, and as such, they cannot accept that you do not think as they do. Of course, these ignorant have no reference whatsoever to what Plato has formulated thousands of years ago in his allegory of the cave. There is no such thing as the absolute truth. This concept can be seen in a way as contrary to the religious teaching: in religions, especially monotheist ones, God is the source of the absolute truth and the sacred message he has sent cannot suffer any controversy. This is really the very basic level of reading of the religious message. Most religions have allowed for some interpretation and flexibility, and this should open the doors for tolerance.

There is a great example against the absolute truth which we can learn from physics. Remember, I am an engineer by training. In the physics of light, there are two major theories to describe the same phenomenon, but in a really different way. Both have led to real-world technical applications. The waves theory has been very useful in stroboscopy and the quantic theory is behind lasers! Of course, scientists have found bridges between them… but in essence, this is showing that there is no absolute truth, and if we are convinced of this, we will listen much more to our fellow citizens and we will show more openness to opinions that can conflict ours.

This reminds me of one of the best courses I have ever had in my life. It was not an engineering course, but rather a soft-skills one, and it really helped me on the path to tolerance. It was a course on how to better speak in public and how to deliver a proper message. The coach asked us, a small group of twelve people, to comment on events from the news, and he picked the two persons that had diametrically opposed opinions to debate. He asked them to come on stage. However, each one had to defend, not his own opinion, but the one of the other person, meaning the one he is firmly against! Imagine yourself trying to find arguments against what you think and imagine yourself defending this in public against someone defending what you do think! Once you have witnessed that or practiced it yourself, no matter how strong your opinion is or can be, you will listen to the people opposing you, you will try to understand their arguments and you will probably be more incline to find solutions that will content all parties… This is a fantastic way of teaching tolerance, and, without tolerance, there can be no peace and there can be no democracy!

Tolerance holds however a major paradox, as stated by philosopher Karl Popper in 1945. It can hold the seeds of its own disappearance. Quoting Popper from "The Open Society and its enemies": "Unlimited tolerance must lead to the disappearance of tolerance. If we extend unlimited tolerance even to those who are intolerant, if we are not prepared to defend a tolerant society against the onslaught of the intolerant, then the tolerant will be destroyed, and tolerance with them." I fully agree with this statement and believe it applies as well to democracy. A democratic country cannot accept parties that are fundamentally non-democratic as their motto is exactly to end democracy! For instance, religious fundamentalists are willing to play the democratic game until they get elected. Once they reach that point, they will ban the man-made constitution that allowed them to be there to replace it by the divine revelation!

DEMOCRACY

Dear so called "Free World" leaders, thank you for willing to bring democracy to the whole world's population. I am sure you are doing this because you care, you care for the many very humble subjects of the many humble countries that do not compete in the $30k+ GDP/capita arena…but, have you thought a second about what people in these countries really want? They do not necessarily cry for democracy. They might not even know the word or what it means. What they really care for is some wellbeing, very basic wellbeing … We are not talking about having access to the high speed internet or the latest technologies in heart surgery…No, we are concerned about having drinkable water at the tap (thousands die per day from drinking non-potable water), we are concerned about having decent food, some education for the children, some jobs for the older. For all this, democracy in not necessary, it might even be a problem to overcome in some cases. Indeed, in non-educated environments, democracy could be confused with anarchy. Democracy is not something that you import and impose on people. Democracy needs numerous structures and institutions; it needs a lot more than what you currently find in the countries where you want to force democracy to the stage of leading them to chaos.

The road to democracy is long and difficult, and there are no short-cuts. You've got to have justice, you've got to have education, you've got to have public health, you've got to have a decent GDP/capita. I do not know of a success story in the emerging countries that was built on democracy. Algeria almost went to total chaos when they claimed they were holding democratic elections in the nineties! I know however of a great success story that was carved by a tough and visionary leader for years, and that is Singapore. It was not built in a democratic environment, but everybody is happy with it, and Singapore ranks today amongst the best countries in the World in education, health care, low corruption, doing business… Look at Dubai and the UAE in general. How democratic do you think it is? How happy are the people that live there, both nationals and expatriates? It is one of the most striking success stories of the Millennium and people in Dubai love their ruler, Sheikh Muhammed bin Rashid Al Maktoum.

It is true that these two examples are those of very small countries. They would never compare to the biggest democracy in the world, India… From a few million people to a billion here. India is said to be a democracy. Does that make it better for the Indians? Is this the good model? I am not convinced, and, contrary to what American economist Jeffrey Sachs is saying in his book "The end of Poverty", I do not agree that democracy is a perquisite to development… Today, what is needed in many developing countries are charismatic leaders that can be autocratic and spend more time on the real job of making things get better rather than loosing precious days on playing the democracy game! Of course, they face many temptations, and I will come back to this in the corruption section. History has shown that no matter how enlightened a despot may be, he would more often than not lose his "light" with time…Interestingly, the "Mo Ibrahim" foundation together with the "Jeune Afrique" Group organized in 2015 in Accra (Ghana) their inaugural "Africa Report Debate" on the theme: "Is Democracy getting in the way of Development"?

Even in developed countries, how democratic is your model of democracy today? In ancient times, democracy worked because of the small populations and people had a direct access to the rulers they elected. Today, the media play an important intermediate role. They are the third party that provides that access, and as we are living in a material world, there is no free lunch! It is business as usual. Accessing your consumers, sorry, your voters, requires millions in advertising money. Political leaders need to do a lot of fundraising. If you do not have the money, no matter how brilliant and capable you are, you do not get a chance to be elected… Is this the essence of democracy?

Let us be more specific, do you know how much money is required to "make" an American President? A senator? A congressman? Do you know who provides the money and for what? A paper of the New York Times commenting on the first phase of the 2016 campaign is claiming that 158 US families have provided half of the total money involved! They mainly come from the finance and energy industries, and are, as the paper says" overwhelmingly white, rich, older and male" … Are we sure that all citizens are equal? Aren't these people "buying" extra voting power? Aren't they expecting any return from the candidates they would have helped? A paper from the Economist says that the total cost of US elections in 2012, including congressional races, topped $7 billion! Time Magazine and the Guardian tell us that the 2016 Presidential elections will eventually cost $4.4 billion in TV advertising alone! This is far more than the spending in any other major democracy by several orders of magnitude… why this much?

I know that I am probably losing a lot of sympathy by saying this, so bluntly and directly, but I want to expose sincerely what I think, and not melt into the conventional streams of thought, the politically correct that many of those supposedly great thinkers expose to us on occidental media! You did not forget I am and Arab and a Muslim, right?

Let us go back to democracy, and for this, I would like to quote Boutros Boutros Ghali, who probably left office at the UN with some frustration: "Democracy within the family of nations means the application of its principles within the world Organization itself. This requires the fullest consultation, participation and engagement of all States, large and small, in the work of the Organization." This of course, was not really the case and the relationship between countries is not democratic! Surprising? Well, the facts are here: there are five permanent members of the security council at the UN. The most powerful nations? The most respected? The most intelligent? The most democratic? The fairest? The most populated?

I am afraid the answer is no to many of those questions. Many of them are subjective too… What means more powerful? What means more democratic? The problem with this anti-democratic de facto situation is that it leads to anti-democratic decisions and a lot of frustration around. Indeed, when you are grown enough to be a permanent member of the Security Council, you are entitled to a right of veto, and the good news is that you can use it as many times as you want, no matter what the others think or do.

My big frustration as an Arab is that I have seen this veto right being used so many times by the same country and for the same reason: resolutions condemning Israel for some other action against the Palestinian people, or its neighboring countries such as Lebanon and Syria. Why is it that the whole world's community thinks that such acts deserve to be condemned and the USA take this very small recognition from them? What an injustice! What a shame for those pretending to install democracy in this world! You lose all your credibility when talking about democracy in doing this. With the latest US decision to proclaim Jerusalem as the capital of Israel, making the two-states solution more complicated if not impossible, we had a caricatural vote at the security council: 14 nations condemning this decision and a US veto making it void… Amongst those who have asked for this meeting, you can find close US friends such as the UK or France. As reported by "Foreign Policy" in its web edition, Nikki Haley, the US Ambassador to the UN warned diplomats on their vote to come: "Trump is watching you"! She has twitted and sent e-mails, and she even announced in a plenary session that was broadcasted that the US will not forget (the names of the countries voting against them!).

In my opinion, it is easier to make the UN work on real democratic concepts than even a small country. Indeed, in such a small circle as the UN, we are talking about a very manageable population, and where each individual participant is well known. No risk to have problems counting the polls, messing around with the envelopes, or giving voting certificates for some dead people… But maybe do you feel that such evil countries as North Korea, Iraq, Iran and others should have no voting rights and definitely not those that you have. This would mean in a country that you would need to take out voting rights off many of the population. We should make it a WASP (White Anglo-Saxon Protestant)-only thing after all…

Just to finish up with these thoughts on democracy and the double language that we unfortunately have on this topic, I would like to mention an environment which is profoundly non-democratic and where success can be found too: the business and enterprise environment. Nobody has tried to organize CEO elections yet… Decisions in a company are often ultimately made by one unique person in a very dictatorial mode. Of course, this person can have advisors, a board of Directors, consultants, staff, subsidiary managers, you name it… but ultimately, he or she will decide to the best of his mind. The sanction is generally not immediate, but it will at some stage show up in the economical results of the company. It will have an impact on the social climate, on the global image and so on. Somehow, this is working…and it normally keeps working if the boss is good, or if the company has an exceptionally good product that will cover up for management errors. Is anybody sure that Coke could have never done better, or Disney?

Today, in the countries' scene, there are those who have the oil and do not necessarily need a "good management". It gets more critical when the wealth needs to be shared with a large population: see Nigeria or Algeria… The game is more complex, but there is no direct sanction for the "managers" because we are not operating in a completely free trade environment. Indeed, if you carry on the analogy with a company, a failing manager will see his company collapse because he will not be able at some stage to compress his operating costs below a certain level as employees will not accept reductions in wages and the equipment will not continue to operate without maintenance. The complete failure will lead to employees leaving to another employer and the company stopping all production. However, with the very stringent rules that have been put on populations movements, especially from the south to the north, the people living in a failing country have no other choice than staying there! They will "reduce their wages": they will suffer poverty, malnutrition, illnesses, death, and they will have no other choice. Imagine a company where you can make all the mistakes that you want and still have your entire workforce obliged to continue to serve!

If you want to help democracy, if you really want to help it, then, make the world free of restrictions on populations' movements. Today, we are talking about this global village that the Earth has become. Goods, money, services can cross the borders easily, but not people. Those in the poor areas and having "bad managers" will have no choice. They will have to accept less and less. Because democracy on a global scale will necessarily lead to a more even distribution of wealth and this is not necessarily what you are looking for!

In a real free world, not only for trade and for northern countries merchandise to start better invading the south, in a real free world, we will see a very natural phenomenon which will consist of a tendency to reach an equilibrium state where everything is evenly distributed, maximizing the Entropy of the system… For those having studied some physics, this will be a very normal thing! Indeed, if you look at what is called the diffusion phenomena, a salt concentrated in some part of a liquid will tend to "diffuse" in order to reach a homogeneous concentration. However, with the rules as they are today, we are rather going for some reverse osmosis, a great technique used to make drinking water from sea or brackish water, and where pressure is used to concentrate the wealth, sorry the salts, on the more concentrated side of a membrane.

I do not want to finish up here leaving you with the thought that I am an enemy of democracy. Certainly not! I am in favor of a democracy that works, not of systems that pretend to be democratic while they miss the most basic attributes of democracy. Quoting Sir Winston Churchill, "Many forms of Government have been tried, and will be tried in this world of sin and woe. No one pretends that democracy is perfect or all-wise. Indeed, it has been said that democracy is the worst form of Government except for all those other forms that have been tried from time to time…."

EXPATS VS MIGRANTS

These two words basically mean the same thing: they are used to describe people who have left their countries to live in another country. They generally do it in the quest of a better job and quality of life. In recent years, because of all wars, catastrophes and unsuccessful democratization brought to some countries, we see more and more people fleeing their countries for brighter destinations. However, in this case, a more appropriate word would be refugees… For Syrians alone, there have been more than a million in 2015! Yes, a million people that have "benefited" from the democratization efforts of the international community in Syria. The people that were armed to fight Bashar Al Assad turned out to be worse… In any case, the outcome was to have millions of lives traumatized forever and millions on the street searching for a new home. Statistics from the UNHCR (the United Nations Refugees Agency) talk about some 70.8 million of displaced people in 2018, a staggering high figure, and the worst since the Agency's inception in 1950. Of them, close to 26 million were refugees. In 2018, 25 people were forced to flee every minute!

If we go back to those who exit their country because of a job, how would you call an American working in Dubai, a French in Shanghai, or a German in Tunisia? That would for sure be an expat… Similarly, how would you call an Indian in the US, an Algerian in France, or a Syrian in Germany? Well, probably a migrant? Related to these categories of migrants and expats, we can point out the high class of business travelers. A paper from The Economist is telling us about the sad, sick life of the business traveler as evidenced by a 2015 study from researchers at the University of Surrey and colleagues at Linnaeus University (that is Sweden!). Let apart the envy-inducing tales or posts the business traveler might have, researchers have found that frequent travel had negative effects on the psychological, emotional, and social life of the travelers. They are also physically exposed to speed aging, heart strokes, vein thrombosis and radiations! One even worse situation that this study does not mention is that of the business traveler from the "wrong" part of the world, the guy that would be qualified as a migrant rather than an expat when he moves outside his country. This traveler is exposed to a severe discrimination named "visa"! Indeed, if you are a holder of an American or a European passport, there is a very large number of countries where you can travel without having to worry if the immigration police will let you in. However, if you come from an Arab or and African country, chances are that you will have to seek visas for just about any location you would like to visit! Here, you are not only exposed to further stress, and paperwork, and expenses, but you are especially exposed to a lot of humiliations. You might be a well-respected businessperson in your country, but your visa gets rejected.

The issue is that you have no place in the world where you might get an advantage! Being an Arab, one of the most striking facts for me is that a visa is required in most all other Arab countries (for my Tunisian passport), while no such visa will be required from the holder of a "good" passport. To travel to many other Arab countries now, getting a visa is a lengthy process. Getting a multiple entry visa or a long-term visa is almost impossible, and some countries have started simply rejecting all requests. What "Arab world" are we talking about? This is pure imagination. The image of a whole bunch of poor people from upper-Egypt willing to travel to Libya for a job is still in my mind. We were taking the same plane to Tunis from Cairo and I was observing the airport agents counting the amount of money they were taking with them as, at that time, Kaddafi has requested that they carry at least 1000 US dollars to be granted access. That sum is more than a half-year salary, if not a whole year, for many of them. I was observing, clueless, this humiliating scene, and thinking of all the sacrifices these people were doing for a job, for a more decent life.

According to Henley & Partners, a consultancy publishing a visa restrictions index, in 2019, Japan and Singapore are topping the list of the "best" passport, with visa-free access to 190 countries (out of 218 in the list). They are closely followed by Germany, South Korea, and Finland (188), and then by Denmark, Italy, Luxembourg, France, Sweden, and Spain, (186). The US come only 15th with 184 countries accessible without visa. The "good passports" are mainly from wealthy countries, either European or South East Asian. If we look at the worst now, the ones that offer their holders the least freedom to travel, at the bottom of the list, we have Syria, Somalia, Iraq, Pakistan and Afghanistan… all of them recent "operations" territories of the "war on terror" fights and the "democratization" efforts.

In recent years, and before the Covid-19 pandemic, the media have been flooded by the so-called "migrants' crisis in Europe". The Old Continent's rich countries were struggling to find a solution to this major influx of refugees, mainly Syrians, but also Afghans, Eritreans, and others, fleeing their war-abated countries to seek new horizons. For France or Germany, would a few hundred thousand people be much of a problem? After the floundering of the Libyan regime, my small country of 10 million people did not have much choice but accept an influx of over a million Libyans. That was close to 10% of the population. With the recent Syrian crisis, it is believed that some 2 million Syrians or more now live in Egypt. Tunisia or Egypt are not especially rich countries. Their population suffers from a lot of unemployment and other material issues. However, they quite naturally managed the humanitarian issue of giving a shelter to populations who have lost almost everything. It is true that it is probably culturally easier for them to mix. They come from similar backgrounds, both on the language and often on the religious side.

Unfortunately, what we see today in Europe is that we seem to be forgetting what is making us humane, the very essence of civilization. The debate was not much on the inacceptable humanitarian situation of these refugees, but rather on the politics and economics of having a quotas' policy inside the European Union for accepting these people. We have seen pictures and videos of Hungarian police treating them like animals, of a journalist kicking children, of several eastern European countries refusing to be part of the pool that will provide them with a new home. We have also heard several speeches that were asking for a religious discrimination among migrants: Muslims were clearly not welcome; Christian Arabs could still be acceptable.

After Germany eventually decided that it would be accepting higher numbers of refugees, a French right-winger politician, M. Devedjian (I know, this does not sound like a typical French last name, he is himself of Armenian descent) managed to make a stupid and racist joke in 2015: "Germany took our Jews and gave us Arabs". True, both are Semites, and both are often the focus of a lot of "attention" from the extreme right wing. I thought France had laws to reprehend racist and anti-Semite attitudes… but M. Devedjian is a former Minister and member of the Parliament. This, maybe, gives him complete immunity!

By the way, have you heard of the "Calais jungle"? No? It has been all over French media… It is quite bizarre I must admit. Calais is in France. It is on the way leading to the UK through the channel tunnel. It is far from the equator. It is quite hard to imagine a jungle at that kind of latitude. A forest perhaps, not a jungle! But what does "jungle" call to your mind? The wild? Wild animals? The absence of law? I find the association of these two words to designate migrants' camps rather racist. It tends to suggest that these people are wild animals, as that is what the inhabitants of a jungle would be. It tends to suggest that there is no rule of law in this location. It should be pointed out that one of the major camps around Calais was erected over a dump. It hosts over a thousand people, and it is the only of 9 camps to be equipped with showers, electricity, and toilets… but don't be in a hurry for the shower, the average wait is 6 hours… Well, for sure, it is a jungle, but these people did not necessarily want it that way. This is a slum in one of the most advanced nations in Europe and the world.

It is not any better in the US! When a Presidential candidate that made it to the supreme job publicly announces that Muslims should be banned from immigrating to the US, how shall the world react? Is this an acceptable statement in a country that claims to defend democracy and human rights? Does he also want to ban the millions of Muslims that currently live in the US, with a major part of them being American citizens? He has also accused Mexico of sending "rapists and drug runners" across the US southern borders. He blamed Blacks and Latinos for violent crime across the Country. He even got award-winning Hispanic journalist Jorge Ramos removed from his press conference in Iowa…He now wants to build a 2000-miles separation wall along the Mexican border, which he would ask Mexicans to pay for and he also wants to deport millions of "illegals". Do you agree to what M. Trump is saying? Or do you consider him to be a racist that does not represent the American people? Unfortunately, the polls do not seem to tell that you are rejecting his position, and this would mean that you are rejecting Muslims and Latinos… Do you expect them to love you? Do you expect the world to believe you when you say you are a country of equal opportunity and freedom? I would just like to respond to M. Trump by quoting a funny post I have seen on social media. It says that two thirds of his wives were immigrants (no, he was not into polygamy, but he had some problems making up his mind!), and this is once again showing that America needs immigrants to do the jobs natives won't do…Once M. Trump was in office, one of his first moves was to issue a decree banning visitors from several Arab and Muslim countries. When his decree was suppressed following some legal actions, he went on to impose the ban of laptop computers and tablets on direct flights from certain countries, as a punishment to those he was not able to ban? I was quite admirative to see the reactions of certain judges that had the courage to fight this presidential decree, and of people that demonstrated in the streets against this same decree. This shows that America can indeed be "great again" if it builds on its openness and diversity, not the way M. Trump wants it.

RICH MAN, POOR MAN

With this little reference to one of your favorite seventies TV series (see, I have some culture about your movies industry!), I wanted mainly to speak about a 2014 Oxfam report on wealth distribution (Oxfam being an international confederation of charitable organizations focused on the alleviation of global poverty). Entitled "Working for the few", this report warns of the increasing concentration of wealth and power in the hands of a few people. Linking this to the previous chapter, of course, this is clearly the major driver for migrations. Wealth, security, quality of life, that is what people go seeking abroad. If they have it at home, there is no reason why they will be leaving a familiar environment and people that they love to move into a country where they are seen as alien, as foreigners, as intruders, as potential terrorists and where in most cases they are not necessarily welcome!

In 2014, the wealthiest 85 people owned 1.9 trillion of US dollars, as much as half the world's poorest population, i.e., 3.5 billion people! 1% of the world's population owned more than the remaining 99%. They owned more than half of the wealth… and the situation shows no signs of improvement. It has worsened over the last years. Indeed, we seem to be caught in a vicious circle, by which wealth gets more and more concentrated. As a French proverb says: money calls money… The richer you are, the richer you will get. With money, lots of it, comes power, the power to influence politicians, the power to do serious, though legal lobbying, to protect one's interests and sources for more revenues and wealth. As pointed out by French economist Thomas Piketty, the author of the best seller "Capital in the 21st century", "as long as the rate of return exceeds the rate of growth, the income and wealth of the rich will grow faster than the typical income from work" and this will increase inequalities. To confirm this trend, the 2019 Oxfam report says that it is now only the 26 richest (down from 85 in 2014) that own as much as the 50% poorest on this planet.

It should be obvious however that this is a dangerous trend. More inequalities will lead to social eruptions, and this was the major driver of what happened in the Arab world and was called the Arab Spring. Richer countries are not spared: this is what happened in France with the "Gilets Jaunes" in October 2018. The concentration of money and power in the hands of a few, a few that use all their influence to skew the rules and even place themselves above the rules, leads to more advantages to the richer and more burdens on the poorer. This is also leading to a deteriorating health and educative system, the basis of any democratic society. In the Arab world, the whole countries started collapsing.

Another comment from the Oxfam report is that most of the wealth is concentrated in occidental countries. This is another view on the inequalities: there are those that one can see in a given country, amongst the population of that own country, and, at the world's level, there is also that major discrepancy between countries, the richer and the poorer. The same mechanism applies. Those who have most of the wealth asked and got more free trade, easier regulations to have the world as a plain leveled field as they claim. Equal opportunity for all! Of course, when you have that kind of field to play in, but you initially kept all the balls for you, you win, and the poorer can only lose, once again! You will tell them that it is their fault. They do not have a proper administration, they do not have well trained people…In fact, they were bust before it started.

The good news in this report (and its regular updates) is that there is enough wealth in the world to really alleviate poverty, to provide for the basic needs of the whole world's population. Yes, it should be possible to provide free education and free healthcare for the whole world. Yet, this is a farfetched dream as there is no will to do that. Those who are supporting these ideas do not have the power, the lobbying, and the resources to make it happen. Those who could make it happen see no interest in doing so, rather the opposite! There could be simple and reasonable measures that could help: clamp down on tax dodging by corporations and rich individuals, shift taxation from labor and consumption to capital and wealth, ensure adequate safety nets for the poorer… these measures, in my opinion, should not be considered only at a country's level, they should also be considered between nations, to re-equilibrate wealth at the overall level.

Widening world disparities are a serious threat on the world stability. However, we do not see governments and international institutions acting in this direction. Yes, for sure, poverty alleviation is in principle on the agenda of the World Bank, of many other reputable institutions, and I am sure that many people working there are convinced that they are contributing to this noble goal. In practice though, pushing bluntly for more free trade, for deregulations, for a planet where multinationals will dictate the law is a very dangerous trend. It is transforming the world's population into an amorphous mass of consumers absorbing a uniform set of formatted products. The salad bowl where everyone could preserve some identity is transforming into the melting pot where everyone would lose its individuality and indigenous culture.

Is this a world where democracy can thrive? Is this a world where human rights are respected? Is this a world of humanity at all? Or is it a world of masters and slaves, of a few producers and a huge mass of consumers, a world where dictatorship is no more political and military. That is too obvious and no more acceptable. Dictatorship is economic and the winner takes all. This is the "dream" democratic liberal world you are designing for all of us as a model. It is your world; it is not mine…

WAR ON TERROR

It is fantastic to see how 9/11 has opened a whole new world of creativity in the fight against "terror". People started being held in a no-law zone: Guantanamo. Many ended up there after having been kidnapped. Some were tortured too. But let the American public feel good. You did not do the job yourselves, you subcontracted, according to various sources…There are still plenty of torture experts around the world, and unfortunately, with the Arab spring, many are getting unemployed!

I really do not understand this war on terror. How do you assess your results today? Is the world a safer place? If you follow up the news, the world news, not just what happened in your direct neighborhood, you will hear daily killings of hundreds of people in Pakistan, in Syria, in Iraq, in Afghanistan, in Nigeria, in Kenya… All those places that you supposedly cleaned from terror.

Maybe the error is in the definition of terror, or, of the expected outcome of your war on terror. Your objective was not necessarily to eradicate it, but to let those "under-developed" people enjoy it, rather than you and your close friends. And it is a plain success. Look at those professional self-killing bombers, they are now happy to show up their "art" in the streets of Karachi, Damascus, or Bagdad! So why bother? No more terror in the territories where you are having your morning jogging. The New York metro is safe… Of course, there are some "collateral damages" as your military might say when a bomb you throw kills a little more than the target "audience": the people of France can testify for that as they are probably the one Nation in the Western world that has most suffered from terror at home in recent times. Meanwhile, the nations you have helped against terror are enjoying fireworks every day, free of charge!

Your war on terror has spurred large territories to become no-law zones. The most pathetic even called themselves a state: the "Islamic State"! This is non-sense. They do not have a single attribute of a State. Why do your media call them so? Why aren't your communication experts opposing this? Are you happy with this new label for terror, directly associating Islam and Statehood in the name? Exit Al Qaeda, welcome the Islamic State... This words' association is misleading and designating an obvious enemy for the masses in the western world: all those who happen to be Muslim, or Arab because there is always this confusion between Arab and Muslim, all of them, all of us should I say, are suspects!

The irony of this, if I can speak of irony, is that "Islamic terrorism" has made more victims amongst Muslims and Arabs than in any other religious or ethnic group. The terror is in my neighborhood, thank you! Your war on terror is a complete failure. It has created thousands more of frustrated, humiliated, ill-minded people that are willing to fight against you, your values, your hegemony... However, before they can make it to the Big Apple, they get their training in the outskirts of Baghdad or Damascus. With the failure of Libya, which you caused by ousting Kaddafi with no clear replacement scenario (as admitted by President Obama who said that Libya's aftermath was the worst mistake of his presidency), they can now enjoy the same thrills in the streets of Tripoli, Ben Ghazi and several other locations. Then, they come to practice in Mount Chaambi in Tunisia, my home country. According to the "North Africa Journal", the North Africa/Sahel region (including Egypt) has claimed over 13 thousand deaths in 2015 from critical incidents, with Libya heading the list with over 5 thousand and five hundred. Reacting to the deteriorating security situation, local authorities have arrested over 33 thousand people in that same year, with Egypt being the more proactive here in arresting militants, political activists, and others with a total of more than 11 thousand.

Of course, you can just forget about visiting these "war zones". You will simply notify your citizens to avoid these hot spots. There are still plenty of other places for tourism. Why go spend your money in Arab or Muslim countries. The vicious circle however, is that, with less money coming in, less wealth being created, more spending on arms and security, less resources for education and healthcare, the people living in these places will see their quality of life deteriorate (if they ever had such a thing, ask people in the Gaza strip!), their purchasing power plunges, their morale annihilates. They will blame it on their governments, and also blame it on you, on the occident in general, they will blame it on the whole planet and will be a much easier pray for the real terrorists... and here is the catch twenty-two!

Your war on terror is creating more terror. It is dividing the world into a safe harbor that wants to further protect itself, and a war zone, creating more and more terrorists. It is not treating the problems at the source, in a rightful way. Even if you chose not to go to these uncertain territories, look at all the new constraints you have now to travel. Boarding on a plane is becoming a terrible thing to do. Travel is becoming a nightmare: take off your shoes, your belt, your watch, get that computer out, throw all liquids beyond a hundred milliliters, scan your luggage, scan your body… When are we going to have to scan our brains?

Despite, or because of all this, we are becoming more stressed and paranoid every time we have to fly. I am learning to become fatalist. Whatever should happen, will happen! Determinism you say? Forget about that… faith, yes!

WEAPONS OF MASS DESTRUCTION

This is one of the big jokes of the Century. It is in fact a weapon of mass confusion and misleading. "Oops, sorry guys, we found nothing in Iraq. We had wrong intelligence" … too late! Once a flagship of the so-called Arab World and the Middle East, this country with rich history and culture is in deep chaos since you went there for war! Who cares about the epic of Gilgamesh and ancient Mesopotamia, of Babylon and its suspended gardens, of the magnificent Bagdad of the Abbasids? Americans probably think that Aladdin and its fables are just a creation of Disney…

By the way, who is the Nation that had one of the biggest stocks of chemical weapons amounting to over 25 thousand tons? Who is the only nation that used nuclear bombs against civilians? Not only once… it needed to make sure that a Plutonium-based bomb was as good, if not better, as an Uranium-based one. Both were A-bombs, based on "breaking" the atoms, or nuclear fission. It is true that you were not able to test the H-bomb, based on nuclear fusion, in Japan. The thermonuclear bomb was ready only a few years later in 1952, and your "Ivy Mike" dug a 50-meter-deep and 1.9 km diameter crater in the Eniwetok atoll in the Pacific Ocean, 190 miles west of the more famous Bikini atoll. Nobody cared about all the pollution and harm to the environment that these atmospheric "tests" did at that time. Who knows for how long radiations will still be affecting that portion of the Marshall Islands, and affecting the cells of the local fauna and flora, not even speaking about humans?

You have managed to name your small toys in a way that is almost poetic, making them sound close and familiar, not really the deadly weapons of mass destruction they were: "Little boy" for the uranium gun-type atomic bomb of Hiroshima, and "Fat man" for the plutonium implosion-type bomb of

Nagasaki. The death-toll in Hiroshima was initially estimated around 140 thousand people but later corrected to some 200 thousand, including all the cancers caused by the gamma radiations. Nagasaki had a lower "score": only some 70 to 80 thousand for the first estimates... Some say that these figures are conservative as they do not necessarily properly account for the radiation effect of the bombs, which provides a longer-term "bonus". What a great scientific experience! What a fantastic firework!

Of course, some people in Hiroshima or Nagasaki did not like it, but, hey, you can never please everyone. After all, this put an end to the war in the Pacific Ocean and opened a new era: the cold war. Why Cold? Because there was no war at all, but a massive accumulation of weapons of mass destruction. By whom? Iraq? Iran? Syria?

Several years later, there was a new playground to test new toys: Vietnam. The Asians did not like Napalm? Is it more ecological than atomic bombs? I am not sure what is the worst for the planet. True, it is not green energy. I know, that was long ago. Nobody really cared about ecology, or the earth, or sustainable development. There was no Al Gore to preach against global warming. It was just local warming anyhow. Very local, but warm enough from the prospective of those who experienced it, not to make them care about rising water levels, but rather about preserving their lives!

OK, now you found no such weapons in Iraq, but you are telling us that the very Evil Iran is full of them, and they are willing even to have nuclear weapons. Unacceptable! Just a reminder... who armed Iran for so many decades, during the rule of their beloved tyrant, no, democratic ruler and friend of the West, the Shah? Who gave the Savak, his strong political police, probably worse than the eastern German Stasi, the tools to "manage" the population? Did someone realize that it was years of tough stronghold on Iran that led to the revolution that pushed the country in the hands of the Ayatollahs? You know, in Tunisia, we have a saying: "keep the bad better than you get the worse". It probably has no translation in Iranian: they now have the worse, but this is not necessarily a reason to prepare for war against them. For almost ten years, western countries and Arab monarchies of the Gulf have pushed Iraq against Iran, in a remake of ancient times wars between Arabs and Persians, which can be traced back to 2700 BC and the Sumerian king Mebaragesi. Then, Iraq, getting too strong and too arrogant, got hit for weapons of mass destruction it did not have. And now, you are preparing a similar feast for Iran. Nice screenplay, very popular too. Who wants Mullahs and Ayatollahs playing with nuclear arms? No one will be secure... Honestly, I do not feel threatened, but you certainly do. I wonder why!

To conclude on this "weapons of mass destruction" thing, I believe it is the product of fantastic marketing that enabled to get the public opinion accepts non-acceptable things. Today, can we get a ranking of the nations with the highest numbers of such weapons? Being the number one, can you start fighting number two, which is Russia, or the following ones which are European? What was done against North Korea? No, you are not fighting the guys with the biggest potential for mass destruction. You are very selective in your approach. You are choosing the ones that you will be able later to reconstruct…after destroying them… at their expenses too. This is a win-win game for you: sell the arms and sell the concrete!

Let us just get a little more specific from previous chapter. Nuclear Weapons… This is a big taboo! Under some non-proliferation rule you want to impose on the world, no one that you do not agree with is allowed to develop any nuclear applications, be they for non-military use. I agree with you on one thing though. Anyone developing nuclear technology is suspicious of developing military applications. I doubt countries working on this technology would refrain themselves from doing so. However, one can note that all countries considered to be on the evil side: Iraq, Iran, North Korea have all been "prosecuted" for trying to develop nuclear technology. You have led the World and the UN Security Council to impose sanctions on these countries to have them drop any nuclear ambitions.

I still remember that Israel even got your help, at least your silence, to conduct a raid on the Osiris nuclear reactors of Iraq, who was on the western side at that time and who got the technology from France. It was a great deal for the West: sell the reactors for a lot of money, get cheap oil to pay for it and destroy it later to protect the US major ally in the middle east from any hypothetical or potential threat. What worries me today is that Israel is once again threatening to hit another "evil" country in the region, supposedly trying to develop some nuclear competency: Iran. We have seen more and more declarations of Netanyahu saying Iran has crossed the red line and threatening of an air strike in some future. I wonder why no one is complaining about having Israel be part of the very POSH circle of nuclear-able countries.

In a video published by Davos' World Economic Forum, one can find a ranking of the countries with the most nuclear warheads as of 2015. They start with North Korea, at 8, which is the lowest. Then, Israel, with 80. Both followed by India and Pakistan at around 100 something, the UK at 215, China at 260 and France at 300. The real serious stuff is shared by the US with 6970 warheads and Russia with 7300. Who is really heaving massive weapons of mass destruction? No mention of Iraq, Iran, Syria or Libya here… and by the way, Iran is still under US sanctions and President Trump has undone what the Obama administration has started in relieving the constraints on Iran while it was giving up its nuclear program…

Being an Arab, I see more threat in Israel having nuclear weapons than Iraq or Iran… in the recent history at least, we have all witnessed Israel hovering into Palestinian territories, killing innocents, in what was called "a war" where the other party had only "gadget" weapons and stones! Don't get me wrong, I am not an advocate of Iran or Iraq having access to nuclear weapons. I am just saying that Israel too should be prevented from having this access, but this is not an issue in the international institutions that obey your desires!

If I go back to what has happened in the near past, while the whole world media was focusing on Iran, and while all imaginable sanctions have been imposed on it because it was insisting to pursue its nuclear program, North Korea has announced several successful underground nuclear tests! What did you do? What did the whole world do? They are there now. They have the bomb, and they could be threatening their southern neighbor and potentially many others in East Asia. Your historical ally there, Japan, is getting very nervous… Why didn't North Korea get as much attention as Iran, while it is understandable now that they were way more advanced than Iran is and while this is certainly known to your intelligence services. Why was priority given to Iran over North Korea in the prosecution of the Nations aspiring to become nuclear powers? It is true that there is no oil in North Korea…

For sure, if we want the world to be a safer place, we want nuclear weapons to be managed by responsible people… however, history is telling us that nobody is perfect! Anyone heard of the village of Palomares in Spain? A small fishing village that "received" three American H-bombs in 1966! This is reported in the March 2009 edition of Time Magazine. Well, the US were not bombing Spain, no! In fact, the B-52 bomber of the Strategic Air Command carrying 4 H-bombs collided with a tanker during mid-air refueling. 3 of the bombs ended up near Palomares. The fourth one fell into the sea. Serious ground contamination resulted from the accident. Sounds like James Bond "Thunder ball" right? Fortunately, Palomares did not experience a nuclear blast! As reported by the BBC in 2015, John Kerry in his capacity of Secretary of State agreed to have the US clean-up the contaminated Spanish costal soil.

Interestingly, there is a little David trying to combat the Goliath of the nuclear armed states: the Marshall Islands, this tiny Republic of the Pacific

Ocean, has filed applications in the International Court of Justice in 2014 against those 9 states, including the US, UK, France, Russia, China, India, Pakistan, Israel and North Korea, in a move to draw public attention on the necessity of removing nuclear arms. It is accusing all these nations of not fulfilling their obligations and commitments to lower their nuclear arsenal. It is worth noting that, by this action, the Marshall Islands are not claiming any financial repair for all they suffered from the American nuclear testing program. Some sources claim that, for several years, the US have fired the equivalent of 1.7 times the Hiroshima bomb every day! It is true that in 1954, "Castle Bravo" exploded with 1000 times the power of the Hiroshima bomb. The test was not completely mastered as the neighboring atolls of Rongelap and Utirik were contaminated. It was not only a question of some more coral that would become radioactive! These atolls were inhabited, and their populations had to be displaced. The test had some other unplanned consequences: jellyfish babies! This is not a joke. Contaminated mothers gave birth to babies with no arms or feet, and a translucent skin. They died immediately at birth. Several decades later, it is hard to simply forget the harm to the people and the environment!

Want to hear about the latest on weapons of mass destruction? I read a stunning paper on The Guardian and could find more on the web (including the site of the American Institute of Physics), relative to the use of climate-altering technologies. Spy agencies from the US and Russia were the major contenders in this quest. According to US scientist and expert Alan Robock of Rutgers University, the CIA is funding major research on such technologies. The published reports talk about climate change and the ways to manage it, which looks like a noble purpose. However, Robock talks about CIA folks calling him to understand how one could find out if someone else was trying to alter your climate… The use of weather as a weapon was normally banned in 1978 under the Environmental Modification Convention (Enmod). It should be pointed out that the US had experimented with seeding thunderstorms during the Vietnam war, not to cool down the Vietcong from the heat of Napalm, but rather to make major supply routes too muddy to pass for foot soldiers. This reminded me that, when I was a student in Davis (California), a fellow agriculture M.Sc. student from France was approached by the CIA to work for them. They needed people who would be able to predict crops productions from satellite observations. If you can act on the weather, you might flood people to get rid of them or you can starve them as well. If you can manage their grain supply, you can manage their politics. This is not conventional war. It is much more powerful and insidious. This is real power, the power of God as many people say or think!

Another point I wanted to highlight is related to the defense budgets.

Indeed, to be a serious contender in mass destruction, you must have some weapons… and to have those costly toys, you have to spend some money. Guess what? Which is the nation spending the most on its arms and army? The US of course! And the figures are just staggering. According to various sources, the US defense budget has soared from around $290 billion in 2001 to some $600 billion in 2015 to nearly $1000 billion in 2019! Some sources say that is more than 20% of the federal budget, more than what is spent on Medicare and more than the next 13 nations combined budgets for military spending.

If you look in more details on how that money is spent, you will find that the major part is on "operations" followed by personnel pay and housing and by weapons procurement… some other items are smaller but would be by far bigger than the whole military budgets of nations such as Iraq, and that would be the spend on research and development (R&D) for instance. "Better" weapons for a better future? Oh, by the way, "operations" means war… Let us focus a bit on R&D… this is a frightening one for the future, a future that could resemble that of the "Terminator", where machines gone wild would be killing us, humans (not only Iraqis or Syrians by the way…). Several prominent researchers, philosophers and entrepreneurs like Stephen Hawkins, Noam Chomsky and Elon Musk have been warning against the dangers of embedding artificial intelligence into weapons… I am not sure your DARPA (US Army's research division: Defense Advanced Research Projects Agency) has been listening. When one sees what is public domain from Boston Dynamics, a robots manufacturing firm, acquired by Google and sold to Softbank in 2017, which has a whole array of animal-like and also humanoid robots, one can wonder what is cooking in the R&D kitchen of your army, with such humongous budgets!

But why be so gloomy while your defense industry is promising us fantastic breakthroughs for a near future, a future where the US will have a decisive technological advance as they claim. Indeed, the latest news from Lockheed Martin's president, Marillyn Hewson, is that they will be launching a hypersonic plane (not a passengers' plane of course, a Mach-6 fighter plane yes!) that will have a speed six times that of sound, making it much more advanced than anything else on earth. And, as one good news does not come alone, she has also revealed that her company was developing a laser which could be used for war. She was optimistic that her firm will be able to deliver arms that were often imagined and shown in science-fiction movies but were never actually industrialized! Great news isn't it? In May 2020, the Daily Mail (of the UK) reported that the US Navy has demonstrated a high energy laser attached atop the warship USS Portland. It was able to shoot down a drone as can be seen on videos available on the web. The system was developed by Northrup Grumman, an aerospace and defense company. Wonder why nobody is asking to stop these weapons of mass destruction's developments!

If we go back to those other nations that top the world's ranking in military spent, the second is China and the third position is disputed between Russia and Saudi Arabia (rankings vary depending on the reference, whether you rely on the "International Institute for Strategic Studies" or the "Stockholm International Peace Research Institute". France and the UK come next…Interesting to see that Saudi Arabia is in the world's top five. At least, the money they get from their oil does not go far away and is recycled mainly in US manufactured weapons. For this industry, the arms manufacturing industry, conflicts, and wars are a benediction. Of course, most of the firms operating here are westerners, and most of those are American. When they see a missile strike, that is a million dollars turnover more! Imagine all the dollars in a single day fight in Syria or Yemen … I can spot many millions just watching my TV set!

So, who is benefiting most from all these wars and insecurity around the planet? The Stockholm International Peace Research Institute (SIPRI) has crunched the numbers and it shows that, between 2010 and 2014, the US were the world's leader in arms exports, with a global market share in excess of 30%. It is closely followed by Russia at 27%... The top 10 list includes, in this order, China, Germany, France, UK, Spain, Italy, Ukraine and Israel… These are the countries that benefit the most from overall conflicts. When it comes to arms production, and because of the huge consumption of the US military themselves, SIPRI shows that the 2014 top 10 list includes 7 American companies, the 3 others being European…

THE NEW MIDDLE EAST

Sir Henry Campbell-Bannerman is a pure British product, for sure! You do not know Sir Henry? You bet! I did not either, until recently… He is not as famous as Winston Churchill or Margaret Thatcher, but he held the same position, long ago… Sir Henry used to be the British Prime Minister in the early twentieth century. Some say that he commissioned a report in 1907, a secret document that became partially known to the public only recently. Why should I bother about this today? Well, it is talking about Arabs, and it has probably strategized their fate for the recent history and the years to come…To be honest, I did not find much evidence of the existence of this report or its content. People that believe in this theory claim that it advocates strongly for the division of the Arabs, as they would be a real danger if they were able to unite.

This is a theory I have heard from a friend of mine, who is very pessimistic about all that is happening in the region these days… He does not believe at all in the so called "Arab Spring". According to him, all of this has been fabricated in the bright minds of some powerful right-wing US think tanks that are maneuvering to keep the Arab word in the worst possible position to continue gently pumping the oil! He sustains the idea that the war against Iraq was the initial step of this whole scheme. He has been doing business in Iraq from the seventies. Despite the fact that Saddam Husain was a dictator, he says that he was a visionary leader that managed to bring back to Iraq several of the competencies the country had abroad. He put in place a program that helped get many of the diaspora highly educated people go back to their country and contribute to build its institutions. My friend tells me that Iraq in the eighties and early nineties was certainly one of the most advanced, if not the most advanced Arab country, from any angle you would analyze it: education, health, institutions, public administration, art and culture… This country was getting to a level where it could become a threat to American interests in the Middle East, interests which are often interlinked, or at least perceived as such, with Israel's interests. The first serious strike was therefore for Iraq. Look at it today, years after the first US bombing on Baghdad. It has become routine to hear in the news that there has been another bombing, killing another fifty or so people, and nobody would care… the Iraqi oil is flowing in the right direction, and that is all what matters…

Now that Iraq was down, and now that several of the Arab dictators were wearing out, it was about time to introduce some more chaos there, to keep them busy and far from building any tangible force. It started with Tunisia as a test. The geopolitical implications are not that risky, but this could validate a "prototype" revolution. In any case, Tunisia is a small country, with no oil, no "sensitive" borders… the movement was then spread to Egypt, the "real" thing, the massive country in the Arab World. It was continued to oil-rich Libya and then, to Israel-neighboring Syria. Some small episodes in Bahrain and a wider conflict in Yemen would also help make the Petro-dollar monarchies understand they will always need the US big brother to contain any potential risk. This new Middle East has now the "perfect" configuration for easily exploiting its resources and having it under full control of the West and more specifically of the US.

You might say this is science-fiction, you might say this is the usual conspiracy theory, you might say this is total nonsense, but I can tell you this is some of what even intellectual and prominent people think in our part of the world. Do you believe this is bringing friendly feelings?

ISRAEL

It took me years to just accept to say this word! It is tough… the whole environment you live in when you are in an Arab country is anti-Israel: education, media, friends, family… to give you a picture, it rings in my mind just like Afghanistan would ring in yours, or may be Al Qaida. If you say Menahem Begin, I hear Moammar Kaddafi… It is evil. It is the evil that is using state terrorism to kill Palestinians. It is the evil that took away their land, their lives, their dignity. But in fact, why would I have to feel concerned? I am Tunisian, I leave thousands of miles away, and nothing happening in the Middle East is directly affecting my life! Why should I bother? What is at stake? Well, I am an Arab, and the Palestinians are too. Somehow in my sub-conscience, I feel we are brothers. We have things in common. And after all, there is big injustice in what they are experiencing. Is it different from Apartheid, to paraphrase the book title from President Jimmy Carter? This is probably one of the big issues that is building anti-Israeli and anti-American feelings in the Arab countries, even in educated environments. This is how fanatics emerge… this is how people start mixing things and building hate.

Of course, by learning more on history and politics, by confronting ideas, meeting different people and simply being realistic, I ended up accepting the existence of Israel. I ended up understanding that Israelis are not all terrorists, or fanatics, or killing Palestinians and taking their land (I know, it is the other way around in the western world, but, remember, I am telling you about my perspective here!). I ended up thinking that there could be two countries leaving in peace and harmony if each party accepts some concessions. But this is certainly not the dominant feeling in the Arab World, and this does not seem to be shared by the close circles around Donald Trump either. It is already challenging for someone like me, who thinks being rather well educated and rather close to western thinking and culture. Imagine the guy, with low education, with not much exposure to other people or cultures and who can only see massive aggressions on Palestinian people not being prevented nor even condemned. You are pushing the guy in the hands of Al Qaida and of Bin Laden's friends.

Your media talk about "terrorist" acts killing and injuring civilians in Israel, about artisanal bomb shells being sent on some village on the border… My media talk about massive airstrikes killings tens of civilians, of massacres in refugee camps such as Sabra & Chatilla. Your media talk about retaliation of Israel on Palestinians. My media talk about retaliation of Palestinians on Israel…They also talk about all the vetoes that the US have opposed on UN resolutions condemning Israel abuse. Why did the French, the Brits, the Chinese, the Russians all accept and the US still using their Veto? Is everyone wrong in his assessment? Is the US acting from a dogmatic position?

The Trump presidency has made things worse and people in the Arab world felt more injustice: moving the US Embassy to Jerusalem; blessing more colonies and the annexation of Palestinian land, ignoring all international resolutions on the matter; "punishing" the UNESCO and the UNRWA, two United Nations institutions accused of being unfriendly to Israel; Menacing the International Criminal Court because of its asserting jurisdiction over Israel, saying the United States will "exact consequences" for any "illegitimate" investigations; proposing a totally biased peace plan dubbed "Deal of the Century" asking for little to no concessions from the Israelis and very harsh constraints on the Palestinians and unveiling the plan together with Benjamin Netanyahu while ignoring Mahmoud Abbas… Quoting Alon Liel, former Israeli ambassador to South Africa, from a paper he published in Feb 2020 in "Foreign Policy": "Trump's plan for Palestine looks a lot like Apartheid. In the heyday of South Africa's apartheid regime, the country's white minority government planned to create 10 so-called homelands – also known as Bantustans – where black South Africans could live far away from the cities it hoped to keep white". He certainly knows what he is talking about, being fully aware of what South Africa was and what Israel is.

There is also certainly a lot of confusion that is maintained between Israel, Zionism, Jews, Shoah… I am not sure who is benefiting here and who is propagating this. The outcome is that in many simple minds, in the Arab world, being a Jew means being a Zionist, and being an Israeli is being an enemy… this eventually leads to the fact that anyone showing any sympathy or understanding for Israel is a traitor in the Arab world. You are not allowed to accept Israel, not even to think of it as a State! Some of our newly elected representatives in Tunisia wanted to pass a bill in our future constitution that will penalize any normalization with Israel. This is complete non-sense! But it was at stake, and people were seriously discussing it.

What would that mean? That I could be put in jail for having an Israeli friend? Or for selling goods to someone in Israel? Or for flying to Israel? I do not even know if it would be possible for me to travel there with a Tunisian passport... in any case, I am not interested, not now. I still have very mixed feelings; I have no problems with Israeli people. Indeed, like a French singer has pointed out in a nice song, "we do not choose where we are born". Therefore, I cannot blame someone for being an Israeli and I hope he will not blame me for being an Arab. But as a State, I still have some problems of acceptance, just like I would have had with South Africa during apartheid time. Remember, Jimmy Carter has written a book entitled "Palestine, peace not Apartheid"! This is a former american president saying loud how the Palestinians are being unfairly treated in what most western media will describe as the only democracy of the Middle East.

It is too bad that Yitzhak Rabin got killed. He was not an easy guy. He was not a feeble guy, and he was certainly not the least showing passion for Israel, but he was a Statesman and he walked the peace talk with Arafat. He was on his way of signing a real and long-lasting peace with the Palestinians, for the good of both Israelis and Palestinians, and all Arabs. And he got killed... by a fanatic Jew! At least this time, it was not a fanatic Muslim, and this showed that fanatics exist in all religions, and they are equally dangerous, no matter the religion. It was really sad it ended up this way! No one took over from Rabin. No one had the courage nor the legitimacy with the Israeli people to continue the job and get the peace.

We all know what had followed. More killings... More hate...

At some point, even the Israeli army started to question the Netanyahu policy which seems to be leading to another "Intifada" (uprising in Arabic, but this word has been used worldwide in all languages related to the Palestinians protests). Haaretz, one of the major newspapers in Israel cited General Major Herzl Halevi, head of military intelligence, in November 2015, who declared that the frustration felt by young Palestinians was driving them to desperate acts. The last months of 2015 have witnessed a lot of killings, on both sides. However, as usual, the death toll among Palestinians is in the range of ten times that of Israelis. The first have committed several desperate knife attacks. They are of course not allowed to carry any firearms. At the opposite, Israeli settlers, who live in territories that the international community qualifies as colonies and clearly not belonging to Israel, are allowed, and encouraged to carry rifles and colts... They sometimes use them against their Palestinian neighbors. However, both populations do not get equal treatment from Israeli forces. When a Palestinian commits an aggression, he is often "terminated", without necessarily an initial quest to arrest him. When an Israeli settler commits an aggression, he might get arrested, but never killed at once. Even when arrested, he would often manage his way through…

Israel claims to be the unique democracy in the Middle East. Is it really? What does the Palestinian population of East-Jerusalem think of it? I refer you to a paper by Professor Shibley Telhami in the Washington Post: "How Israel's Jewishness is overtaking its democracy". Based on a Pew Research Center poll, the paper demonstrates that more than half of Israel's Jewish population wants Arabs to be expelled out of the country, a statement that is stronger with the younger population, and especially with the Dati (Modern Orthodox) and then the Haredi (Ultra-Orthodox). More strikingly, an overwhelming majority says that Jews deserve "preferential treatment" in Israel, which is simply contradicting the notions of democracy and equal rights of citizens, unless all Israel's citizens were Jews. Like their Jewish counterparts that feel their Jewish identity comes before their Israeli one, the 20% Arab citizens of Israel identify themselves with their ethnicity first. Once again, it seems that the two-states solution would be best. Without it, meaning without an autonomous and recognized Palestinian State, Israel cannot have its Jewishness dominate its democracy without creating serious discrimination and injustice feelings amongst its Arab population.

Do democracies accept and favor settlers in colonies in territories they do not own? Of course, this was done in the past by the UK, France, Germany, Belgium, Spain… well, mainly by European nations, who thought they were somewhat "superior" to the rest of the World's population. This has faded away in the twentieth century and those colonized nations got their independence, at least politically speaking! Today, the UN and most nations recognize that Israel is unduly colonizing territories such as Syria's Golan Heights, and Palestine's West Bank. But nobody is doing anything about the construction programs that Israel continues to carry in these territories to eventually impose them as becoming part of its land. It is surrounding East-Jerusalem by new developments meant to further isolate it from the West Bank. Worse than that, in a poll conducted by Nielsen in 2016 in the US for the Center for Middle East Policy at Brookings, 16% of Americans support the idea that the US should support maintaining occupation, and another 13% the idea of annexation without equal citizenship! Talk about democracy and human rights…

In a move regarding the import of goods from Israel into the European

Union, the latter has requested that the origin be further specified to distinguish what is produced in Israel from what is produced in the colonies. M. Netanyahu and his government reacted severely saying the EU should be "ashamed" to act in this way and imposing a "discriminating" legislation! Isn't he ashamed himself to continue occupying these territories and managing them in an Apartheid mode, where Palestinian rights are not respected, despite several UN resolutions? During Apartheid, South Africa was under embargo… This small act of bravery from the UE is far from being as strong, and still, it is being questioned!

The same "omerta" (you know, the Mafia's silence rule!) seems to reign over American politics. No single US President, or presidential candidate can allow himself to criticize openly Israel or its politics. This would be a clear case for dismissal. It is often interesting to see the addresses Presidents or Candidates, or other political figures have at the AIPAC gatherings…the American Israel Public Affairs Committee is a strong lobby group created in 1951 to support Israel and the Zionist ideology. For the 2016 election, Donald Trump, Hillary Clinton, Ted Cruz, and John Kasich all took their oral examination at the AIPAC! One of the candidates went on promising that he will recognize Jerusalem as the Israeli capital and that he will cancel all the signed agreements with Iran, which Israel has resisted so much (and he won the election! And did what he promised) … When looking at their speeches at AIPAC, you might wonder if these candidates are running for office in the US or in Israel.

Interestingly, one Presidential candidate, Jewish Senator of Vermont, Bernie Sanders did not do the AIPAC roadshow. Moreover, he took an interesting public stand for the rights of Palestinian people, that no other major candidate has ever taken, just days before the New York primary! Sanders considered that Israel's invasion of Gaza in 2014 in response to rocket attacks was "disproportionate", that the US and Israel have "to treat the Palestinian people with respect and dignity" and that "the US cannot continue to be one-sided". Sanders talked about Palestinians unemployment and poverty and condemned Israeli settlements construction in the West Bank. Well, this is quite unprecedented, and this is much closer to what people in the Arab streets think.

America will have to understand that Israel and Palestine are two sides of the same coin. They will exist together or perish together. I profoundly believe that the unilateral and univocal support of Israel is not in its best interest on the long run. The US is maintaining this illusion now with a yearly 3.5 billion dollars of taxpayer money going to the military support of Israel. Wouldn't it be nicer to spend that money on development and welfare?

PALESTINE

Just like I had a problem with saying "Israel" when I was a kid, your media, western media, seem to have a problem in saying "Palestine" these days… they can talk about "Palestinians", about "Palestinian territories", about "Gaza", about the "west bank"… some, more courageous, could even talk about "occupied territories" but no one would mention "Palestine" as a state! For western media, Palestine is a mirage, it does not exist. It cannot be considered as a nation or a country, even though the French parliament, after the Swedish, the British and the Spanish ones, has passed a law to recognize Palestine.

It is interesting to look at a definition that used to be given in Wikipedia (it has changed now!): The word Palestine can have several meanings depending on the geographical, historical and political context in which it is utilized! This is probably a unique case in the several countries definitions in the online encyclopedia… if you type France, Britain, Italy, Rwanda, Nepal or Chili, the first thing you will get is that it is a country, not something which definition depends on the context! It does not say that Italy if you are talking food means pasta or Brazil if you are talking sports is football! No, it says that they are countries… For Palestine, depending on the context as explained above, you can end up with: A historical and geographical region of the middle-east that designates the region composed of Israel and the occupied Palestinian territories; Another definition includes the above plus south Lebanon, the Golan heights (Syrian territory occupied by Israel) and part of Jordan; A State that the Palestinians are claiming since 1988 (why 1988, I thought this claim to date back to much older!) and which is recognized by several States, UNESCO and the UN as an observer State not as a member State.

Nowhere will you find that it is a country… you will also find a mention of the "Palestinian Authority", which is not a government nor an administration… as there is no State, how could there be an administration, but it is an "authority". What does that really mean?

To further confirm this awkward situation, my favorite address book application does not allow to register a person from Palestine! Is Microsoft boycotting Palestine as well? Indeed, at a gathering in Egypt, I just met people from various places, including Palestinians living in the West Bank and in Jerusalem. Their business cards give addresses in Palestine. When I tried to input this information in "Outlook", I was not able to find "Palestine" in the countries list, and I was not allowed to create it! The only option is Palestinian Authority, but, to my understanding, that is not a country?

In any case, if you look at it on a map, what is Palestine really today? If you consider the territories that are not directly administrated by Israel in this region you have two disjoint pieces of land: the Gaza strip and the West Bank. This is supposed to form a nation or a country or a state called Palestine. It also has a President, except that this guy has lost power over Gaza for years, to the benefit of Hamas, an Islamist political organization, thanks to all the actions performed by the Israeli administration leading to the radicalization of the population.

A young woman which I recently met has explained to me that she was originally from Nablus, in Palestine, but she is the holder of the Jordanian nationality now. She also has an ID that allows her to go to the West Bank and visit relatives that remained in Nablus. Of course, crossing the borders and the Israeli controls to Jerusalem would take her ages all the time. At the most recent feast, the Aid, she (and many others) had to wait 12 hours to cross… Still, the most amazing thing is that, with that ID, she was not allowed to go to Gaza! If she wanted to do so, she would have to go to Egypt and cross from the Egyptian border. Israel is preventing her to cross the few miles from Jerusalem to the Gaza strip. It looks very much like the pass system applied during Apartheid time in South Africa. Why is nobody in the international community complaining?

Palestine holds probably one other record, which is not necessarily one that would make its inhabitants feel good. It is that of density of population. According to a paper on the New York Times by Eduardo Porter, this density is still going to double to 1626 per square kilometer, three times that of densely populated India! Apart from all the other constraints they have, this is certainly not helping them enjoy a proper living…

In the minds of many Arabs, the 20th century history of Palestine looks like a Kafka's novel. I recently red such an "amusing" story: imagine one day, while you have done nothing special, someone knocks at your door. When you open, the guy pops in and tells you that he has lived here long ago, in this land, at a time where the building itself did not even exist. The realtor promised him he can come back, and the municipality has granted him the right to "return". You say "no", try to push him out, but before you even know it, the guy is already installed in one of the rooms. The next day, you call your neighbor to help you out, but the guy, who already served himself from the fridge and sat at your table fights back. Soon, his cousins, nephews, uncles, and aunts join in and occupy all your rooms. You wife and children find themselves pushed to move out and ask some neighbors for hospitality. Once again, with the help of some neighbors, you try again to get back your apartment and the new guy manages to take the garage from one of them and a cellar from the other. You get angry and even more nervous and the guy eventually locks you into the toilets. Your wife gets locked in the bathroom. You cannot communicate without stepping into "his" part of the apartment. You are not given food and are not allowed to go out without his prior permission. When you set fire to the WC, the firemen come quickly to fix things and summon you to keep quite…

As rightfully pointed out by Sophie Bessis (Historian, Jew) and Mohamed Harbi (Historian, Muslim) in a post in French Newspaper le Monde (Nov 17th, 2015), we should ask the so-called "International community" to immediately enforce the UN resolutions regarding Israeli occupation and to recognize a Palestinian State based on its frontiers of 4th of June 1967. Such moves will take a lot of resentment out the minds of millions of Arabs, and will help combat the radicalization of many, often seen as an act of last resort. You cannot imagine how much the double standards adopted in foreign policy by the West in the Middle East and especially regarding the Israeli-Palestinian problem are planting the seeds of violence and hate. Even today, we can witness many demonstrations in the streets of Arab nations, calling for more solidarity with Palestinians. These are probably the sole demonstrations that were allowed and even encouraged during the reign of dictators and which can enjoy the same popularity with the outbreak of democracy.

In a study published early 2016 by the World Bank, written by Shanta Devarajan and Lili Mottaghi, titled "Why MENA (Middle-East North Africa) needs a new social contract?", there are frightening statistics on what is going on in Palestine: "48 590 Palestinian homes have been demolished in the occupied Palestinian territories since 1967; in 2015 alone, 552 Palestinian structures have been demolished in the West Bank and occupied East

Jerusalem; 80 000 Bedouins live under the constant threat of demolition in 35 villages that Israel does not recognize in the Negev; and 94% of Palestinian building permit applications are denied"… I have been directly quoting this report, with its own vocabulary, just to say that the words and the terminology used are not that of an Arab, nor a Palestinian, but those of an impartial international institution. How would one qualify this behavior from Israel towards the Palestinians? How would you expect these people to react? Where is this international community, so prompt to defend many causes? Where are the occidental media to simply relay these basic facts? Don't you think these would certainly move public opinions? I strongly believe that people, all over the planet, look for justice… Unfortunately, they are not told the full story about Palestine and Palestinians!

IRAQ

It has been well over 20 years since the first war against Iraq. I still remember that flight from Paris to New York (and on to San Francisco) where one flight attendant asked for an ovation to "our boys" coming back from Iraq. I realized that the plane was full of Marines. I did not applaud... I was against that war, I still am, just like 90% of all Arabs, except probably of the happy few that own several oil pits themselves.

Do I like Saddam? Of course not... sure, there are thousands of my fellows who see him as a Hero, the guy who defied the United States, the guy that threatened their interests in the Middle East. I am not one of those. I see Saddam as a Dictator, as a stupid narcissist guy who put his fellow citizens in hell. But I wonder, how is life in Iraq twenty years down the track? Is it a democratic country? I doubt! Is it a safe country? Clearly not with the average 10 to 20 people dying daily. The news do not report the death tolls anymore. There are better scoops now, with new war zones heating up! Iraq has been destroyed as a country and as a nation. Ask the average Iraqi person how their life is now?

And how it compared to their lives under Saddam's rule. Sure, they did not have democracy, they could not speak out and certainly not criticize him or his family to the risk of being killed. But they had a great education system, good enough healthcare, excellent infrastructure, and a decent living... The average Iraqi could go to the market without the risk of being shot. He had a very good standard of living compared to the average third world citizen... What has changed for him today? Does he feel it is a positive change? We have already seen a population under embargo, decided by the US after the first war. That was a humiliating and totally inhumane situation. Hospitals ran out of drugs, people were starving, war demolished infrastructure could not be retrofitted… yes, that situation probably fabricated a huge number of US lovers in Iraq and other Arab countries. Don't you think so? OK, agreed, it was not really "lovers", but rather crazy enemies, who had nothing else to lose. And you wonder why the average Arab guy does not like the US?

You are right! It was an error not to finish the job, and, once you have gone into war against Saddam's Iraq, you should not have left him in place. The collective punishment of the Iraqis was not a good idea, and you "corrected" this with the second war, that removed Saddam, because you could then install a democratically elected leader! Even Saddam was given a "fair" court case and he ended up only being sentenced to death… Could have been worse, but you did not allow your new friends to torture him! Just kidding… I don't know if that trial was fair, I don't know if it was good to sentence him to death… what I know is that Iraq today is certainly not a dream place to be. With Saddam gone, the country's unity has also disappeared. You opened the Pandora box of identity quest and regional separatism that lead Iraq to implode! Not a bad plan after all you might say! Who wants a strong Iraq these days?

And by the way, where is the oil now? Is production back on track? Does it benefit the average Iraqi to improve his standard of leaving? Did corruption disappear? Who is extracting the oil, and who is reconstructing the infrastructure? It is a good game: experiment your new weapons to destroy, send in your companies to rebuild, and do not forget to send a global bill for the whole. Do they have the choice not to pay? It is a good job to be the policeman of the world, when there is no one else to dispute the job.

The problem is that, when you multiply instable regions, you multiply the risk of having terrorist training camps: poverty, injustice perception, all of that provides the ferments for a "good recruitment". No security, no rule of law, and some "friendly states" that provide the financing and the arms. By all these actions that were supposed to be under the umbrella of "war on terror", you have actually created "terror factories" for the whole world. People go there like on pilgrimage. They get indoctrinated, brain washed, and tested! Those who survive make up a real menace on modernity, on the values that surprisingly I share with you! This makes me dislike you too, not for the same reasons than the previous guy, who has more of a dogmatic view, but because you are always making things worse for me! I am the one living close to these guys…

One more thing about Iraq: you know, recently, I was helping my 9 years-old son with his History courses, and this has reminded me of one thing: Iraq is the home of modern mankind history. Iraq is the land where writing has existed for the first time. It started in the form of cuneiform signs on clay tablets. This is the inflexion point between prehistory and history, roughly at 3500 BC. This is the start of human civilizations. Iraq is Mesopotamia. It is the fertile crescent. It is the land between the two rivers, the Tiger, and the Euphrates. What a miserable destiny, when we see what Iraq stands for today, while it was the icon of Civilizations, home to Sumer, to Assyria, to Babylon and its suspended gardens, one of the seven marvels of the Antique World!

IRAQ-IRAN WAR

On 22nd of September 1980, Iraq declared war on Iran, invading it by air and land. This was a rather ambitious move, as it was notorious that during the Shah's reign, Iran had one of the greatest and strongest armies in the world. May be Saddam thought that the country was disturbed with its new Islamic revolution, and it was about time to get some chunks of it. There was certainly also the fear that there could be some contagions to the long-suppressed Shia majority in Iraq.

This was reviving an old tradition in the region, as the Arabs and the Persians have never stopped fighting each other, despite the fact that they were supposed to be united by the same religion, Islam. But yes, do not forget, the fights between "Shia" and "Sunna" in Islam are probably worse than the fights between Muslims and Christians. It is dramatic to see how dogma, brain-washing and wrong understanding of faith can make people so stupid and ugly.

This is a war, almost forgotten now, which was a wrong war, and which has led to over a million victims. Yes, probably one of the most atrocious and lengthiest in the second part of the 20th century. Yet, it was a war supported by the West, and supported by many Arab nations in the Gulf. No matter who started it, for which reasons, wrong or right. What mattered was that this war was against Iran. Iran was the evil at that time, as no one had really a clue of what this new Islamic republic was, and this was a new villain to demolish.

The US knew that the new Iran was not a friendly country, with what happened at the American Embassy in Teheran, and the West knew by transitivity that this was not a friendly country either. The Russians had a similar case with Afghanistan, and probably saw another potential risk at their borders. What would happen to the "Caviar" industry of the Caspian Sea?

Iran had therefore no friends. It was a threat to everyone, even to Israel, who was also complaining about this newcomer to the Middle East scene. A country with a strong army, a strong speech and a religious orientation that could only bring trouble, inspiring the Lebanese Hezbollah and other Shiite groups scattered in the neighborhood!

Iran was the country to abate, and Iraq was ready for the task. What a nice world we live in! Almost everyone helped Iraq against Iran. Saddam Hussein was a hero. He was the safe defense against these crazy Islamist Mullahs and their black painted theocratic state. Western countries were all telling us: What did you say? Saddam is not a democrat? Saddam is torturing his own people? Saddam has installed a dictatorship in Iraq? A nepotistic regime? Well, that is his own country... We cannot intervene in internal affairs. Today, Saddam is our friend. He is making a great job and lots of sacrifices in fighting Iran. Let us not be picky and annoy him with human rights at home, and all those small issues that can disturb his attention and make him lose focus. After all, he needs a quite country and supportive people to properly manage his war, which is our war!

Everyone supported Saddam, our friend, our savior... forget that he caused the death of a million... you created another evil, at State level while Bin Laden was for the guerilla moves. This one had an organized army, with state-of-the-art weapons, provided by your factories in the West, paid for with the petrodollars of the Gulf, and his ego was growing bigger!

The Iraq-Iran war was good business too. How many missiles, how many fighter jets, how many tanks and guns and grenades have you sold? It was a recurrent business. The war lasted several years, 8 to be precise... for nothing! How many growth points did it add to Iraq's GDP? Or Iran? Or neighboring GCC countries? All that money was funding arms factories in the West, while it could have built more roads, more hospitals, and more schools in the Middle East, to fight the biggest evil of all, ignorance!

This war has spread the seeds of what will come next: The isolation of Iran, the invasion of Kuwait, a stronger Hezbollah, and so on. A wrong war with disastrous consequences and a war that you sponsored and supported. Oh yes! You're right... Who am I to even think I can tell if it is right or wrong? You decided that it was right, and that is what the media conveyed and what people think.

THE GULF WAR

Many indices seem to show that this war could have been avoided. It was a fabricated war, a war that the Bush administration needed desperately. What for? The trigger was simple: Saddam Hussein invaded Kuwait, a small oil-rich neighbor of Iraq. How did he have the courage to do so? Some say he has informed the US Ambassador of his intentions and was given some kind of a green light. No matter if this is true or not. He did it…and this was wrong. Kuwait is a sovereign country. Iraq cannot pretend to simply annex it.

If you look back in history, for how long did Kuwait exist? It is not just a creation of the British colonizer, who took off the oil-sunk enclave from Iraq, just as he did for Brunei from Malaysia…Today, Kuwait is a recognized country in the UN. It is one of the GCC (Gulf Cooperation Council) countries that enjoy the best social and political environment. This was a very bad move from Saddam, but, may be the immense international backing of his war against Iran, which was as much unjustified, made him think he could afford such insanities, if not with the support, at least with no adverse reaction, from the West.

He was wrong! This was a heaven's gift to the Bush Administration to destroy what was becoming a threatening regional superpower that could jeopardize the oil economy in the GCC, and thus American interests, but also the security of Israel, as Iraq ended up having a strong, well-trained army after all the years fighting Iran. It was also an army that had significant weaponry paid by all the allies in the Iran war, but certainly no arms of mass destruction as was claimed and relayed by all western media, in a huge propaganda that seemed to be coming from another age, from World War II! Collin Powell (that American general that became Secretary of State) recognized that there was wrong intelligence and Iraq did not have those arms… a bit too late?

Later, Bush son finished what his father did not have the time to accomplish. Indeed, after the first war, Saddam was feeble but not totally vanquished. The second war killed him like a rat. I still recall those images of a bearded dirty man that was extracted from an underground cave and presented like a mere criminal to the media. It also finished demolishing what used to be one of the best and strongest Arab nations to transform it into a dangerous playground for terrorists.

This war has probably had one of the worst psychological effects on Arab masses. Many of them did not support the move against Kuwait, many of them did not like Saddam the Dictator, many of them did not know much about Iraq, however, when this all started, and with this man standing against the dominant power of the West, shouting that he would fight for the Palestinians' rights, many of them started supporting him unconsciously. Many of them saw him as the one that will restore their lost dignity. In recent history, the Arab masses have all been colonized, humiliated. They were feeling that this was the savior that will take off their slave's chains… All this "dream" collapsed. They were pushed back to their sad reality. They were nothing in this big world chess game. They are the losers and there is no hope that this will change. This was setting up the ground for what has come later, and which we all do not like: ISIS…

You might think that my allegations are wrong, that I am taking this too far, but look at what Tony Blair has just admitted in his CNN interview with Fareed Zakaria. You trust CNN, I hope? This is a reliable all-American news TV, right? You trust Tony Blair as well? He is that former UK Prime Minister and long-term US ally. He was in power when the second war against Iraq was proclaimed and he totally supported what George W. Bush wanted to do there. Surprisingly, 12 years later, Tony Blair said that there was wrong intelligence that supported the decision to invade Iraq. He partly apologized for the consequences of that decision, admitting the link between overthrowing Saddam and the emergence of ISIS. This late Mea Culpa is seen by several western media as insufficient. Some say that he is voluntarily "forgetting" that the whole story of "weapons of mass destruction" owned by Iraq was largely sexed-up, that its procurement of uranium from Niger was even totally invented. He is also forgetting to tell his people and allies that he has lied on his real intentions back in 2002. At that time, he was claiming that he was working on a diplomatic solution to the Iraqi problem while a memo sent by Colin Powell to George W. Bush on the 23rd of March 2002 mentioned that "Blair is with us" (for the war in Iraq).

With the Chilcot's report released in the UK in 2016, some voices asked that Tony Blair and George W. Bush be prosecuted before the International Criminal Court (ICC) for this unlawful invasion that has claimed the lives of hundreds of thousands and left Iraq in a disastrous situation, and these voices were not that of an obscure third world Marxist leader. No, they were from prominent legal people in the Western World. One can find such a call in a paper published by French newspaper "Le Monde" by Serge Sur and Julien Fernandez, two public law professors. In his statement on July 6th, 2016, Sir John Chilcot clearly said: "In 2003, for the first time since the Second World War, the United Kingdom took part in an invasion and full-scale occupation of a sovereign State. That was a decision of the utmost gravity. We have concluded that the UK chose to join the invasion of Iraq before the peaceful options for disarmament had been exhausted. Military action at that time was not a last resort. We have also concluded that the judgements about the severity of the threat posed by Iraq's weapons of mass destruction – WMD – were presented with a certainty that was not justified; despite explicit warnings, the consequences of the invasion were underestimated. The planning and preparations for Iraq after Saddam Hussein were wholly inadequate; the Government failed to achieve its stated objectives. M. Blair had been warned that military action would increase the threat from Al Qaida to the UK and to UK interests. He had also been warned that an invasion might lead to Iraq's weapons and capabilities being transferred into the hands of terrorists. M. Blair told the Inquiry that the difficulties encountered in Iraq after the invasion could not have been known in advance. We do not agree that hindsight is required. The risks of internal strife in Iraq, active Iranian pursuit of its interests, regional instability, and Al Qaida activity in Iraq, were each explicitly identified before the invasion. The invasion and subsequent instability in Iraq had, by July 2009, also resulted in the deaths of at least one hundred and fifty thousand Iraqis – and probably many more – most of them civilians. More than a million people were displaced. The people of Iraq have suffered greatly. After the invasion, the UK and the US became joint Occupying Powers. For the year that followed, Iraq was governed by the Coalition Provisional Authority. The scale of the UK effort in post-conflict Iraq never matched the scale of the challenge. Whitehall departments and their Ministers failed to put collective weight behind the task. In practice, the UK's most consistent strategic objective in relation to Iraq was to reduce the level of its deployed forces. The security situation in both Baghdad and the South East began to deteriorate soon after the invasion". These were his own words… What else to say?

The Gulf War has not been a "clean" war. It turned eventually to be an occupation of Iraq, and the American forces on the ground were accused of many abuses, not to mention what private security company Blackwater did as well. Some of the sad and dirty remains of this war are the Abu Ghraib prison torture, the Haditha killing or the Mukaradeeb wedding party massacre… The latter refers to the bombing of a wedding party in a village close to the Syrian border, in May 2004. It killed 42, among which 13 children. The US military considered mistakenly it was a legitimate target. The Haditha killing happened after a bomb blasted a Marines convoy in Iraq in November 2005. 24 civilians were shot at close range by US troops. Many have compared it to the Vietnam's My Lai massacre. It was only after a Time Magazine reporter revealed the case that the military carried an investigation, which eventually led to nothing!

Of all these war "collateral" damages, may be the most known to the public were the prisoners torture and abuse cases in Abu Ghraib prison. Horrific pictures can still be found on the web. A famous one, that of prisoner Ali Shallal Al Qaisi, has made it to the cover of "The Economist" magazine of May 6th, 2004, with the headline "Resign Rumsfeld", calling for the Defense secretary's resignation. Only two military personnel were eventually sentenced to prison: Charles Graner and Lynndie England had so many pictures of them (not selfies, at that time, it did not exist!) with naked Iraqi prisoners in humiliating postures that it was very hard to pretend they did nothing. Several humanitarian organizations, including the Red Cross, Human Rights Watch and Amnesty International stated that the abuses were not isolated cases but part of a real strategy the American army had in such detention centers.

How do you expect this behavior to impact the ordinary people in Iraq? And in a wider scope, in the Arab world? This can only increase resentment towards the US, and by extension, to the Western world. Combined with long refrained frustration, and the remains of the quest for repair from the colonization times, this eventually provides a fertile ground for those recruiting troops that will fight to restore the dignity of Arabs as they might think. Abu Ghraib has certainly fabricated many of the future Emirs of ISIS. They do not necessarily care about Islam or religion at all. That is only a means to disguise their real objectives and recruit some feeble minds. What they care for is revenge… As reported by the "The Telegraph" on the 27th of May 2009, President Obama changed his mind on the release of more photographs of what happened in Abu Ghraib, rightfully saying that "The most direct consequence of releasing them, I believe, would be to inflame anti-American public opinion and to put our troops in greater danger". The problem is that anti-American public opinion has been steadily growing with all the "mistakes" made in Iraq, cumulated with what is happening in Palestine, with or without the photos…

IRAN

This is one of the worst enemies of the West as presented by the media for over 40 years. Currently named the Islamic Republic of Iran, the country is ruled by Ayatollahs, which are the clerics of Shiite Islam, clerics being absent from Sunnite Islam. Ayatollahs are seen to be so dogmatic and ruthless that the term has had some success being used as a strong substitute to dogmatic or stubborn!

Also known as Persia, Iran is the second largest country in the Middle East, with a population of nearly eighty million, not all of them being fanatics waking up every morning in the quest of making a nuclear bomb, as your media are relentlessly suggesting! All we heard for decades is the discussion on stopping Iran from developing nuclear technology and using it for military purposes. It is true. Iran is not your friend. Iran has been voicing many reprehensive speeches against the USA, against Israel; against the West…However, unlike some closer allies of the US in the Gulf region, Iran respects better gender equality, as pointed out by "Business insider": Women in Iran have the right to vote, drive and travel alone, unlike Saudi Arabia.

It is true that life is tough in Iran today. It is far from being a democracy. It is far from respecting human rights. It is far from freedom of speech and it is imposing a very rigorous and old-fashioned vision of Islam. But let me ask a question: who made it this way? Who killed a nascent democracy in this country back in the fifties? Guess what declassified CIA documents, revealed by the Guardian (a British newspaper!) are telling us? Yes, it is you. It is the Americans and the British who threw away Mohammed Mossadegh, the democratically elected Prime Minister in 1953. The CIA has admitted it was behind the Iranian Coup, the MI6 is still not willing to admit but evidence from the CIA seems to show their implication as well.

I thought you were the champions of Democracy, willing to bring it to any tiny piece of land on Earth, for the good of all human beings. Democracy, peace, and love! Am I wrong? Well, it is clear that you do not much like leaders who are too nationalist. There is a long list of them that you did not like: Nasser, Chavez, Castro… Mossadegh, was also one of them, but, at the difference of many, this one was democratically elected and he had democratic ideals! What is wrong with him then? What was wrong with him is he was a serious threat to your strategic economic interests in the region. He was jeopardizing the West's oil interests in Iran. He nationalized the British Anglo-Iranian Oil Company… I agree with you, never heard of… Its latter name is BP, British Petroleum, the biggest company in the UK and one of the top five oil companies in the world! For sure, this should ring a bell, or you must be an alien.

In the fifties, Iran was on its way to enjoy democracy, but it committed the crime that you could not tolerate. Forget about human rights, independence of nations, all those nice buzz words…no! Your economic interests were at stake, and this has cost Iran its democracy and probably some barrels of oil as well. The CIA and the MI6 installed a pro-western Monarchy in Iran and your companies never stopped pumping the oil. To maximize your benefits, you helped Iran's dictatorial regime build a strong army, which was a good way of not wasting all the money you paid them into development projects, better get your arms factories work at full load… and you helped this new ally build a strong political police, the sadly famous Savak, which helped maintain the stability of this regime, a regime that forgot they had a population to feed and to educate.

You put the seeds of what was meant to happen: a revolution! This one was an Islamic Revolution. Probably the first of its kind, and it took everyone by surprise. It shows the power of spiritual forces against tyranny! Yes, in the introduction about Iran, we did not yet mention that Persia was also home to one of the world's oldest civilizations back three thousand years BC. At its pinnacle under the rule of Cyprus the Great, it became the largest empire the world had yet seen. Before being an Islamic land, Persia was home to Zoroastrianism, the religion or philosophy founded by Zarathustra, and which is one of the oldest monotheist religions that influenced Judaism, Christianity, and Islam. The approach was a simplification of the pantheon of ancient Iranian gods into truth and lie, good and evil… same story isn't it! Who is good and who is evil is in many instances a matter of prospective!

Persia is also the home to the frame story of the world famous "One thousand and one nights" folk tales, which are often referred to in English as the "Arabian nights". This collection of stories, which probably originated in Persia from an Indian background before being translated and completed in Arabic, has influenced authors as diverse as Henry Fielding, Flaubert, HG Wells, Proust, Borges, Salman Rushdie or Naguib Mahfouz! If you are not familiar with the famous Scheherazade, and the infamous Shahryar, you would certainly know that Sindbad was a sailor, that Aladdin had a magic lamp and that Ali Baba was in trouble with forty thieves, all stories embedded in the "Nights"! Persia has made genies and flying carpets part of the world's common fantasy. Yes, you should know by now, it is not Disney who did that…

Going back to real life, what geopolitical role is Iran playing in the Middle East and its never stabilizing map? It is fueling the Houthi rebellion in Yemen and helping them against the Saudi-led coalition. It is also supporting Hezbollah in Lebanon and potentially Bashar Al Assad in Syria. Another source of conflict with Saudis will be the oil. Iran sits on the world's fourth largest reserves, and it needs to push its production high, as it needs the money to recoup from years of economic stagnation. This would come at the expense of Saudi Arabia, either by further pushing the oil prices down or by eating up Saudi market share. The cold war that exists between Iran and Saudi Arabia can easily transform into a real war. You played it right. You are intelligently reviving this old Persian/Arabic rivalry, and the good news is that you will provide the arms. No matter who wins or loses, you are a winner in all cases.

LIBYA

This is another evil country! Actually, used to be…when it was ruled by the "Revolution Guide" Kaddafi. Now, it is not anymore. It is chaos, just like a lot of what has come out from the so-called "Arab Spring". Of course, you would not want to go there now. Too many weapons still in circulation, unless you want to go for some nice ammunition shopping. Yes, you can get a new Kalashnikov or an RPG at mind-blowing low prices! Everything is on sale. Not necessarily used, but the offer is so much higher than demand. It is flowing to the neighboring Tunisia on one side and Egypt on the other side, nothing scary, but does not really help stability in the region. Does it help democracy? Why had the West and its allies to pour all those weapons in Libya? Was it an NRA sponsored move? Were you fighting for the legitimate rights of every Libyan to have weapons? I thought they were all evil, just yesterday…

Getting back to the former Libyan leader, at least, he succeeded in putting Libya on the map! He was famous, and so was his country, before the Arab Spring broke through and you got to know of Tunisia and so many others… he had his own marketing ways. Indeed, there are serious reasons to dislike the guy, I agree, and in any case, he is dead now, but at least, he was fun. Watching a Kaddafi public address was as fun as watching the Simpsons! You will hear so many strange statements that you would not know if he was serious or making a joke! When you hear him seriously assert that Shakespeare is of Arab origin and that his name was initially Sheikh Zoubeir, you really wonder how heavy he is on ecstasy or pot!

There was one interesting story about him that I was quite surprised to read: according to Jean-Jacques Servant Schreiber (the founder of the weekly news French magazine, l'Express) and his book "Le Défi Mondial" (the

World's Challenge) written in 1980, Kaddafi was the actual troublemaker behind the 1973-74 oil crisis. He was the one that first said enough to the oil super-majors that were taking the biggest portion of the oil profits, leaving so little to the producing countries… He was the one who was behind that re-equilibration of the balance in distributing those huge profits. At least in theory, because then, what was supposed to belong to the countries and their people ended up in the pockets of a happy few. Corruption took it all!

Libya was also famous for its "man-made river", a pharaonic project that took water from deep wells in the desert to feed coastal cities… I am not sure the economy was right or better than water desalination from a never ending resource that is sea water (deep fossil water is actually finite!), but the project has allowed so many western engineering and construction companies to make money that it is indeed a good project. Never mind the embargo that the US declared on Libya at that time. Business is business, and Libyan money is as good as anybody else's.

Post-revolution Libya is shaping up anyway. There are difficulties of course. People are divided. Tribal grievances have surfaced back, some violence is still happening. The State needs to be established, but money can cure it all, and oil money is not scarce in Libya. Had they had a visionary leader 20 years ago, the country could have been a real paradise, especially that it can rely on a huge marvelous coastline, still scattered with ancient roman ruins. Yes, Libya has some history! It also boasts a huge territory, mostly desert for sure, but Libya is three times bigger than France, the largest country in the European Union, and is one of the largest countries in Africa. Most of its little population, estimated at around 7 million in 2016 lives by the coast. Just like neighboring Tunisia, Libya was home to the Berbers. Phoenicians established trading counters and ancient Greeks some city-states in eastern Libya in a region that became known as Cyrenaica. Several other old civilizations have ruled the country at some stage. This includes Persians and Egyptians. It is however under the Roman Empire that Tripolitania, the region around Tripoli the current capital, became most prosperous, with a city called Leptis Magna which became one of the three major cities in the south of the Mediterranean Sea with Carthage and Alexandria. The city gave birth to a Pope known as Victor I.

From the history of Libya, one can see its current fragility as a State. Indeed, we have already mentioned two notable regions or provinces: Cyrenaica and Tripolitania. There is a third one which is Fezzan, the south western part of Libya, mainly home to Tuareg and Toubou nomadic tribes. These three provinces were not always united under one ruler and have had at large portions of time a different history, even under the long-lasting rule of the Ottoman Empire. After the Italian-Turkish war, Italy turned Libya into a colony where it sent over 150 thousand Italians and killed half of the Bedouin population. After World War II, Great Britain administered the Tripolitania and the Cyrenaica provinces while the French administered Fezzan, all before King Idris proclaimed the independence of the United Kingdom of Libya in 1951.

Going back to more recent history, as President Obama eventually admitted, there was something wrong in what was done in Libya. There was no plan for the day after Kaddafi is taken away. OK, Kaddafi got killed and the people "liberated"! What's next?... Chaos; No State able to control the whole country; Militia ruling different parts, according to tribal affiliations, and plenty of oil, plenty of arms… the perfect theatre for ISIS to sneak in and that is exactly what they have done! Many Libyans have left their country, to settle in neighboring Tunisia amongst others. At some point in time, the number of Libyan immigrants in Tunisia was said to be over the million, which is close to 10% of the population of the country. Not easy for a recovering country and economy to cope with this massive influx…

This is also creating a serious security threat in the region, at the doors of Europe, making life very hard for all neighbors such as Egypt, Tunisia, Algeria, Chad, Niger or Sudan. Indeed, all the candidates for Jihad, for smuggling, for drugs in the region have been joining this new Eldorado where there is no police and no army to enforce any law. On top of that, plenty of arms are available to equip yourself, plenty of oil is available to travel long distances, and plenty of desert is there to help you hide. Libya has also become a platform for desperate people from sub-Saharan Africa willing to cross the sea to Europe. The business of illegal immigration is now booming. You can find "agents" with full service: hosting, official papers fabrication and transportation to the promised land from a coastline that is no more controlled!

SYRIA

Is Syria still a country today? Will it survive as such after all this is over? Or is the plan to split it in pieces, giving birth to Kurdistan on one hand, and enlarging Israel on the other hand… Do you really care? You started supporting the rebellion against Assad, the son! Indeed, the Syrian regime has created a new model of governance, the inherited Presidency! Bashar El Assad took over from his late father, Hafez. He inherited the throne. No Syria is not a Monarchy, not anymore… It is a Republic, and, yes, the son took over as President. No, he did not win elections. In our part of the world, we save on elections. Why loose taxpayer money? Why the spent? It is costly, it is uncertain… better organize things in a predictable and efficient way.

OK, lets us go back to the revolution in Syria. You eventually discovered that those guys whom you were training to take Bashar down were fundamentalists, not really the kind of people you would want in power. A journalist from the French magazine "Le Point" said that you had a plan to create a 15 000-soldiers' independent army, and for the purpose of training these "new Syrian forces", you have dedicated 500 million dollars. The first cohort, named the 30th division, was back to Syria in July 2015…

Initially, it was Russia who has helped Assad resist, against your actions and those of the Europeans. We had in Syria a new cold war "ambiance"! Each of you was using it as a battleground, or, should I say, a playground for your favorite old game with Russia!

Today, the media are telling us that you were not completely wrong and the people you wanted to support deserved it and still deserve it. They are not the real fundamentalists. They are "light" fundamentalists. There exists a third party which is the real threat, which you are not supporting, but which is equally fighting Assad! That is ISIS. However, if I refer to the old saying "the enemy of my enemy is my friend", then, it seems to me that your trainees are objectively associated with ISIS in the fight against Assad. They are buying their oil too… with the same transitivity principle, if they are friends of ISIS and they are your friends, you become friends of ISIS…This is getting confusing!

You are saying that the first are nice while the second are evil, and you are supporting the first and fighting the second. You are making targeted strikes to manage this situation, and you still want Assad out, while he is fighting both of them! Your media have done a lot of Russia-bashing when M. Poutine decided he will be involving his military forces in Syria, because he decided that he will be supporting Assad and attacking indistinctly all fundamentalists, be they "light" or not! Many in the Arab World feel that he is probably right. Fundamentalists are fundamentalists! Better find another alternative to Assad… In any case, if you have no real solution to replace him, as was the case in Iraq and then in Libya, better leave him alone!

Add to that the Israelis on the Golan heights. They are colonizing this territory since the 1967 war. They took it from Syria and never gave it back. Why not? Well, first, no one is asking, at least, nobody serious is really insisting. And it has some good water resources and a nice view on the neighboring plains…

Add to that the Kurds, and all the stories of support from the Turkish Kurds to the Iraqi Kurds… in the parts of Syria, Turkey and Iraq that informally make up the Kurdistan!

There does not seem to be an issue! Not in the short term at least. This country, or what is left from it, has been in total chaos and civil war for years now. The balance of power does not seem to go in a given direction. The external forces help maintain all belligerents alive and provide good customers to the arms industry, your industry? If all these wars did not exist, one would have to invent them! Otherwise, these precious industries would collapse and yield to more unemployment in your economies…

Meanwhile, the flood of migrants out of Syria is just becoming horrendous. They are fleeing war, malnutrition, non-education… They are looking to simply live. This migration juggernaut is now headed for Europe, after having flooded several neighboring countries such as Egypt, Lebanon, Jordan, Turkey… a report from the World Bank says that more than 12 million Syrians – half the population in 2010 – have fled their homes. They face life-threatening security incidents, deteriorating livelihoods, lack of access to basic needs and severe unemployment, leading to tremendous budgetary pressure…"A preliminary World Bank-led assessment of damage in six cities in Syria showed an estimate of $3.6-4.5 billion as of end 2014. The report focused on damage in Aleppo, Deraa, Hama, Homs, Idlib, and Latakia, over seven sectors - housing, health, education, energy, water and sanitation, transport, and agriculture - and it is not improving!

On top of that, the report says "Syria's neighboring countries (Turkey, Lebanon, Jordan, Iraq, and Egypt) have borne the brunt of the economic impact of the war. The cost to the five countries is close to $35 billion in output, measured in 2007 prices, equivalent to Syria's GDP in 2007". Clearly, the whole region is paying the price, and getting no support for it. These countries found themselves in the middle of a mess they did not ask for, and which the West has heavily contributed to.

What else to expect? Well, terrorism in Western Europe could be another side-effect of all this Syrian mess… In a paper dating back to early 2015, the Brookings Institution was warning from the return of western foreign fighters from Syria and Iraq. Large numbers of people are involved: close to a thousand French, over 500 from UK, Germany, and Belgium… The killings in Paris have inaugurated a new way of carrying terror actions. What is frightening about it is that it is making it so easy and cheap: a few crazy chaps willing to die, and a few Kalashnikov machine guns can have a death toll of over a hundred.

Of course, by Syrian standards, these numbers are nothing. That has been their average tribute paid to revolution every week since the start of their Civil War. Hundreds of thousands of Syrians have died since the start of the fights against the Assad regime. They have had air strikes, bombs, tanks, machine guns, missiles, innerving gas… they have had it all. Only nuclear weapons are missing. The population got trapped in between many fighting factions, and they have lost family, friends, homes, goods… What is the situation of the children not having access to education, nor healthcare for years? Here again, World Bank assessment is that 13 million children are out of school in Syria, Yemen, Iraq and Libya. This is a real disaster and a time bomb for the future. The damage to the human capital will take much longer to heal…

What a sad outcome for a nation who has probably witnessed in the early days of humanity the birth of agriculture, and later on, the start of the Bronze Age. Syria is at the crossroads of several commercial routes. It has witnessed the presence of many different civilizations and cultures: ancient Egyptians, Hittites, Assyrians, Canaanites, Arameans, Persians, Greeks, Romans,

Byzantines, Arabs, Crusaders, Mongols, Ottomans, French… In the history of the Arab world, Damascus became famous during the Umayyad period as it became the capital of the growing Muslim empire, before the Abbasids left it for Bagdad…

The brutality and stupidity of the ISIS militia reminded us also that Syria is home to Palmyra. They engaged in destroying this ancient city, which was part of the Roman empire. Its queen, Zenobia, self-proclaimed an independent empire within the Roman empire but was eventually defeated by Aurelius in 270 BC. Palmyra fell into the same hands that made Raqqa hell for its inhabitants. Palmyra's treasures got destroyed but ISIS cannot erase history. Palmyra got eventually liberated, by Bashar Al Assad's army with the help of Russia and the world applauded to this liberation…

All this rich history, this mix of cultures and religions, does not seem to be of any help today. The West seems to be determined to remove Bashar Al Assad, and makes it a priority, while the first priority on the ground should be to get people back to a normal life. He is certainly not a great democrat; his regime was probably severely corrupt and his family taking a major portion of the wealth created in the country. But look at what is looming now as a replacement! Is that really what you want? How in the world would that be a better option for the population? For the neighboring countries? For the world? Things have gone too far now. Someone will have to fix the mess!

YEMEN

One other of the countries that was making the news almost on a daily basis since the so-called Arab Revolutions… Yemen is now chaos. Each day brings its toll of dead people. A bombing in a Mosque or near the Presidential palace: a hundred dead, forty dead, fifteen… I am not sure if you would qualify it as evil or not. Nobody really seems to care. It is a small neighbor to oil-rich Saudi Arabia but does not represent a serious menace on the oil economy. They can continue killing themselves. There will be fewer fools at the end.

And yet, if you look back into history, Yemen is surely the deepest-rooted country in the Arabian Peninsula. It has a rich history and has seen the birth (and death) of many civilizations. Some local legends claim that Cain and Abel (the sons or Adam and Eve!) are buried in the city of Aden. Their story about jealousy and anger can be found in the Torah, the Bible, and the Quran. The harbor city of Aden lies in the crater of an ancient volcano. It gives its name to the Gulf of Aden, at the cross-roads of Africa and Asia and dates back at least to the 7th century BC under the Kingdom of Awsan. Before the Yemenite reunification, it used to be the capital of the South Yemen republic in the seventies.

The current capital, Sanaa, is also an ancient and famous city. It is one of the oldest continuously inhabited cities in the World. According to local legends, the city was founded by Shem, the son of Noah. The oldest known copy of the Quran was found in Sanaa in 1972. The city is located 2300 m above sea level, at the crossroads of ancient commercial routes. It has been inhabited for more than 2500 years and its old fortified city contains several architectural gems that have been classified as World Heritage by UNESCO. It boasts probably the first skyscrapers built by men. The houses are several stories high and decorated with elaborate friezes.

Another famous city in Yemen is Marib, which was probably the capital of the ancient kingdom of Saba (or Sheba), cited in the three monotheist religions. Marib has a 3000 years old temple, and the oldest dam built on earth, dating back to around 1500 BC. Saba was known mainly for its queen, who went to Jerusalem at the end of the tenth century BC to meet the king Salomon. Saba had rival kingdoms in the neighborhood, like Hadramout and Qataban, but probably the most surprising in this area was Himyar. Starting around 100 BC, the Himyarite kingdom conquered Saba, Qataban and Hadramout, and reigned over most of Yemen until around 525 AD. Surprising because, around 380 AD, the Himyarite kings decided to abandon polytheism and convert to Judaism, making Himyar a unique Jewish kingdom in Arabia. At the beginning of the 20th century, there were still thousands of Jews living in Yemen. However, with the creation of Israel, many of them were flown there but it was not easy for them to integrate...

As we were just describing, Yemen is full of history and the home to many nice legends that will speak to anyone of Jewish, Christian, or Muslim background... It could also be the next Star Wars or Jurassic Park destination with the island of Socotra. This unique place is home to an incredible flora that seems directly inspired from a Science Fiction movie. The "lost world" of Socotra is home to around 800 rare species of flora and fauna, some dating back to more than 20 million years, and with a major part of them that cannot be seen anywhere else on the planet. One of the big stars of the island is the Dragon's blood tree. Another bizarre one is the desert rose or bottle tree...

Despite all of this, Yemen is the poorest country in the Arabian Peninsula, and the second most populated, with a population close to that of Saudi Arabia, in the range of 26 million. That makes it a real threat to the "peace" of oil-rich monarchies and oil extraction! Since antiquity, Yemen has been a territory of confrontation of neighboring super-powers: Persia on the one side, Byzantium on the other side, Ethiopia on the third one with its Aksum empire... Yemen is today the territory of an indirect confrontation between Saudi Arabia and Iran. It is the territory of the resurrection of an ancient war: Sunna against Shia.

Indeed, after the fall of the Shiite kingdom that was installed in Yemen, a country that was divided between Ottoman Empire and British rule, in the sixties, Yemen was split in two countries that united only in the nineties, under the rule of President Ali Abdallah Saleh. The country was very much dependent on Saudi Arabia (KSA) aid for its finances. The relationship with KSA got seriously destabilized with the Iraqi invasion of Kuwait...Since the early 2000, the country is subject to insurrections from the Houthis, a Zaydi Shia faction, which represents 40% of the population of the northern part. With the advent of the "Arab Spring", President Saleh was pushed out and a new President was elected. However, the rebellion movements increased, and the Houthis were able to enter the Presidential Palace in 2015. It should be pointed out that these people are not necessarily good friends of Al Qaida in the Arabian Peninsula, the local franchise of Ben Laden's creation. Al Qaida is rather Sunnite and Salafi, while these people are Shia and closer to Iran ideologically.

All this trouble at its southern frontier has eventually led Saudi Arabia to conduct a strong military action in Yemen, starting at the end of March 2015. It was supposed to be a quick war to "reinstate" the legitimate power in place in the country. KSA gathered an "Arab coalition" to give this war some international accreditation. However, years later and thousands of dead and injured and displaced people later, this war seems to be still on-going. It is not making the headlines anymore, but it is having dramatic consequences on the population. The Houthis have been reacting even in Saudi territory, and there is a group that claims they will be liberating Najran, Aseer and Jizan, provinces that KSA has annexed in 1934 and that no Yemenite government ever dared to claim back. The old demon of secession has also been reactivated and the South is once again willing to separate from the North. And above all this, this complete chaos has offered a fertile ground to the local Al Qaeda branch to develop, as well as Daesh to start a franchise, as could be noted from terror acts claimed by each of these organizations! It is spurring competition among villains to dispute this new territory. Al Qaeda seems even to have been able to control the port city of Mukalla at some point in time.

According to the World Bank, before the war, more than half of Yemen's population lived in extreme poverty (below $1.9 a day). After the war, the numbers have dangerously increased, and it is estimated now that over 20 million people in Yemen can be considered poor. Humanitarian needs were estimated mid 2015 at about $1.6 billion, but no one was willing to help… in 2017, the situation got even more apocalyptic: half a million people have been hit by the worst cholera epidemic ever as reported by the New York Times or the BBC! A child dies every ten minutes from malnutrition according to UNICEF…

And what is happening to all the beautiful UNESCO World Heritage of Yemen with the Saudi bombing? As you might expect, there are several "collateral damages" … Over thirty sites have been damaged or completely ruined since the start of this "war". As reported by Fanny Arlandis in the

French newspaper "Le Monde", the temple of Nakrah in the antique town of Baraquish is among the "victims". And so is the medieval fortress of Al Qahira. In the capital Sanaa, over 5000 of the 9000 old traditional houses have been hit by air strikes. In May 2015, the museum of Dhamar has been destroyed and over 12000 objects dating back to 3500 BC have disappeared. In the western world, no one voiced his anger to see all this happening, as the main protagonist is the Saudi army, while everyone has commented the destruction of Palmyra in Syria and Nimrud in Iraq by ISIS. Some claim that the Saudis are clearly targeting specific historic sites in Yemen as a way of directly attacking the collective history and memory of their today's enemy. The city of Saada, the birthplace of Zaydi Shia, has been especially bombed, and so was the dam of Marib, even though it had no strategic military value. Some other people claim that Wahhabi KSA is chasing all pre-Islamic monuments. At the same time, Al Qaeda has been targeting the tombs of Sufi saints, in a move to erase all traces of Sufism in Yemen. The Houthis on their side have destroyed the unique Christian cemetery in the country as well as an Indian mosque.

This war in Yemen, which is no more a civil war, has many flavors of a war on the very identity of the Yemenite people, on their history and it is actually targeting what is probably the oldest civilization of the Arabian Peninsula, but no one seems to care! No oil and no money. No one is interested in the misery of what is also the poorest country in this region.

The only concern for the global community as pointed out by some consultancies is Bab El Mandeb and its potential closure! What is Bab El Mandeb? It is the strait that separates Yemen on the Arabian Peninsula from Djibouti and Eritrea on the horn of Africa. It is an important junction in the global crude oil trade, as well as LNG (liquefied natural gas) with over 3.8 million barrels per day crossing in 2013. People can die in Yemen, that is not a real issue, but hey, no one should mess around with the oil flowing so close…

QATAR

This small rich Arab state is one of the numerous oil and gas gifted countries in the Gulf. It is a peninsula of roughly eleven thousand square meters, inhabited by an estimated 2.9 million people in June 2020, of which only some 300 thousand nationals, all the rest being expatriates… and there is even another category that you will not find in many places: the "bidoun", which in Arabic means "without" … Indeed, several thousands of Qatari-born people have been denied the nationality. For some, it has been revoked as a political act in 2005, Qatar took off their nationality from some six thousand people belonging to the Al Ghafran clan of Al Murrah Bedouin.

Qatar is now famous for its major media asset, the Al Jazeera TV channel, that people called at a point in time the Arab CNN, and its sporty off springs, the BEIN channels that have negotiated football rights all over the planet, and also for its "Cheikha" Mozah, the mother of the ultra-rich Cheikh who is investing all over the world. She was the first lady when Qatar started becoming famous, but Sheikh Hamad, her husband, resigned in favor of his son Tamim, for some unknown reasons. Maybe he was just being cautious, knowing how power has changed in the past in the Emirate. Indeed, Cheikh Hamad himself has removed his own father, Cheikh Khalifa, back in 1995 while the latter was travelling abroad. His father has removed his cousin, Cheikh Ahmad Bin Ali, in 1972...Cheikh Hamad probably preferred to anticipate!

Coming back to the wealth and Qatari investments around the world, there is some confusion on whether it is the Emir's personal wealth or his family's or the country's wealth through a sovereign fund… there are countries where these things happen, and they are not often considered to be democracies! That does not preclude them from being well thought of in the

West, especially in the US or in this particular case, in France, where Qatar's money has been flowing steadily…

Qatar has managed to secure the organization of the FIFA World Cup of football for the year 2022! To win the bid, Qatar promised to build fully covered and air-conditioned stadiums…That's expensive! But, as one recent satiric French show "les Guignols de l'Info" has mocked, nothing's too expensive for the small Emirate: buying the "Paris Saint Germain" football club, buying several landmark real estate properties in the French Riviera… nothing really except getting the Pope go out on St Peter's square and pray "Allah Akbar"! Do not worry, it did not happen, and will probably never happen! There are, fortunately, things that money cannot buy…

Qatar now, in my part of the Arab world, the poor one, is perceived as being one of your instruments in the region and clearly a strong support of the Muslims Brotherhood movement. It does the job that the US want to do but do not want to show… Qatar is seen as the provider of the arms in the war in Libya. It is seen as the provider of financing for several of our Islamist parties and associations… It is seen as the little toy that the US is using in the region to play the game. They get some prestige against pouring a lot of money. Many, in the streets of this part of the Arab world also see Qatar as the traitor that maintains good ties with Israel, conforming here to the policy that the US is dictating to them.

To be honest, I have seen Aljazeera initially as the Arab CNN. It was the first and only Arab channel to have that free tone to tackle political and economic information in the region. I really enjoyed it… But then, I started discovering that, despite the fact that Aljazeera conveyed a lot of information with no compromise, it never dared criticize the Emir of Qatar! Is he so good that all he does is perfect? Or is it one of those non-written rules, which eventually meant that there is a bias in what Aljazeera is serving in the homes of Tunis, Cairo, or Tripoli… Many agree that Aljazeera, in conjunction with several social media internet sites, has positively contributed to the Arab uprising and revolutions, but there is now a shared perception that Aljazeera has mainly played the card of the fundamentalists. It has probably helped "Ennahdha" Islamist party in Tunisia more than anyone else. It is playing a similar role in all Arab countries. The question is: how does this benefit to Qatar? Or to the US? Or to Israel? This is the suspicion that you will now find in the Arab street. I am sad to see that Qatar is starting to gather a lot of hate… Wrong or right, this is the perception, and in our modern world, perception is the truth!

I am sad to see this because I have had the opportunity to meet in Tunisia a Qatari minister. We were a small group of people having breakfast with him, and I initially went there mainly pushed by curiosity, not really expecting much. I must admit that I was impressed by the guy. In his late forties, he was a lawyer by education, a jet-pilot by training, and had a perfect knowledge of so many geopolitical intricacies. He was also very sharp, very direct…which is not always the image we have of the culture in this region of the world, where you would not really say things so bluntly. He was very curious to know what we had in mind to develop the country, the projects we could think of in relation to Africa… He insisted that we should develop a common vision already within the country, and then, be able to sell it to attract investors. His speech was very simple and very true and full of business sense. It reminded me that Qatar was also having some great successes in the Telecom business through a company called Ooredoo, in the banking sector with QNB, and in the hospitality sector as well.

This leaves me with a lot of mixed feelings towards Qatar. It is displaying so many contrasted images and opposite signs! On the one hand, it is developing fast, securing a top three worldwide position in the GDP/capita race; it is embracing modernity with a twenty-first century capital city; it is opening to the outside world with huge investments abroad and significant media, sports and telecom assets… On the other hand, it is still adopting a very backward approach of Salafi Wahhabi Islam; it is corned by so many human rights institutions regarding basic freedoms in the country, the treatment of Asian immigrants or the situation of the "bidoun"; it is still a place for crony capitalism, corruption, and money laundering… It should not be this difficult to play it right though. It is only a matter of will, and all the positive ingredients are there!

UAE

Or maybe should I say Dubai! You might have not heard of the United Arab Emirates, nor its capital Abu Dhabi, but you have surely heard about Dubai, and all its Guinness book of records achievements. Dubai, it is the tallest man-made building on earth, Burj Khalifa; it is one of the most eye-popping buildings, Burj Al Arab; it is one the most intriguing reclamation projects, the Palms islands. Dubai has a skiing slope in the desert (yes, really, you can ski, with outside temperatures of over 30° Celsius). Dubai is an incredible blend of nationalities and ethnic groups making up 80% of its population, leaving 20% or less for the locals. Dubai is business, Dubai is leisure. It really has to be seen.

When you get there, you can have a feel of what a visionary leader can do. The vision is there, and execution is even better. You might say this is an oil-rich country, and money is the key. Then, why isn't this happening in so many other places in the world, which are definitely richer than Dubai? Dubai has managed to bring that money in. It is providing an environment that thrills people and investors. This is the country that makes me feel "I am proud to be an Arab" because yes, Dubai and the Emirates are an Arab country. Usually when you are thinking of Arab countries, you have the image of poverty, of poor education, low service level, unpredictable environment. This is certainly still the case in many of the Arab nations, despite the Arab spring…

The UAE has an interesting position between Asia on the one hand and Europe and Africa on the other hand. It has had the vision to leverage this geography to become a unique logistics platform and more generally, a business hub between these regions. It has developed free trade zones, an extraordinary Ports infrastructure, either by sea or by air, with the latter becoming the home of the largest airline carrier in the World, Emirates. Dubai airport is said to have become the biggest in passengers' traffic overtaking Heathrow (UK), JFK (US) and Narita (Japan).

The country has managed to put itself in a virtuous loop and keeps growing and improving as time goes by. In a way, it might have had the inspiration from the Singapore model, and it has further built on it. It is building on a vision of excellence, of hard work, and the provision of an open environment that attracts talent. Yes, this is happening in an Arab country, and an Arab and Islamic country. This spirit was one of the key factors of success of the US as well. It has been the magnet that pulled much of the worldwide talent to the American Dream!

In February 2016, the Ruler of Dubai and Prime Minister of the Emirates has appointed a State Minister for Happiness headed by a woman. In a Twitter post, Sheikh Mohamed said that this Minister would "align and drive government policy to create social good and satisfaction". This move came as part of a larger government reshuffle which has seen the creation of a State Ministry of Tolerance, also headed by a woman, while a third woman, aged 22, became Minister of Youth… How will all this translate into reality? I am not sure. In terms of image and communication, it is really efficient, and it is doing the job of contributing to modernize the image of the UAE on the institutional and social levels. It points out that the ultimate goal being sought for the population is welfare and wellbeing. It is not just about economy, money, and infrastructure. Those are the means, not the goals. The goal is really about people and how they feel. The first country to have raised this issue, and maybe it is tied up with the essence of their religion, which is Buddhism, is Bhutan. This small kingdom of South Asia in the Eastern Himalayas has a population of less than a million. It has been promoting the concept of "Gross National Happiness" (GNH) instead of the traditional GDP (Gross Domestic Product) used in economy. As put forward by Dragon King Jigme Singye Wangchuck "GNH is the bridge between the fundamental values of kindness, equality and humanity and the necessary pursuit of economic growth". I definitely subscribe to this philosophy that focuses more on spirituality at the expense of the more western materialism!

PAKISTAN

Once a close friend of yours, turned into a villain where your drones were killing an average ten people a day… I might be exaggerating a bit, but this is certainly what Pakistanis, most Pakistanis think of you today… I read in a 2014 issue of "Time Magazine" a post from a lady from Islamabad, questioning what the magazine has written on "the overwhelming success" of drones, and reminding the readers of "the crisis posed by the killings of Pakistanis in defiance of international law". This is exactly what I was discussing the other day with a friend from Karachi, who now lives in Saudi. He told me that most of his family has left the country because of insecurity. He explained to me the growing resentment against Americans in the population, which is feeling since 9/11 and since the various wars against Taliban and Osama Bin Laden that it is being collectively punished for a crime it did not commit.

Pakistan is probably the unique nation that was born to be Muslim. With the independence movements to free British India, there were leaders like Nehru and Gandhi but also Mohamed Ali Jinnah. The latter was advocating for the concept of two nations, one to host Hindus and one for the Muslims. In 1947, Pakistan and India became two independent dominions within the Commonwealth of Nations. However, with a badly defined status for Cashmere, they ended up fighting each other there. There were also major populations transfers: millions of Hindus going to India and millions of Muslims to Pakistan. An important issue was facing the newly born Muslim nation at the onset: there were two parts of Pakistan, the occidental one, speaking mainly Urdu and the oriental one, speaking mainly Bengali. The two parts were separated by 1600 kilometers of Indian land! That does not help build a nation, and what was meant to be eventually happened in 1971: the oriental part separated from the occidental one, proclaiming the new state of

Bangladesh, with some help from the Indian army…

One can see that the birth and childhood of Pakistan were not easy. It is however a major nation in South Asia today with a territory bigger than France or Germany and a population of roughly 200 million, making it the second Muslim nation after Indonesia, and one of the most populous nations worldwide. The country has had extended periods of military rule since its inception, and is still suffering from problems of illiteracy, poverty, overpopulation, corruption, and terrorism. The armed forces are very important, ranking among the top 10 in the world, in a nation that is part of the very select club of nuclear powers.

What is wrong with Pakistan today? Why has it become a CIA operations territory, where people believe that even some suicide bombers were manipulated by intelligence agencies, and are not really those fanatics that we want the world's public opinion to think… I must admit that I have very little knowledge of this country and all its complexities. It is for me a big nation. I somehow see it as a "Muslim" India. The people I have met in France, Dubai or KSA were hard workers, and many of them very clever. The ones I have met were not the typical fanatic guy either… However, all we hear in the news is quite frightening. There is not a day where you do not hear about a suicide bombing, an ethnic or religious fight, in any case, a drama that has claimed the lives of tens of people. And this is reported quietly in the news, no more emotionally at all, as if that is normal life in Pakistan.

In any case, it is so remote, they are so different, who really cares? They can keep killing each other… Still, Pakistan is in a very geostrategic region. It is at the crossroads of Iran, Afghanistan, Russia, India and China. And it has an important population. What will happen next? Today, the friendship with the US seems to be at a dead-end. Will China get involved? There are already talks of concessions and military zones… will the country eventually manage to get some stability?

DRONES

It seems that Google has a serious strategy to use Drones for goods delivery. It has abandoned the idea of internet everywhere through Titan Aerospace drones, but with "project Wing", it has delivered burritos in Australia with drones, as reported in 2019! This is following up an initiative from Amazon who said it will be using drones in the future to deliver books! What a wonderful, peaceful world we will live in… Culture, education and well-being will be dispensed at your door by high tech companies. Your grandchildren will probably wonder how we could live in a world where no drones existed to provide us with such essential services…

The less disciplined will probably also be misusing drones to do some graffiti scribbles, as reported by Wired, the tech magazine, making a headline on "the age of Drone vandalism"! We owe to Katsu, a graffiti artist and vandal, the marvelous invention of a "Spraycopter" which is a quadcopter equipped with an automated spraying can. He managed to reach one of the most viewed NYC billboards and put a red tag on Kendall Jenner's face. A new advertising method for Kelvin Klein? If they are not happy, they might consider hiring a protective drones' squad for their billboards… A machine war in your neighborhood?

Some other people are claiming that drones will bring a great revolution in the world of project management for industry, construction and real estate. Drones will be able to report progress through fantastic aerial views and we will be able to follow up execution handily. However, if we do not start thinking very fast on how we would regulate drones' flights above us, they will soon be as numerous and annoying as flies or mosquitoes, much bigger in shape though!

Some other applications are for the sporty ones. You can pilot your drone with your mobile phone to make it film your latest sports performance, be it bicycling in a fantastic scenery or rafting down a whitewater rapid. Of course, keep your drones off airport zones. In March 2016, many French media were commenting the fact that an Air France Airbus A320 almost collided with a drone while it was readying to land in Charles-de-Gaulle airport. It is estimated that the drone came as close as five meters from the left wing of the plane at an altitude of 5500 feet. This was scary! No one talked about any terrorist attack…In December 2018, several flights were canceled at London Gatwick airport because of drone intrusions close to the runways.

Meanwhile, the truth is that today, the sole real application of drones, if I forget about those gadget mini-drones that start to sell for kids in the wealthy world, the sole application of drones is in the military world, and it is completely shifting the paradigm of war. Indeed, just like in a 2015 Si-Fi movie starring Harrison Ford, that showed mankind recruiting youngsters who were the best at video gaming to save us from another Alien invasion, war though a drone camera is as unreal as a video game…

With the humongous success of the Predator, which development program has cost over $2.3 billion, General Atomics, an American private company working especially for the US army, is now proposing a more advanced version named Reaper. The drones have evolved from surveillance tools into engagement weapons. They can carry Hellfire and Stinger missiles as well as laser-guided bombs. As they have become customers of this fantastic technology, France and the UK have announced the commitment of 1.5 billion pound to a development program. At least, Dassault Aviation, Thales, BEA systems and Rolls-Royce to cite a few will also benefit from their respective governments investments in the field…

Hey, see that terrorist there in his pickup truck in that desert village in Afghanistan (or whatever Something-istan, who cares)? Wait, there are at least four of them, they are disguised, the back of the truck is surely packed with bombs and arms… Shoot before they escape! The young guy behind the joystick in his Nevada army base presses the button. Gone with the truck, and the people riding it, and yes, there were some collateral damages to the people around… Wait a minute, those were not terrorists, in fact a group of women going to a wedding? Too late. What a mess. I need a break. Too much time behind the screen and my head is dizzy now! Those are the sole regrets that your young soldier might have.

The media keep telling us from time to time that such Al Qaeda general or that ISIS commander has been "terminated" by a selective American drone bombing. What would happen if some other nation decided to go for that CIA operative or NSA director in your neighborhood? Would it be a legitimate war or a terror act? Do you think it might be a "normal" counter-reaction, if they had the capability to do so? I still remember all the narrative that was used during the war against Iraq. You performed "chirurgical" strikes, very much targeted to military installations, as the media kept saying. They sometimes admitted for "collateral damages". Clearly, no one was listening to those Iraqis on the ground saying: "stop your chirurgical war, we do not have social security"!

Is this war as you do it now? Or should it be called state terrorism? In any case, it is the end of war as theorized by Clausewitz. No more values, heroism, virility… Welcome to the zero-risk war, to the virtual war, to the coward war, which looks like a training exercise, at least on your side… the poor guys in their Afghan desert will probably have a different view. I doubt that they will be future customers for Google or Amazon! All they have had from drones are bombs. They will certainly be hard to convince that they can get books or pizzas delivered by drones…

AFGHANISTAN

Did you know that they used to love bikinis in the sixties? Women were wearing short dresses back then in the streets of Kabul! A nice amateur photo collection, shot by Professor Bill Podlich from Arizona during a two-year stint with UNESCO in Kabul, has been published by the Daily Mail of the UK. The journalist, Peggy Pemberton, chose this title "Life before the Taliban: Fascinating photos show short skirts, flash cars and no burqas before Afghanistan plunged into hell"! This sounds totally surrealistic today as all we see from Afghanistan on TV are Taliban bearded men, Burqa dressed women or whatever is underneath the Burqa, and killings, and explosions, and a totally faltering state with international forces fighting terrorists in some caves in the mountains…

It all started after the Soviet invasion in the eighties. Afghanistan was not making the news before that, not much… Now, even the "dumbest" person on earth has heard of it. OK, your red neck fellow will still need to be able to put it on a map, but they would know it is not their next holiday's destination!

When the Soviet Union invaded Afghanistan, it was supposed to be an easy one, a promenade… It ended up being a nightmare for the Russian soldiers, it was somehow their Vietnam! And all of us, in the "free world" were happy to see how those valorous "Mujahidin" were striking back the Red Army. By the way, did you notice that "Mujahidin" has the same Arabic roots as "Jihadists"? It all comes from "Jihad" … At that time "Jihad" was welcome and admired on all western media. It meant resistance! It is true that its target was the older evil enemy, the "East", the Soviet bloc, the bad guys that you were opposing in the world's domination battle, the tenants of the socialist system, which had its appeal in some third world countries. You were both fighting as dogmatically as we see religious fighters doing today.

The war in Afghanistan was not a "declared" East-West war. It was the Soviets against the Mujahidin. It was David against Goliath, and at that time, no one was qualifying those Mujahidin of terrorists. Their guerilla actions were against those Bolsheviks, and thus, it was a good fight, a legitimate fight…

Some people trace back the "birth" of Osama Bin Laden to this period. He was one of the "instruments" used against the Soviets. He was a creature of the CIA. I have no proof for sure. It is clear however that the Bin Laden family is a wealthy Saudi family, they were close to the Bushes, and the actions Osama started his "career" doing were "right"! They were in symphony with the West's policy in Afghanistan at least. He has certainly contributed to defeating the Russians there, and this is an achievement in its own!

Who trained him and his people? Who provided the logistics? Who provided the arms? Who provided the money? The red army is no easy enemy. Their pulling off from Afghanistan shows the evolving of the forces at stake and the dramatic power that small groups of people, not only armed with a strong faith, were able to achieve. This was the start of a whole new era in the history of terror, of non-governmental armed groups that were able to defeat one of the world's strongest and most organized armies! Thinking of it this way, this is a rather frightening prospective. This was also the beginning of a much troubled and obscure era in the history of Afghanistan: bye-bye bikinis! Welcome the black burqas. The dark age of ignorance and radicalism, thanks to the West?

Today, Afghanistan has become synonym of terror in the West. However, the people suffering the most from its new status are probably Afghans themselves. Regular bombings and terror acts happen in the country, a country which has been through a civil war before falling under the rule of the Taliban. The US eventually ousted them in 2001 to "place" a new President, Hamid Karzai. Formally, it was an international coalition under the command of NATO who was in charge of installing democracy in Afghanistan. Instead of becoming a model democracy, Afghanistan has become the first world producer of poppy, from which opium and heroin are extracted. The 30 million population of Afghanistan enjoyed a life expectancy of 45 years on average in 2011! It might have improved by a couple of years now, but that is definitely much lower than what one would expect in the 21st century, right?

Indeed, if they survive the harsh conditions, the drugs, the daily terror acts, the Afghans can still suffer from some "mistakes", just like the one that saw a "Doctors without Borders" hospital being shot by the crew of an US AC-130 aircraft in October 2015 in the city of Kunduz. 42 people were left dead. As reported by the New York Times, "even after Doctors without Borders informed American commanders that a gunship was attacking a hospital, the airstrike was not immediately called off". Of course, after a 3000-pages report, the Pentagon eventually decided to punish sixteen military personnel. They were facing "administrative sanctions". Well, it seems that their career will somehow suffer from this, probably not as much as the 42 people that were wrongly killed…

The only time where people will get a break in Afghanistan is harvest time. With the spring, the flowers blossom and the poppy bulbs are ripe for being scraped. The Taliban, who have not completed disappeared and who run whole regions of the country still today, let go their Kalashnikovs for some more peaceful tools. They go on the fields and "help" the farmers get the precious, but deadly gum. This is one of their best financing means, and funds are the rule of the game. If you have the money, you are the king and you can buy the hopes of thousands of people that live on less than a dollar a day. Desperation leads to manipulation. Add a little smoke and some spiritual varnish, and you have all ingredients to produce highly motivated little soldiers… The poppy culture provides some $3 billion in Afghanistan, mainly in the Helmand Province, under Taliban rule. It is not at all helping improve life conditions for the masses. It is fueling this planetary mess that has been fabricated by some Intelligence Agencies. During the harvest, not only do the Taliban collect money, lots of it, but they also have a chance to see new faces and make recruits. Tough times ahead for the Afghan army, which is getting NATO support only for training and which suffers from desertions and lack of professionalism.

SAUDI ARABIA

What comes first to your mind when you hear the name of this country? Oil? OPEC? Lawrence of Arabia? Bin Laden? One of the oldest and most reliable allies of the US in the Middle East? The country where Islam was born? The country where women are not allowed to drive (until 2019)? What image do you really have of Saudi Arabia?

I have been to KSA, the Kingdom of Saudi Arabia only two or three times in my life. Despite the fact or because of the fact of being an Arab, I did not get the best treatment at the airport! I must admit however that I have met several Saudis who were very nice and gentle people, many of whom having been educated abroad, and well aware of what is going on in the world.

It is a country of many contrasts. The "system" seems to be rather archaic and not willing to change. When I say the "system", I mean the apparent social, legal, political system. On the economical side, Saudi Arabia has huge ambitions, and despite a falling oil barrel price, still has the muscle to perform. The Petrodollars can do a lot: Infrastructure, industrial plants and even agriculture. Did you know that the biggest milking cattle breeding farms are in KSA? There are two such farms of some 50 000 cows together. By any standard, this is huge! At what cost of fodder are they developing them? that is another story… The newest initiative when it comes to agriculture and food security is pushing private Saudi companies to secure farm land abroad, in Africa for instance, and develop them, at the condition of bringing back home half of the production.

Saudi Arabia is rich, it has huge oil reserves. However, not all its people are rich. Compared to its neighboring countries with a very scarce population, countries that can afford to offer housing and many advantages to their nationals, because the wealth is such and the number is so small that the rulers can easily manage to make everyone happy by covering much more than their basic needs. Compared to its neighbors then, KSA has an important population. It is by far the most populous country of the so-called Gulf Cooperation Council, GCC, and this makes it difficult to simply spread the wealth among the 30 million people… There are unfortunately still a lot of poor, uneducated people in KSA, and despite all the "Saudization" programs that exist to impose a higher employment of nationals in public and private firms, companies are still using huge numbers of expats, at various levels of the organizations.

What is the perception of KSA in the Arab countries, or at least, in the Maghreb countries? There has always been a perception that it is a vassal of the USA. Many people believe it is a strong ally to the US in the region, second only to Israel. Having said that, this means that people did not necessarily have the best feelings towards KSA. What mitigates this kind of hard feeling in the Muslim world is that KSA is home of Mecca, the religious capital of Islam, the hometown of the prophet Muhammad, and this creates some empathy. This makes KSA one of the most visited "tourist" destinations in the world, because of the pilgrimage! I know it is not famous for its sandy beaches or its cocktail bars, but the huge influx of people willing to accomplish the religious rite in Mecca makes it one of the world's favorite destinations, worth 12 billion dollars a year. One thing that people do not necessarily know about this pilgrimage is that it existed before Islam! There was already some kind of ritual that helped Quraish, the prominent tribe of Mecca before Islam (and the tribe to which the Prophet belongs), establish it economic power in the region.

One important problem with Saudi Arabia is its approach to religion, to Islam! Still today, the country is dominated by the Wahabi reading of Islam, a very tough, rigorist approach, that does not seem to be compatible with the needed modernization of society.

The Wahabi approach to Islam in KSA has to do with the history of the reigning family. Back in 1745, Mohamed Ben Saud engaged in consolidating his power by the sword, and using an alliance with a man preaching the use of a "tough" and rigorist Islam, Mohamed Bin Abdel Wahab, thus "Wahabism"… Much later, in 1902, Abdelaziz Bin Saud also consolidated his power by the sword against the Rachidi tribe. He established the Kingdom in 1932 and self-proclaimed to be a king. He married several daughters of other tribes' chiefs to further install his authority and had 45 sons (I do not have the girls counts, not important after all some would say!).

In 1945, on board of the US Quincy warship, he signed with President Roosevelt the pact that positions the US as responsible for the security of the Gulf region in exchange of Oil. Responsible does not mean that it will finance it though! In fact, this made KSA become a major customer of the US military industry. From 2010 to 2013 alone, its purchasing budget was of 86 billion US dollars. That is a huge spent which corresponds to roughly 3 million dollars per Saudi inhabitant. That is more than a million dollars a year per person! It could have been a nice poverty relief policy if it were not helping the American arms industry grow, and probably the pockets of a happy few as well…

Back to our story of Abdelaziz Bin Saud, at his death, his son Saud became king in 1953 and was replaced by Faycal, another son, in 1964. The latter was probably one of most famous Saudi kings, because of the oil crisis of 1973-74, and because he was also in good shape while in power! After him came a succession of brothers who were already aged and not in good medical condition when accessing power. With the new king Salman now, a new generation is starting to make it to the limelight as the real power is in the hands of his son Mohamed Ben Salman, MBS, who is in his thirties!

However, things do not seem to be changing on the social side, at least, not fast enough… How can we accept that still these days, a woman can be beheaded in a central place of a major town in the country? How do you accept this from what you consider a close ally? I am not even talking about democracy and dictatorship and other governance matter. I am simply talking about human rights and justice and the way to perform this. Even if we accept that the death penalty still has its place in our 21st century world, it must be performed in a "humane" and discrete way. Having this punishment executed with a sword in front of the "mob", this is really a picture of the middle ages that is being shown.

In the year 2015, social media have been relaying an amusing job opening from the KSA government: they were looking for an executioner. Indeed, in the first part of 2015, the death penalty figures in the country were already exceeding the total numbers of 2014, and there was a need for more recruitments to help keep up with the beheading need. Great job creation! I wonder what the qualifications for this nerve depressing job should be. Is any experience in a slaughterhouse required? What should be the psychological profile of the candidates? You should not be fainting at the view of a blood fountain. May be a few years with Daesh can be considered as a bonus: some mass executions and some refinement in burning, drowning and slaughtering their poor victims are real assets. What are the benefits that come with such a job? Free drugs to anesthetize your consciousness?

One big irony is that KSA has been chosen to head the United Nations Human Rights Council in 2015. A clever French cartoonist has depicted this with a character representing KSA holding the head of a beheaded character representing the United Nations council mentioned above! If the international community continues to accept this, of course there will be other Bin Ladens… I must here apologize to the Bin Laden family. This is a well-known and reputable Saudi family whose name has been totally slaughtered, being associated with terrorism at an international scale! Osama Bin Laden and Al Qaeda were used to explain 80% of all our problems by western media!

CUBA

Now that we have made our tour of Arab or Muslim evils, which are certainly the majority on your bad guys list today, let us have a look at those who were more under the limelight for you in the sixties till the end of the century: the communist Latin American states. Those were the older personification of Evil in the minds of the north American public, and they were a neighboring threat to America's model and well-being. At the forefront, we can certainly find Cuba, and its military junta, and its missiles once pointed to the US…

Cuba is where Christopher Columbus landed during his first discovery trip in 1492, after Hispaniola, where he sank his flagship, the Santa Maria. It is the biggest island of the Caribbean and was a Spanish colony for roughly four centuries. At the start of its independence war, in 1895, Cuba got some help from the US, and ended up moving from Spanish rule to US rule! With the Paris treaty of December 1898, the Spaniards renounced their possessions of Cuba, Guam, Porto Rico and the Philippines, which all moved de facto under US sovereignty. Porto Rico got annexed by the US and became part of it. The Philippines became a protectorate. The US eventually left Cuba only in 1903 after having secured the installation of a military base in Guantanamo Bay.

In 1934, a military junta led by Fulgencio Batista managed a coup that led to a pro-American regime in the island. Having lost power in the democratic game, Batista orchestrated a second coup in 1952, and took over Cuba. Being close to the Mafia barons in the US, Batista made Cuba one of the platforms of money laundering, gaming and prostitution… It is only in 1959 that Fidel Castro, a lawyer by training, managed to take him down. The US were among the first nations to recognize the new government of Cuba, but relationships soon deteriorated after Cuba nationalized several foreign assets, including those of United Fruit Co.

The US were not comfortable with the Cuban regime, which expropriated several American economic assets and developed links with the Soviet Union. They tried to throw it down with the failing attempt of the famous bay of pigs' invasion, organized by the CIA, under President Kennedy's administration. This event became a major embarrassment for US foreign policy, one of many related to Central and Latin America, as we will see in the following chapters. The CIA is said to have been involved in 638 schemes or attempts of killing Castro as depicted in a 2006 documentary on British public television.

The consequence was what became known as the Cuban missiles' crisis, and that was the closest to real war the cold war became! Indeed, Fidel Castro convinced Nikita Khrushchev, the Soviet Leader of that time, to help him deploy nuclear missiles pointing to the US, less than 100 miles from Florida. That certainly did not help the bilateral relations between the US and Cuba, which brilliantly earned its title of Evil! It also made the US extend the Cuban blockade it has started in 1960 to include almost everything one can think of. It is the most enduring trade embargo in history, despite its yearly condemnation by the UN General Assembly since 1992.

What about these days? What is happening? Great news! The big island sitting next to you in no more evil! Why?... because Barak Obama decided so. After decades of embargo, and hard life for the Cubans, you simply decided that time was up! Cuba has changed… Fidel, the "Lider Massimo" is gone. His less flamboyant brother Raoul has taken over before leaving the scene himself in 2018. The arch-symbol of anti-Americanism, of communist revolutions, the Che, is also history… Soon, nobody will know nothing about him, except for the cool look of his bearded face photograph printed on millions of tee-shirts. Fortunately, he has the wrong beard to become the idol of Daesh fans!

Soon, Cuba will be no more Cuba. No more pictures of the 50's dream cars. No more that image of a vintage city of Havana, trapped in an era without technology, without air-con and glass walls, but rather an era of glamour, romance and cigar smell! Life will probably be much better for the Cubans, they will be entitled to more 21st century comfort, they will have less and less restrictions and will start to enjoy some freedom. It is true that they had a dictatorial regime, but, would you agree that the embargo you put on Cuba was also part of the fence that took off their freedom and wellbeing?

One satiric French TV show had this message for Cubans: "your salaries will increase, so that you will be able to buy new cars, PCs, mobile phones…you will have to pay for your current free Medicare. You will live elsewhere than in the city center or on the beach front, that will be for foreigners…you will eat crap. You will be afraid of the future. Your language will disappear. Your music will melt down in the common mainstream. You will not be able to smoke your cigars anymore. You thought you had a dictator; you will have banks! In no time, spending the day on a chair in the street will be suspicious. With the TV programs, you will be stupid in five years. Welcome to the free world!"

It is also interesting to note how easy it was for you to remove Cuba from the list of the countries supporting terror. What did they really change? you decided that they have learnt their lesson. They are ripe… Viva Cuba Libre!

Sure, this was the outlook during Obama's time. With the Trump presidency, things will probably take a bit longer…

PANAMA

When I decided to talk about Panama in this book, there was still no "Panama papers" scandal... I will come back to that later. I had in mind to talk about Panama as an example of US destabilization action in Central and Latin America. It is also featuring one of the numerous CIA puppets turned into a villain. The name is Manuel Noriega. A native of 1934, Noriega was born in Panama City. He received military education and got intelligence training from US institutions. That generally bodes well for being "friends" with the CIA, and indeed, Noriega is said to have worked for the Agency from the 1950's for thirty years. He was one of its most valuable resources, being a key element in channeling weapons and money to US-backed counter-insurgency forces throughout Latin America, and especially Nicaragua and El Salvador...

However, Noriega was not satisfied of being simply the US-supported military dictator of Panama, he was also a major drug trafficker. Not marijuana no... he was more into Cocaine, dealing with the insane Medellin cartel. In many third-world countries, rogue regimes have been dubbed "kleptocracies" to remind of their corrupt nature. In Panama, Noriega probably invented the first Narco-kleptocracy of the world, with the blessing of his friends at the CIA, an Agency that had a Director called George H. W. Bush at periods overlapping with Noriega's tenure...

In a December 1988 report, that is public now and which I have freely downloaded from the web, prepared by the Subcommittee on Terrorism, Narcotics and International Operations of the Committee of Foreign Relations of the US Senate, one can read in the executive summary: "The saga of Panama's General Manuel Antonio Noriega represents one of the most serious foreign policy failures for the United States. Throughout the

1970s and the 1980s, Noriega was able to manipulate U.S. policy toward his country, while skillfully accumulating near-absolute power in Panama. It is clear that each U.S. government agency which had a relationship with Noriega turned a blind eye to his corruption and drug dealing, even as he was emerging as a key player on behalf of the Medellin Cartel". The said subcommittee was chaired by Massachusetts Senator John F. Kerry.

It is true that in 1988, Saddam Hussein and Osama Bin Laden have not yet emerged as the super stars of Evil they have become later… At that time, the US-declared Evil was communism in all its forms, and there was a lot to do in Latin America, with so many dirty wars going on to take out whatever leaders that were not on the right side! Today, I would say that Saddam and Bin Laden are to be added to the ever-growing list of "serious foreign policy failures of the United States". They were created, nurtured, and helped to become what they have eventually become, and they were eventually taken down, just as Noriega was.

Indeed, history (if I make a parallel between Panama & Iraq) has repeated itself, as Noriega's story as a US-backed dictator ended up with the US invasion of Panama at the end of 1989, early 1990 under George H. W. Bush's administration. The war was called "Operation Just Cause". Here again, the Pentagon's marketing experts have been much better than the Panamanian people who simply called it "La Invasion" (no need for a translation!). The General Assembly of the United Nations did not consider this cause to be so just and voted to condemn it as a violation of International Law, but a UN Security Council draft resolution asking for immediate withdrawal of US forces was vetoed by the US, France and the UK. It is easy when you make the law and that you have friends to support.

Your excuse was that the 30 thousand plus Americans of the Panama Canal had right of self-defense. I have forgotten to mention that the Canal was of great US economic interest and was an asset that the US have held until the end of the twentieth century, before they had to hand it over to Panama… Your troops were stationed there! The story of the Canal starts with a French entrepreneur, the same that succeeded to make the Suez Canal. He might not have been the first to come with the idea, but he was the one who started its execution in 1881, through what was then Colombia's province of Panama. Ferdinand de Lesseps was unfortunately not able to repeat his Egyptian success story. The snakes and mosquitos of Panama ate up all the funds he was able to mobilize for this new engineering adventure, and the failure of the project turned into a scandal which almost brought him and fellow entrepreneur Gustave Eiffel to prison! The US acquired the French interests in the canal, and helped Panamanian rebels separate from

Colombia, promptly recognizing the newly formed Panama State, and signing with its government a treaty granting the US the rights to build and indefinitely administer the Canal. The Theodore Roosevelt administration has de facto managed to take Panama from Colombia and turn it into an American protectorate. The US managed to get a zone ranging five miles on each side of the canal to become under its direct ruling, with police, army and courts…This has lasted from 1903 till 1979 when the Carter-Torrijos treaty was signed.

The Canal is an important economical resource to Panama. The other major contributor is the financial system. The services sector contributes close to 80% of the GDP of the country, making Panama one of the best economies in Central America. However, it suffers from a very bad wealth distribution. The Panama papers scandal, besides revealing several aspects on offshore economies and tax evasion of the super-rich, has put this small country on the map for many around the World. Many of the world's dictators have been using tax heavens to hide their wealth. Panama, Belize, Caymans Islands, or the British Virgin Islands are all suspect locations for businesses now. But what about Delaware? Is it any better? Is it all transparent and safe? So many of your icon companies are registered there… Sorry, I forgot, Delaware is in the US. It cannot be bad!

NICARAGUA

This country is another landmark example of the US hegemony policy in Central America. It used to be another Evil place under the Sandinistas... No matter that these revolutionaries, committed to Socialism, have pushed out the corrupt Somoza family that run the country for decades. For the US, being socialist meant they were no good! And being socialist in the neighborhood of the US means you have to disappear...

The US intervention in Nicaragua and in Central America in general dates back to the "Banana wars", in the late 19th century, early 20th century... these wars or conflicts were mainly to preserve US economic interests in the region. In the case of Nicaragua, it was occupied by US troops from 1912 to 1933, until the Franklin D. Roosevelt administration decided to promote what it called "the good neighbor policy", putting an end to US-military intervention in central America, at least temporarily... In fact, during this occupation period, the idea of a Canal through the central American isthmus was envisaged in Nicaragua by the US, and they had to hold on to the land around it! They eventually changed their minds for Panama, taking over from the French...

During US-occupation, the leader of the armed resistance was Augusto Cesar Sandino. He reached an agreement with the Government in place after US-troops left, but was soon after assassinated, opening the way to the Somoza dynasty dictatorship, which ruled the country until 1979, when it was overthrown by the Sandinista revolution.

What happened then in Nicaragua can probably be qualified as a proxy-war for the still active cold-war between the US and the Soviet bloc... the leftist Sandinistas were supported by the latter, while the counter-revolutionaries, the "Contras", were financed and trained by the US, under Reagan's administration. The Contra-war eventually led to several other civil-war outbreaks in neighboring El Salvador and Guatemala. What is still remembered from this period is especially the Iran-Contra affair, which was a political scandal in the US. While Iran was under embargo, senior officials in the Reagan administration authorized arm sales to Iran to finance the contra-war, while extra funding for the contras was prohibited under the Boland Amendment…This is not to mention the violence that characterized the contras' action. They were responsible for several human rights violations, brutalizing the rural Nicaraguan population, and destroying several social assets such as schools, hospitals and cooperatives. They have also embarked into serious economic sabotage, and the war led to the death of some 30 000 Nicaraguans. I am not saying that the Sandinistas were any better, but what I am saying is that the US have supported and armed a faction of the Nicaraguan population into a civil war which was deadly both for the people and the economy, and I really doubt that the motive was to bring democracy and welfare to that population!

Interestingly, the International Court of Justice ruled in 1986 in favor of Nicaragua and against the US in an international law case, considering that the US were responsible of many violations of customary international law. The court even decided a compensation for Nicaragua. However, the US later blocked enforcement of the judgement at the United Nations Security Council. Easy when you have a veto right! Regarding the Nicaragua situation, the US used (and abused) it five times… who cares that so many people in the rest of the world think it is unfair! The rules are for all the others to obey. The case was brought before the General Assembly of the UN and it was eventually passed on November 1986. Two countries only aligned their votes to the US: Israel and El Salvador, both benefiting from significant US funding. Even your closest friends in the Western World could not show support for what was being done in Central America. Even so, the US chose not to pay any compensation to Nicaragua… Imagine another country resisting to comply with UN-resolutions! They will be called villains and would have to cope with severe sanctions all over, if they escaped any direct military intervention!

FRANCE

France is my second country you know! Yes, I am an Arab, but we, the Arabs of the Maghreb, are also part of something called Francophone World: 200 million people sharing the practice of the French language. These are some of the remains of the colonization period. France had many possessions in Africa, and independences in the continent only happened in the late fifties and sixties. We feel therefore close to our northern neighbors, even though many of those voting for Mrs. Le Pen, which inherited the extreme right-wing party from her father, would not want us to be so close. Lately, a TV and radio activist even suggested that France should deport its 5 million Muslims who are in majority of Maghrebin origin. Yes, France is supposed to have anti-racist laws, and in many other cases, the guy would have been prosecuted right away, and certainly banned from the media. However, in this case, as his victims were Arab and especially Muslim, this did not seem to affect his career!

It is funny to see how the relationship with France evolves with time. There is somehow this love and hate movement "Je t'aime, moi non plus"! France is the major economic partner of Tunisia, Algeria, and Morocco. People speak French in any of these countries. Many cross-cultural and cross-religious marriages have happened. Still, some ghosts from the past reappear from time to time, with a resurgence of the independence fights, which were particularly dreadful in Algeria. France used to be the promised land for many of my Maghreb fellows. It is not anymore the only one... Satellite TVs have made people here look beyond, while before that, their only choice was their own country's media or the French...

As I was hearing from a former French Minister, Jean-Pierre Chevènement, France still has the full attributes of a Great Nation. He was saying that it was not anymore as Great as it once was, during the colonies and the "Empire" era. France is one of the permanent members of the Security Council of the UN. It has the nuclear weapon. It has an army that can be reasonably rapidly deployed anywhere in the World. It has an extensive diplomatic network, 31 corporations among the World's top 500. It is the second populated country in Europe and the fifth worldwide power. His regrets were that France was losing the prestige and the luster it once had with the General de Gaulle. It had its own will and international positions at that time. It was not one other nation simply following what the US were dictating.

France has been great in the past at assimilating other cultures. It has had a tradition of a welcoming country and a protector of human rights. This has translated into interesting features such as France being the biggest world producer and consumer of "Couscous", this Berber dish originating from North Africa. The Francophone World extends to more than 200 million persons and links many nations and cultures together.

France was however the European country that experienced the worst terror attacks in 2015: Charlie Hebdo as a starter and in November, the murder of over 120 people in 6 coordinated deadly attacks. The series has continued in 2016, especially with the shocking Nice truck attack on the 14th of July, the National Feast day. In a paper in "Liberation", a French leftist newspaper, JF Bayart, a professor at IHEID Geneva calls it "the boomerang effect". He advises to look for the origins of what happened in forty years of European foreign policy: the Palestinian issue, the non-acceptance of Turkey into Europe and the alliance with the Gulf oil monarchies. I certainly agree with him that the Western attitude towards all these issues has increased the hatred and favored the radicalization in many of the Arab populations.

It has also done the same in second or third generation immigrants into France, people whose parents came during the industrial boom to help the French economy strive. These people were often parked in suburbs that were not the best environment to live in. They did not speak much French, and they were of rather modest origin. Many hold two nationalities now. However, when your name is Karim, Mohamed, or Jawad, it is difficult to be accepted as a "real" French... it does not sound like Jean, François or Pierre... These people are not really at home in France. The problem is that they are not really at home elsewhere. If they go to where their parents came from, the Maghreb, namely countries like Algeria, Tunisia or Morocco, they often do not speak the language, do not have the same cultural background, and will end up being rejected! Easy recruits for Daesh...

France has tried in the recent years to promote many of the second-generation migrants within its government. There are several success stories in the media, theater and especially sports. However, the issues related to immigration are still a major hot topic in the political debate, especially when it relates to religion, and to Islam… In the whole world, with all the tensions that we see, ultra-nationalism, selfishness, and the rejection (if not the hate) of the others are becoming mainstream, and France is not escaping this trend.

AFRICA

This is the continent I belong to. The ancient name of Tunisia, my home country, which is in the northern part of Africa, is Ifriqyia… You've got it! My claim is that ancient Tunisia, Ifriqyia has given its name to the whole continent. Might sound a bit pretentious for a small nation of 10 million, but that is the historical truth! Today, not all Arabs are African, but the biggest number of them is… Indeed, the most populous nation in the Arab World, Egypt, with over 100 million population in 2020 is African. Two other nations accounting for over 30 million each are Algeria and Morocco, both in North Africa. These all are heavy-weight population countries compared to the Arabian Peninsula countries, which is across the red sea towards Asia, and is accounted for as being in Asia. Indeed, the most populous nation there is the Kingdom of Saudi Arabia, with around 30 million. The Arabs, therefore, which were originally from this peninsula, are more African today…

You might not recall, but Africa has seen the birth of humanity. The famous Australopithecus skeleton of Lucy was found in Kenya. There seems to be a lot of anthropological evidence that Homo Erectus, the first human, emerged from Africa. Today however, Africa could be seen as the most lagging continent. Recent history took a severe toll on it: slavery, colonization, apartheid, genocides, civil wars, corruption, instability… you name it.

A Movie like the "War lord" with Nicolas Cage has depicted the very troubled situation of many African countries and the enrolment of children as soldiers. Imagine a twelve- or fourteen-years old boy with a Kalashnikov! Another movie, "Blood diamond", with Di Caprio has shown another facet of the misuse of the fabulous mining treasures of the Continent to fuel wars in any kind of form in so many parts of it. Hollywood did not paint only the dark side of Africa. It has also conveyed a very romantic and glamorous image of it in blockbusters such as "Out of Africa", featuring Robert Redford.

OK, now you know a little better what I am talking about. For the years to come, Africa can be seen as a demographic time bomb or as a huge opportunity for businesses and the place to be for growth. Indeed, its population, which was around 180 million not so long ago, in 1950, is expected to be around 2 billion in 2050. It will have increased more than ten folds in just a century. Sure, Asians will still be more numerous, but countries such as Nigeria, Congo, Ethiopia, and Egypt will be serious heavyweights boxing in the above 100 million population arena. An interesting prospective book, called "Chindiafrique" in French, which is the contraction of China, India and Africa, talks about how important these three zones will be in the coming years, as they will represent by 2030 half of the humanity at 4.5 billion population, with roughly 1.5 billion each. Moreover, these populations, and especially the African one, will be amongst the youngest!

If we look at the current situation though, Africa is still suffering from several plagues: not to mention Aids, Ebola, dictatorships, Boko Haram, Shebab, AQIM and other terror organizations, regional conflicts such as the one relative to the occidental Sahara involving Morocco and Algeria, ethnical conflicts involving Hutus and Tutsis in Rwanda, Africa suffers from poverty and its usual consequences: malnutrition, lack of education, lack of public health… One recent ranking which I found on the web was listing countries by the worst Gross Domestic Product (GDP) onward. Unfortunately, Africa is trusting most of the seats in the "top" 25 of this list.

Indeed, the "top" 10 is 100% African, and 22 out of the 25 poorest countries are African. The only aliens here were Afghanistan at the 12th position, followed by Nepal (23rd) and Haiti (24th). The average GDP/capita of this list is below 600 US$ for 2015. The poorest is Burundi with a GDP/capita of 315.2 $. You might wonder: how much is it for the richest in the World? Well, it is Luxembourg and the figure is a staggering 118 251$, that is only 375 times more… The US comes only 9th in the GDP/capita competition at a "small" 57 thousand dollars.

But can you imagine that these poor people in Africa will be paying the pensions of the 111000 subscribers of Mosers, the Missouri state employees' retirement system? As fund managers around the world are having issues in reaching expected returns in mature markets, they are turning more and more to emerging ones. High risk, high reward as sharp finance people will say. Part of the 9.3 billion US dollars of Mosers have been invested in private equity funds managed by Actis or Development Partners International (DPI), two private equity firms operating in the African continent, and betting on a developing middle-class of consumers…

Africa, just like the Arab World, is still healing from its colonization wounds and recovering from the humiliations of the colonial era. On colonization, I have a very nice quote from one of the African liberation leaders, Jomo Kenyatta: "when they came, we had the land and they had the Bible. They taught us how to pray with our eyes closed. When we opened up, they had the land and we had the Bible!". Africa is facing huge challenges in education, healthcare, infrastructure… Most of its nations are still quite fragile, either with very young democracies, or very old dictators or on-going "coups" from armies that do not know anything else, as they would be perfectly incapable of defending their countries against serious foreign risks. All these armies were able to do was to intervene on a regular basis in internal politics to change the rulers…

In any case, better watch what is happening in Africa! As pointed out by Vijay Mahajan, a University of Texas Professor whom I first met at a private equity association meeting in Cairo, Africa is raising. That was the title of one of his books… He has also written another book called "the 86% solution". What I liked about his ideas was the fact that he has very much his roots and beliefs in the so-called "developing world" which used to be called "underdeveloped world" or "third world" … He sees a lot of potential in "south-south" collaboration and sees a lot of potential for business in our part of the world, which is quite encouraging! At least someone who is telling us "you are important", someone who is talking to us as an evolving consumer, with modern needs, with growing needs, aspiring for a better living… His latest work was focused on entrepreneurs in the Arab world: we hear so little about business practices, business successes, or business at all in the Arab world. It is therefore important to highlight that our world is not just a gigantic oil well on one side, a ruthless desert on the other, and the home of camels, fanatics, terrorists, and burqa-dressed women… there is more to it: there is also business, growing business to keep up with a fast-growing demand fueled by a demography that can be seen as a major potential or a major threat, depending on how optimistic you are and how well managed the situation will be.

And by the way, not to leave you with the only impression that Africa is poor, and struggling… I would like to quote Ellen Johnson Sirleaf, an African lady who was President of the Republic of Liberia and a 2011 Nobel Prize winner. She has so rightfully said: "Africa is not poor… It is poorly managed."

FAITH AND RELIGION

This is a very complex and dangerous topic to talk about. It really exacerbates passions all the time… Have you tried to have a discussion on the matter with your friends, even closest friends? You would be surprised… you might find yourselves fighting each other (at least intellectually) in no time! Look at was happened to Salman Rushdie for daring to write his "Satanic Verses".

Moderate people will often tell you that the subject is very private and very personal. It is a matter of moral standards. It regulates many of your behaviors in society. It is not something that you need to show off extensively and it should not be a reason for opposing you to people having a different religion or no religion at all.

The more orthodox or conservative, and of course the fanatic ones will tell you that religion is everything and in everything! It mixes with your life, it mixes with the State, it mixes with the Law…

I don't know if there are any serious studies that have tried to correlate the religiousness of people with their education level or with their standards of living. Having travelled significantly, I had the impression that the "weight" of religion is heavier in countries with lower income. Somehow, more "developed" societies become more materialist, led by consumerism, and the quest of material well-being. Less developed ones rely more on spirituality to reach their Nirvana! Religion is more present in their lives. They lack so many things they cannot afford; religion is free…

I came across a study by Win/Gallup International reported by The Telegraph. It is the outcome of a poll that encompassed a sample of 64000 people in 65 countries. And guess what? Western Europe is the region of the world that is the less religious, with only 43% of the people that believe in some religion. On the opposite, 86% of the population of Africa is religious. Africa is followed by the Middle East and then Central America… If we look at individual countries, Thailand is the most devout with 94% of the population saying they believe in something, while China is most atheist country with over 60% of convinced atheists! The latter example might be seen as a counter example to the theory I was elaborating here. However, China is certainly an exception from this point of view because of its specific recent political history!

In one of his recent books, "the Disoriented", Amine Maalouf, a French Lebanese writer who is an "immortal" (This designates the members of the "Academie Française" and not the Avengers or the X-men!), says "Religion is important, but not more than family, friendship and loyalty. There are more and more people for whom religion replaces morals… because they have a religion, they believe they can afford not to have ethics!"

Don't get me wrong. I am not trying to combat religion, or to say that it is something that will disappear with development. In many wealthy groups in developed countries, religion is very present too as these people tend to be very conservative. It is a way of being. It is a matter of education. What is often highlighted though is the moral aspect, and, in a way, all religions are the same if you look at it that way.

There is something I learned at a religious education class in my public school in Tunisia, something I owe to a very open-minded professor I had and which I would like to share: He told us that, in Islam, God will forgive you for any mistakes you make with him. If you do not pray, if you do not fast and so on, there is no harm, and this can be forgiven. These "sins" can be cleared from your file… On the other hand, what He will never forgive is the harm that you would cause to others, as there is a third party involved. And this is simply sound judgment! This also means that all religions are somehow the same. The moral principles guiding your interaction with others are the sacred principles that have to be obeyed: do not kill, do not rob, do not lie… the specific rites of each religion are more "optional"!

This leads me to some rational thinking that can be quite disturbing for a dogmatically religious person: how many people belong to one single religion on Earth? Even the biggest one? Less than 2 billion, over a population of 7 billion of the current world's population. How many people born of parents of a given religion will change their religion during their lifetime? 5%? Say 10% and this is large… This would mean that, for any religion, there is no potential to exceed 30% of the world's population. If I say that all other people of different religions are going to hell, whatever my religion, this would mean that 70% of the world population is destined to go to hell, from birth, as they are born with the wrong religion. And this was not their choice. It is simply decided by the fact they were born in a certain environment… Is this Just? Certainly not, as these people have done nothing wrong, except being born with the wrong religion at startup! But, in any religion, God is Just! He cannot fill hell with 70% of the world's population by design… Then, the assumption that all other religions different than mine are wrong is wrong!

Another disturbing fact related to religions is pointed out by Yuval Noah Harari in his book "Sapiens". As he explains some historical facts and how religions have evolved from the polytheist ones to some major monotheist ones, after the failed attempt of Akhenaten in ancient Egypt, he shows the contradiction in monotheist religions of having the duality of good and evil coexisting. To quote him, "In fact, monotheism, as it has played out in history, is a kaleidoscope of monotheist, dualist, polytheist and animist legacies, jumbling together under a single divine umbrella. The average Christian believes in the monotheist God, but also in the dualist Devil, in polytheist saints, and in animist ghosts"

Well, let us keep it private and personal! Let us not judge people on the basis of their religion but rather on what they actually are. Let us not use religion to make people fight each other just like in the middle ages. Let us not use religion to divide, but rather to unite. Let us not use religion to avoid asking tough questions and to impose taboos. One quote from Mohamed, the Prophet of Islam "You have your religion, and I have mine"…
Religion is a precious thing, keep it for yourself!

ISLAM

Many people make no difference between Arab and Muslim. They believe that Islam is the religion of Arabs. I should make it clear here that not all Arabs are Muslim and not all Muslims are Arabs. It is safer to say that most Muslims are not Arab: they can be Malays, Chinese, Wolof, Toucouleur, Indian... Biggest numbers are in Asia. So why I am having this section on Islam? Well, it happens that I am a Muslim. I am proudly among those cumulating what you would probably see as two handicaps: Arab and Muslim! It is also true to say that Arabic is the language of Islam, and there has been a strong historical tie between the language and the religion, leading to what is called the Arabic-Islamic civilization.

Many wrong things are being done in the name of Islam today, and the first victim of all this is Islam itself. I wanted therefore to clarify a few things about Islam, Allah, Muhammad and the Quran, the sacred book of the Muslims.

There is one word that we, Arabs, use to say God: it is Allah. It is not our god in opposition to anybody else's God... However, in occidental understanding now, Allah is always associated to fanatism, to killings made in the name of Allah, to terrorism... Expressions such as "fools of Allah" are often heard on the various media... I would like to ask if you have ever been to an Arab church, where you have Arab Christians praying. Yes, there exist Arab Christians; they represent a significant part of the Lebanese and Palestinian populations amongst others... In their churches, they will be praying Allah! Not the Muslims god, but the Christians' god, the same as the majority of you in the western world...

What else to say about Allah? Oh yes, Insha'Allah: this is a very common phrase you will often hear in the Arab world and also in some non-Arab Islamic countries... Literally, it means "god willing" or "if it's god's will". Most people will use it when talking about the future, and this is quite cultural, and once again, is a trait shared by Muslims and Coptic Christians. Nothing should be certain in the future. You cannot claim you will be doing this or that without adding some uncertainty to the event, showing your submission to God. It is simply the way you should say things. It is sometimes used in misleading ways as it could mean that an event is quite improbable or even if your interlocutor is simply trying to politely say no! In that case, it would mean that what you are asking for will not happen, not because he does not want to, but because God, who is above us all, will have to make it happen, and he will probably not. What a tortured mind you might say! Well, I am not sure it is that bad. It is quite subtle, and it quietly allows avoiding confrontation, which is a quest several other cultures have. Not losing face, not confronting the other...

Anyway, if we leave the semantics to focus more on the symbolic, Allah is the good and the creator of all. In Islam, He has 99 other names, which you can understand as adjectives, and which tell about his kindness and his toughness as the same time. These names are often used to name people and they will take either one of two pre-fixes: Mohamed (being the name of the prophet) or Abd (meaning the "man of" or even the "slave of"). As an example, we will get: Mohamed El Hedi (Hedi meaning the guide, it can also mean calm) and Abd El Aziz (Aziz meaning precious, cherished)… these are examples of the many Arab first names that are derived from the above mentioned list of 99!

Allah is used in expressions that express joy. Typically, "Allah Allah" is used in many songs. "Ma Shaa Allah!", literally meaning "What god wished", stands for "Wow"! this would be a typical expression that a man would tell his friend in a café when seeing a beautiful woman. You can understand that saying so, he is not at all thinking of god "Allah" even if he is using his name…

Expressions such as "Allahou Akbar" are used in a more formal or serious way. They can be used to express sorrow when you hear of someone's death. Another very common expression is "Bism Illeh", which means "in the name of god", and which a good Muslim would use before starting anything like eating or giving a public speech or getting into a car… All these expressions, which refer explicitly to god, are part of the daily language, and people forget that reference to god. They are now used as idioms rather than with that religious background you might think of…

Another famous "name" in Islam that you have probably noticed besides Allah is Mohamed. This is the name of our Prophet. It is also a very common name in the Arab Muslim World, with all its variations: Ahmed, Mahmoud, Hamda, Hmaida, Hammadi… I remember when I was at school, we had systematically one third of the guys with their first name in this category. This shows that it is very cultural, and that there is a strong attachment to the Prophet in many forms.

I have to point out here that all Jewish or Christian Prophets are considered as such in Islam. Mohamed is only the last in the list, but all of Abraham, Noah, Moses, Jesus are cited as Prophets and thus, as highly regarded people with perfect morality and integrity.

It was therefore very much offensive for many Muslims to see outrageous cartoons of Mohamed in some occidental newspapers. Does this contribute to enhance freedom of speech? May be does it contribute to improving the civilizations dialogue and respect among communities? Certainly not! Even the intellectuals, defending human rights and freedom concepts were offended (in our part of the world) and felt very bad about this. Of course, this anger did not lead them to physically attack the people behind this, but not everyone can behave as an intellectual.

I hope this helps you understand all the reactions spurred in the Muslim world by those offending cartoons started in Denmark and continued in France with the now famous Charlie Hebdo, and all the sad consequences that we know, consequences which I strongly condemn, don't get me wrong! But consequences that are not that much surprising from fanatic people.

Looking back into history, and into what Mohamed was and did, I think that there is a lot to be learned. He started as a poor analphabet guy, though a member of the strongest and wealthiest tribe in Arabia. He was more of a self-made man, someone who built his life and personality, not someone who inherited his position in society. Mohamed got married to an older and wealthier woman, Khadija, and he got involved in managing business for her, which is again another great story to remember from those old and misogynous ages.

He got the revelation of the Quran at the age of forty, which is a rather old but certainly mature age, and the first injunction he got from God was "Read", in Arabic, "Iqraa". If there is a symbol I would like to get out of this, it is that the first message of Islam was to read and to learn. It was against analphabetism and ignorance. When we hear all those preachers that are against education, especially of women, against culture and knowledge, we can only see that the "Message" was totally distorted by a horde of ignorant people.

Mohamed's prophecy was not welcome in his hometown of Mecca. Just as a French proverb says, "no one is a prophet in his own country"! He had to migrate to Medina, under circumstances where he escaped death several times, and was protected in a cave by a spider's web. For this, Islam has been asking for animals' protection and respect of all forms of life, be it a spider that you don't like!

Mohamed managed to get a group of followers in Medina, and ended up eventually re-conquering all of Arabia and converting people to Islam. During the period where he was building this new nation, Mohamed was often consulted for many aspects of the daily life, resolving disputes between people and even, inside families and couples. He proved to be a wise man and, besides Quran, which is the speech of God in Islam, he has left an abundant literature, gathered after his death, and known as "Hadith", which means "talk" or "speech" in Arabic. His many positions on various aspects of daily life provide an exhaustive code of conduct that complements and explains what was provided by the Quran.

One important thing about Mohamed is that he is not pictured at all in Islamic tradition. Even the great movie, "The Message", with Irene Papas and Anthony Quinn, depicting the early days of Islam, suggests his presence, but never shows him. I am not sure myself if there is anywhere anything written forbidding to picture him. I really doubt it. It is more of a cultural thing, a tradition, as it has been generally avoided in Islam to show human figures as religious icons. The idea was to avoid any personification of God, and any "godification" of the prophet, to strictly move from the polytheist nature of widespread religions at that time, to a unique God, which cannot be described, except by his virtues and qualities, making Him more of a conceptual icon than something we can easily relate to.

In Islam, no one is related to God, not even Mohamed, who remains a simple human being. The ban of any Mohamed pictures was intended to avoid having him in Mosques and avoid having Muslims confuse their loyalty to God with anyone else. In any case, what was strongly offending in the cartoons that were released was not even having pictures of Mohamed, it was more having him pictured in certain situations that were felt offending. As one young lady pointed out on TV, you would not accept to see your mother or someone you really like to be pictured in such a degrading way.

In the view of many Westerners, Islam is a violent religion and the roots for this can be found in its book: the Quran. If not in the Quran itself, this would be in the "Hadith", referring to what Mohamed has been telling his fellows… An interesting video has been posted on social media, showing an experiment performed by two guys in the Netherlands: they took a book, which is the Old Testament and replaced its cover to make it look as if it were the Quran. They chose some particularly violent phrases and started reading them to people on the street. The first reaction was of course that people felt comforted in their belief that the Quran was legitimating violence, and then people got totally confused when they discovered that the speech was from the Bible… In fact, all these books are dating back to a period in human history where the "codes" were different from what they are today, and one should probably not judge a religion by some phrases extracted from a holy book totally out of context.

Another fact that is often ignored in the Western world is the place that Jesus has in the Quran, and the approach that the holy book of Islam has of all other prophets, recognizing them and integrating them completely in this new religion (for the time!). There is an interesting book by the two French authors of the TV documentary "Corpus Christi", Mordillat and Prieur. Their book, "Jesus according to Mohamed" holds a quite provocative title in the association of the two Prophets names. The TV documentary series that goes with it, "Jesus and Islam", tends to show the numerous similarities that exist between Judaism, Christianity and Islam, and to insist on the very special role that Jesus has in the Quran! I am a strong believer that the three major monotheist religions have much more in common than what their adepts tend to think these days. There is much more to unite than to separate…

The Quran, which means the recital, is a very interesting read in Arabic, though a difficult one. Indeed, the collection of the various verses and their grouping in a unique "mushaf" (book) has been achieved only under the third Caliph Othman, twenty years after the death of the prophet. The text has not been organized according to the chronology of the revelation, and this makes things harder to understand and analyze. It is quite poetic, uses a significant portion of the Arabic vocabulary, and can have different levels of interpretation. This makes its translation complex as translating is already interpreting the meaning in some direction.

This also shows that not many people fully understand what is really in the Quran. Most people and even, most Muslims, are not able to read and understand the original Arabic text. As mentioned earlier, most Muslims are not Arabs and do not understand Arabic. Even Arabic speaking ones are not proficient enough in Arabic to fully understand all the verses, and to understand them with the contextual meaning they have. This has made the job of fundamentalists easier: taking some sample verses that served their objectives, extracting them out of context and interpreting them literally, has enabled them to build a certain message, which is a message of exclusion and violence. It is also a message denying learning, doubt and philosophical interpretation…

I prefer to choose the verses that urge for the quest of knowledge, the pursuit of justice, of love and fraternity, the ones that dictate the proper behavioral and social attitudes that one should have promoting morality, loyalty, and care for the others. And I am not the only one thinking this way. You can read the book of Mahmoud Hussein, on "What the Quran does not say" and what some people are making it say! In Arabic, Islam means "surrender" and it shares the same root as "Salam" which is peace. The way people would great you in Arabic, "Salam Alaikom" means "Peace be on you" … Arabic "Salam" is the same as the Hebrew "Shalom".

THE SALAFIS

Tell me! How much do you know about Greek mythology? It is important to know a little bit of it to understand what is lying behind expressions such as opening the Pandora Box... Pandora is supposed to be the first woman on Earth, and Zeus (you know, the super-god of the Olympus!) has given her a box (probably a jar at that time!) asking her to never open it under any circumstances... Of course, as you can imagine, curiosity was stronger and Pandora opened the box, letting all evil spread on earth. It was too late when she tried to close back the container.

The takeaway from the story is, of course, that we always have to be careful of the consequences of what we do. Sometimes, by performing a very small and simple act, one can trigger a huge reaction with far-reaching consequences.

The other day, I was explaining all this to my eleven-year old son, and I was quite amused of his reaction. He said: "Our Pandora Box was full of hair. When we opened it, we had a Salafis invasion!". He was referring to the fact that these people were not shaving their beards...

The definition of Salafism refers to the Arab word "Salaf", meaning past or predecessor, and more precisely "Al Salaf al Salah", which refers to the "pious forefathers", the first three generations of Muslims, including the direct followers of the Prophet. It is an ultra-orthodox movement within Sunni Islam. To quote Robin Wright, the author of "Rock the Casbah", "Don't fear all Islamists, fear salafis"... Salafi groups are getting a lot of support from Wahhabis out of Saudi Arabia. True, not all Saudis are Wahhabis and not all Salafis are Wahhabis but all Wahhabis are Salafis. In fact, those who are quietists do not represent a major threat. They are mainly willing to enforce what they believe are the strict rules of Islam upon themselves. A more disturbing group is that of the activists. They are very much into preaching and proselytism. Eventually, the dangerous ones are the Jihadists, who have set themselves the goal to act violently to impose their views.

These are people that have a very backward view of Islam. They have alter egos in Judaism and Catholicism in the form of Ultra-Orthodox Jews and various forms of Jehovah Witnesses and peers! These people seem to be trapped in a past where Gillette did not exist as they all have a problem with their beards. They do not seem to be willing to shave them. In my view, they need some image/communications advisors as they are not that handsome with an ugly beard going crazy!

Besides the beards, they will be wearing some undefined garments that are halfway between a big bag and a marathon outfit for a desert road! If you look to their forehead, you will also notice a dark spot, supposed to be their mark of submission to god. Indeed, in Islam, there are five prayers per day, and you have to bend, and knee down, and put your head on the ground or on a prayer carpet. However, my grandmother who was a very devout person that did her five prayers a day every day never had such an ugly mark on her face! Wasn't she religious enough? Or maybe she was not in the show-off, in the commerce of religion. She understood religion as being something for her soul, not something to make people consider her differently. For that, she used the principles of religion in treating people well and behaving nicely to gain people's consideration. This is not necessarily what we see from so many Salafis that do not obey the most basic religious teachings in my opinion.

I will not even comment on the women outfit. They call it "Niqab". It is not the "Men in Black", it's the Women in Black. Did they inspire Will Smith? I doubt it, I doubt they could inspire anyone. They could only inspire some desperate suicide movers. You've got it: that's what terrorists do. If only they had normal wives!

POLYGAMY

This is one of the favorites of Salafis: It means the right to have several spouses… it is a nice feature in societies to avoid extra-marital relations. It is also a means to combat divorce. You don't like your previous wife, get another one. The two have united against you, get a third. The three are not able to make you proper food, get a fourth one! This is something Mormons were very keen on (but have abandoned the practice in 1890 as federal laws were against!), and, probably in your mind, Arabs and Muslims. We should not forget Africans too…

Clearly, this is something that does not put men and women at an equal stand. A man can have several wives, and this "right" is clearly denied to women, even though an equivalent feature, called polyandry, exists in some remote Nepalese, Bhutanese or Indian communities. Polyandry is found in communities where resources are scarce and was intended to preserve the land and limit natality. The justification of acceptance of Polygamy and not Polyandry is that the latter makes it very complex to identify the father of a child, before DNA sequencing existed of course!

In the past, when the death toll of war battles was high, polygamy played even the role of social assistance. Survivors married the widows and took charge of the orphans. Polygamy was also a means of making alliances and uniting tribes. Mohamed himself, the prophet of Islam, married several women, many of which were widows or divorced, and that contributed to gain more people to his cause.

To be honest, my own interpretation of Islam is that polygamy is forbidden. I am not an Ayatollah or an Imam but trust me: It is said somewhere that first of all, there is a limitation to four. You might think this is already too much, and I agree, but in the ancient time where this rule has been given, people allowed themselves much more than that. Therefore, it came in as a limitation already. And then, as an addition, there is a condition that has been imposed, which is practically unachievable: you have to be fair to all of them and you have to treat them equally! How can you do this in practice? It is not formally forbidden, true, but it is so complex to achieve that it should be seen as actually forbidden.

In Tunisia, it has been abolished by law at the independence, and this was the right thing to do. However, right after the revolution, we have seen some people, close to what was then the ruling party, Ennahdha, which is of religious background, ask for polygamy back! I wonder how an intelligent person would want to live in the middle ages when some others have been flying to the moon!

With the recession looming, and the economy at a full stop, who would want more mouths to feed? OK, this is probably not the right angle to look at it, but I was trying to use some pedagogy for these people. If you are willing to use arguments of women rights or, let's say, human rights, it will not work! That is not their world! While Tunisia was the first country to abolish polygamy in the Arab world, and to give women several rights in the 1959 constitution (immediately after independence), in the writing of our new constitution, in 2011, there have been some proposals that the constitution should state that the woman is "complementary" to the man, instead of simply saying "equal"! The latter eventually won, and we placed "equal". This is now posing problems with the inheritance laws. Indeed, according to Sharia, the Islamic law, a woman inherits half of what the man inherits, and that was also what the civil law and practice led to in Tunisia. According to this new constitution, this uneven distribution is now unconstitutional! What will our clever politicians and legislators do?

JIHAD

This Arab word has made its way into the English and French languages nowadays! I am not sure about Mandarin, Russian and Sanskrit! Do you really understand what it means? When we hear it on TV, it is to speak on the various killings made by the so-called "Islamic groups", often in the worst fashions one can imagine. It is assimilated to some form of crusade or religious war… Jihad today is crime. It is terror. It is Al Qaeda, and AQIM, and Boko Haram, and ISIS… Is it Islam? We see so many debates on all these issues, and we see so many people claiming that violent Jihad is embedded in Islam. Being a Muslim is becoming a hard to carry burden, especially in the Western world.

Many serious analysts and commentators have started explaining that most young jihadists are not interested in Islam or the Quran, they are finding in Jihad the thrill of ultra-violence and the expression of their revolt. As commented by Peter Harling of International Crisis Group, "their Islamic culture is very low, not to say inexistent. Actually, those with a stronger knowledge of religion are less incline to join groups such as ISIS". Raphaël Liogier, the Director of the Religions Observatory in France (and Professor in Aix, South of France), completes by saying "these people are looking for antisocial violence. In the 80's, they would have become punk, or left-extremists or right-extremists… They jump into jihad because it is the most visible way to do it today". In fact, we have often found that many of these people were already marginal, have been arrested several times for burglary, aggression, and other urban violence. They have nothing from being devout. They have had no theological background. All they are looking for is somehow to "exist" in society, they want to be noticed and they have no intellectual tools for that, they only have a Kalashnikov.

What does Jihad etymologically mean? It means "to fight" or "to make an effort", and this is not necessarily to be associated with any military or aggressive action. Jihad can be for better living, to relieve poverty. Jihad can be for educating people. I really like a public address in which President Bourguiba, the first President of the Republic of Tunisia, claimed that our biggest Jihad ("Al Jihad Al Akbar") was against ignorance, against poverty and was to fight for development. This is the meaning I like… This is what we should advertise more in the Arab world.

Going back to the 20th century history, and especially the fight of several nations for their independence, you will find that this term has been used to designate those people that have fought the colonizers. A "Moujahid" is a resistant. He is someone who has joined those liberation forces that are seeking to free the country from its foreign rulers. This was the case in Algeria and Tunisia. There was no religious meaning whatsoever attached to it. In Tunisia, and for years after the independence, we got used to Bourguiba, our first President, being called "Al Moujahid Al Akbar", the great "Moujahid", the great fighter…

Later, in the eighties, the Afghan Moujahids were the people that fought the Red Army and kicked it out of the country. They were depicted favorably in Western media. Here however, there started to be some religious connection to their fight. We should not forget that the emergence of Al Qaeda and of Bin Laden was in Afghanistan… against the Russians… aided by the West?

There is also another meaning of Jihad that can be found in Islam. The "real Jihad" is "against" ourselves. It is against the Evil in us. Yes, like in any religion, there is the good and the bad, God and the Devil, the Yin and the Yang, the biggest Jihad is of moral nature. It is in our deep soul. It is a noble cause. It is what should make us better!

Did I convince you to like Jihad now?

AL QAEDA

This is a "wonderful" creation of some very vicious minds... Does it really exist in the form we are told by the media, or not? Do we have any tangible proofs? You know, when I hear Al Qaeda, I immediately think of some of the very old James Bond films. The idea was already there. It is not called Al Qaeda, but rather the Specter! This is the theme and the title of one of a more recent Bond movie, "Specter"... Maybe at the time of the first James Bonds, the Arabs were still considered to be friends, or simply not sufficiently intelligent or aggressive to inspire fear. The Specter was this international terrorist organization, strong enough to dare attack the "free-world" and the eastern bloc at the same time. It hi-jacked nuclear weapons and tried to start world war three!

Let us go back to our modern incarnation of the Specter, Al Qaeda. So much has been said about it, its machiavellic structure that makes it so powerful and so diffuse at the same time, so pervasive in our modern society. Some say that it is not necessarily composed of poor illiterate people, but rather by the elite of the Muslim world! A French colleague of mine told me that I would perfectly qualify: Arab, Muslim, age forty (at that time!), married, with children, rather bright (and not always modest, as you might have noticed), well educated (a Master & a Ph.D.)... This description was written in some very serious European newspapers, and I kept wondering how possibly such a description could fit an Al Qaeda activist. Or maybe the objective was simply to introduce even more confusion, and make sure I was treated such as a potential terrorist. There is no escape! All of us are potential terrorists...

Al Qaeda has become an institution. It has basis in several Arab and Muslim countries. It has a new leader after Osama Ben Laden was killed. It has money, it has media coverage. It has almost become something familiar, that we do not like, but we have become acquainted to. It is also very convenient. Anything that goes wrong has Al Qaeda behind it... Proof? Analysis? Justification you say? Who really needs that? Who cares? It is Al Qaeda... Sure, since the rise of ISIS, the Al Qaeda brand has been somehow fading away compared to its new terrible infant!

How was Al Qaeda born? How did this catastrophe happen? Many people have written about the topic and several TVs and radios have commented. There was a very nice documentary on France 2 TV station. It showed the effective genesis of Al Qaeda. The authors trace back the issue to the 1979 mosque attack in the highly symbolic town of Mecca, KSA, the Muslim pilgrimage destination. They claim that this event has troubled the young 22-year-old Osama (Bin Laden, of course!), and somehow gave him a purpose in his life, defend fundamental Islam...

The Grand Mosque is a massive compound that encompasses the sacred "Kaaba" and can accommodate over a million people at the same time, especially during the pilgrimage period. It is the outcome of an $18 billion renovation project began in 1953 by the ruling monarchy in Saudi and managed by the Bin Laden construction Group.

Indeed, young Osama did not much appreciate the intervention of French GIGN police forces in the city that was supposed to host only Muslims, Mecca. When approached by the Saudi secret service to go to Pakistan in 1980 to help defend Islam against the atheist communist Soviets, Osama naturally accepted as this was giving a meaning to his life. It is difficult to exist in a group of 50 brothers and sisters when you are not the elder... Bin Laden flew to Peshawar to recruit Jihad candidates, financed by KSA, and that is where he met his mentor, Abdallah Al Azzam, the Palestinian born "father of global Jihad"...

When he arrived in Afghanistan, Bin Laden found himself pushed back in the middle ages... He lived in a cave and structured the resistance against the Soviets. Meanwhile, he inherited some $30 million from his father. It took him two years to become a real chief at the borders of Afghanistan and Pakistan. In 1986, while the US were actively trying to destabilize the Soviets, he got US support in the form of Stinger missiles and he was the leader of Arab jihadists that fought under the umbrella of the US/KSA/Pakistan coalition. Zbigniew Brzezinski, the famous American national security advisor, told the Afghans "your cause is right, and god is on your side"!

In 1987, Soviet helicopters attacked the cave where Bin Laden hided, called the "lion's cave". Seven days of combat… He fainted but survived, and the myth became even stronger. He asked to be filmed riding a horse and started building an image just like the Muslim Che Guevara! The Soviets eventually retired from Afghanistan in 1988 and Bin laden returned to Peshawar, with an army and no land to defend. An Egyptian fundamentalist, Ayman Al Zawahiri, willing to "Islamize the Arab world" went to Pakistan that same year. He introduced several other fundamentalists to Bin Laden and, together with Al Azzam, the trio founded Al Qaeda, the "basis" in Arabic. The Americans did not really care as long as the Soviets were getting hit… Azzam got killed in a car bombing a year later, leaving Al Zawahiri and Bin Laden as the sole leaders of Al Qaeda.

Back to KSA, Bin Laden started doing more political preaching, and started criticizing the US publicly. With the 1990 Kuwait invasion by Iraq, he became more aggressive towards the US because of the troops stationed in the Gulf. He went on publicly criticizing the Saudi Royals as well and ended up moving to Sudan, where Hassan Al Turabi just installed a "Sharia compliant" government. Fundamentalists from all around the Arab World were gathering in this new promised land. Bin Laden financed some infrastructure projects in the country, while still presented as the anti-Soviet warrior in Western media.

With the 1993 car explosion in the US, the 1995 tentative assassination of Egypt's President Mubarak, and American intelligence tracing all this back to Sudan, KSA decided to ban Bin Laden from citizenship and to freeze his assets in Saudi Arabia. He decided to go back to Afghanistan in 1996 where he met Mullah Omar in Kandahar and became friends with the Taliban regime. He settled in a small village with Al Zawahiri and found a new disciple to operate Al Qaeda, the Pakistani engineer Khaled Sheikh Muhammad. He had also a "great" communicator in the person of Abu Musa Al Suri, called "the Syrian". The CIA got some intelligence from insiders that Al Qaeda had the size, the modernity, and the money. Members had a comfortable social welfare system: a basic salary plus vacation plus death benefits for those going on Kamikaze acts!

In 1998, the CIA wanted to kidnap Bin Laden, but the Clinton administration did not agree. Meanwhile, Osama was showing in the media Al Qaeda training camps and he was claiming that "Our war against Americans will be much bigger than against the Soviets. They have committed a major sin against Muslim beliefs". A few weeks later, 2 US Embassies were attacked, leaving 224 dead in Nairobi (Kenya) and Dar-es-Salam (Tanzania), both in East Africa. The Whitehouse eventually realized the extent of the problem, and Clinton agreed to kill Bin Laden. Warships sent missiles on Afghanistan and Sudan. The CIA gave $5M for Bin Laden, dead or alive, like in an old cow-boy movie… but it failed to infiltrate Al Qaeda or to get the Afghans give him away.

In January 2001, at his son's wedding, Bin Laden openly requested to act on US territory and during the 9/11 attack, he followed the events on BBC and requested his men to remain seated after the first plane crash. In December 2001, Kabul was taken by US troops. However, he had flown to Jalalabad, and he survived a 56-hours bombing. In 2002, he was up again in the media to claim the Bali attacks. When the Bush administration took power, it presented Saddam Hussein as a Bin Laden ally, justifying Iraq's invasion in March 2003. Saddam got captured and killed, not Bin Laden, and the occupation of Iraq helped create and develop Al Qaeda in Iraq. Al Qaeda was becoming a brand, and it started having franchises. It was only until May 2011, under the Obama's administration, that Bin Laden got killed in his home in Afghanistan. The end of Bin Laden did unfortunately not mean the end of Al Qaeda. It already had solid franchises abroad, in the Maghreb, in the Sahel, in Nigeria, in Somalia, all over…

AQIM

This is the Al Qaeda franchise for North Africa, the "Maghreb" as it is called in Arabic. AQIM stands for "Al Qaeda in the Islamic Maghreb" … in fact, they have a pretty large territory, encompassing Algeria, Tunisia, Libya, Morocco, Mauritania, Mali, Niger and Chad! Yes, mostly desert… that is also called the "Sahel". AQIM has been famous mainly for all the bad it did in Algeria. The country has lived through very tough times and had to fight severe terrorism acts against foreigners and especially against its own population. Of course, international media covered mainly the episodes where non-Algerians were killed. And that is a small portion of what went on in the country.

One of the stars of terror in Maghreb is Mokhtar Belmokhtar, an Algerian national, sometimes referred to as the Bin Laden of the Sahel as portrayed by the magazine "Jeune Afrique". One of the founders of AQIM in 2005, he has been pushed out in 2012 and went on founding another terror group, the "blood signers"… Born in 1972 in Ghardaia, a city in central Algeria, he was not passionate about school but rather appreciative of the Mujahidin fighting the Soviet Union in Afghanistan. He joined them in the early nineties and lost an eye there. Back in Algeria in 1992, he joined the local terror groups, back then called IAG (Islamic Armed Groups), committed several killings, established the contacts with Al Qaeda and managed to transform the local groups into the terror multinational's franchise. When things went sour in Algeria, he moved to Niger, then Mali and eventually to south-west Libya. In December 2015, he rejoined AQIM with his newest formed group, "Al Mourabitoun".

In the recent past, the most prominent actions of AQIM took place in Mali. These people had the arrogance to take entire towns and regions. They even fought against an international coalition lead by France and supported by the whole world! Did they lose? I am not sure… we hear less of them today, but they did not completely disappear, and with all the mess in neighboring countries and all the stock of arms they can amass for little money, the story is certainly not over yet, unfortunately for me, as they are next door. Are you responsible for this? Somehow, yes! How come would you say? Well, AQIM and similar organizations are thriving from the chaos Libya has become. When you (and your friends) decided to take Kaddafi out, which is not something I would blame you for (I am not a fan of Kaddafi), when you decided to do that, you did not calculate all the consequences! You did not foresee how that would unleash all the evil that was "managed" by all the local dictators we had.

AQIM has an extensive history of kidnapping and extortion. It is believed to have had most of it financing from ransom payments… an estimated amount of over $115 million by 2013. Other financing sources include people, arms and drugs trafficking as well as money laundering and smuggling in the region. With its affiliation to Al Qaeda, it has its local "management", and it has increasingly decentralized to provide for more autonomous factions or "katibas"… Lately, it has been focusing on West-Africa rather than the North, with the Grand Bassam attack in Ivory Coast following several actions in Mali, and it has shown that Al Qaeda is still the major terror power in this part of the World that did not see yet the rise of ISIS… In order not to run into ego problems in the leadership part, it seems that Al Qaeda's leader, Al Zawahiri has ordered a regional split with Droukdel, one of the major figures, taking care of Algeria and Mali, Belmokhtar handling Libya and Okacha focusing on West Africa… What a program! This is all happening in my immediate neighborhood, and I sometimes wonder if my fellow citizens prefer this with some democracy, or dictatorships and much less terrorism. You are right, I am excluding many nicer choices, such as having democracy, prosperity, full employment, a GDP per capita above 50 k$ and no violence.

However, looking at the situation on the ground, do you really believe that, in the next five years, we will be entitled to have democracy and no terror in this part of the World?

BOKO HARAM

Let us go a little more south now, just a little south of Niger and Mali! I am taking you on the African tour of terrorist organizations. These guys have the franchise for Nigeria! That is the most populous country in Africa. That is also one of the most dangerous, let alone Boko Haram… Ask all the expats living in Nigeria, or ask Nigerians themselves! One important thing though, and this is something you probably know already, Nigeria has surpassed South Africa in becoming the first African economy! It is the spot to be in. It is the country of promising growth, but it abides by the rule finance people always claim: "high risk, high reward".

Boko Haram has committed several acts of terror in the recent years. One of the most notorious was the kidnapping of two hundred schoolgirls! Seriously, how could such a thing happen in a country that has institutions, that has an army and a police! Yes, it happened in the northern part of Nigeria. The poor girls were not found, and all the media showed videos of what was claimed to be Boko Haram's leader, or one of its leaders, a man who looked like a fool, heavy on drugs, with an hysteric smile, a man who said he was doing this in the name of Islam… Does he even know what Islam means or stands for?

Another abject move from Boko Haram was to use a young 10 years old schoolgirl as a human bomb. The poor youngster was packed with explosives; she was introduced into a shopping mall and exploded there, killing over twenty people and of course, herself. This is horrible. In the name of what cause, in the name of what religion, in the name of what can a human do these things to other humans? These people have lost their humanity. What can produce such monsters?

The problem is not only that Boko Haram exists. The problem is that it exists in a region where it seems that part of the population is supporting it, may be because they have no other choice, because the rule of law of a solid country is not present and because it is a matter of life and death for them. The problem is that Boko Haram seems also not be afraid of an organized army and does not seem to be stuck at the frontier, which they readily cross to Cameroun or other neighboring countries. Terrorist organizations that act so openly without any fear question the very existence of States and power…

It should be pointed out that Boko Haram is also mainly killing Muslims. It is the Northeastern part of Nigeria that is regularly attacked by them. Maiduguri, the capital of Borno State, is one of their favorites. Between June and July 2017, 62 people have been killed in Maiduguri and its environs. One attack that killed 8 and wounded 18 was due to a female suicide bomber that detonated her bomb while trying to enter a mosque.

Another major killer is taking its toll on Africa: it's called Ebola. It is spreading a lot of terror. Oh sorry, it is not another terrorist organization. It is just a tiny virus. Yes, this one is rather similar to what has caused severe hysteria at airports and other places… It is stronger than the avian flu, and all others.

Ebola is said to have killed over 5000 people from the latest outbreak, a death toll that amounts to over 50% of the infected people. This is frightening indeed. Why don't the "big pharma" find a cure? Not enough potential? No wealthy people to secure the ROI (Return On Investment)? Ebola is not new. I read about some Belgian researcher who claims to have discovered the first virus strains in the 70s… Still today, the virus has no cure. It will kill more people, but do not worry, it is far away. It is killing mainly Africans, preferably poor. It is not worse than a civil war, or any of all the other plagues that are taking their toll every day in western Africa…

In some countries, during the outbreak, people's circulation was seriously limited. The economic activities were severely affected. We had a massive media coverage in the whole world, and it felt like there are whole areas in Africa that we should put in quarantine. In other parts of the world, it developed the business of those selling temperature measurement scanners. In just about any airport in the planet, when you landed, you would pass across a group of people measuring your body temperature… I was all the time worried that the little flue I might have could cause me to be put in quarantine if my temperature would exceed by some degrees the allowed limits!

What have we done for Ebola now? Nobody talks about it anymore… the outbreak seems to be past us, at least, until next time. Did we find a cure? Does somebody care anymore? Not really… We are preserving all the thrill for the next time! We do not have enough threats to choose from…

But the biggest scourge facing Nigeria is neither Boko Haram, nor Ebola, it is the lack of toilets as pointed out by Water Aid, an international charity working on improving access to water, hygiene and sanitation! The yearly death toll of the lack of basic sanitation is in tens of thousands. As reported in Nigerian newspaper "This Day", "the country is one huge field where people defecate without shame"…Human waste eventually pollutes water resources and ends up being ingested by the population, causing so many diarrheal diseases such as typhoid fever and dysentery. You know the popular saying in California when things go wrong? Yes, "When shit hits the fan"! Here, it is not a small fan, it is a turbo-reactor, and there is plenty of shit, the production of 180 million people. So you can imagine how disastrous it can be!

AL SHEBAB

As we are on our African tour, let us continue east, to Somalia and Kenya. When talking about Somalia, this is the typical case of a territory with no state power, an anomaly in the 21st century! Somalia has provided the most prominent pirates of the modern times, operating in the Indian ocean, at the "entrance" of the Suez Canal, down at the Gulf of Aden, or the so-called horn of Africa. This is the maritime region between East-Africa and the Arabian Peninsula. At the same time, Somalia is the regional supplier of the local Al Qaeda franchise, the Shebab.

The Arab word "shebab" means the young people. I am not sure they are all young and beautiful. What I know for sure is that this is another situation where a terrorist organization is controlling large territories and fighting against State armies. These people were able to take the port of Kismayo in 2008, displacing over 30 thousand people! These people regularly make incursions into Kenya and commit terrorist bombings against State buildings or malls and highly frequented places. These are another lot of criminals that claim to do this in the name of Islam, and one really wonder who tough them religion and how!

Al Shebab were founded in 2006. Their full name is "Haraket Al Shabab Al Mujahideen", meaning the movement of the youth willing to sacrifice, a whole program... They are a consequence of the civil war that has been tearing down Somalia for already a few years, roughly since 1991, and can be seen as an offshoot of the Islamic Courts Union, a group of Sharia courts that tried to form an administration competing with the transitional federal government and which controlled the country for a period of 6 months in 2006. Somalia is a country that has been topping the failed states index (more gently called now the fragile states index!) from 2008 to 2013 to be second only to South Sudan in 2014 and 2015.

Somalia has a strategic location at the horn of Africa, and it boasts a long coastline, "preventing" Ethiopia from direct access to the ocean! Historically, the country has been at the crossroads of multiple civilizations since antiquity and it was a major trade hub with several flourishing ports. In more recent times, it was partly administered by the British, for the northern Somaliland part and by the Italians for the remaining part, the two regions being united only in 1960 to form the Somali Republic.

With the failure of the autocratic Siad Barre regime in the 1980's, the country fell into civil war with various direct or indirect interventions from neighboring Ethiopia, Eritrea and Kenya, despite the fact that it probably had one of the strongest military forces on the Continent... not to mention a short-lived UN intervention and the implication of an African Union peacekeeping force.

With these fertile grounds, and also some leadership provided by Afghanistan and Iraq-trained ethnic Somalis, Al Shebab is now a force to recon with: around 8000 people, mainly Somalis, but also Yemenis, Afghans, Saudis, Sudanese, Malays, and newly converted Kenyans to name a few. Poverty is a clear recruitment driver from the African Great Lakes region...

With this multi-ethnic recruitment, as well as a media strategy including "jihad rap videos" and twitter posts, Al Shebab are aiming for a wider region to operate in! Having made allegiance to Al Qaeda since 2010, they have the franchise for East Africa, but they do even operate in nearby Yemen. In Somalia, since operation Linda Nchi involving Somali and Kenyan armed forces at the end of 2011, Al Shebab have been forced out of major urban areas and are now based in rural ones. This means they have fewer financial resources than what they used to levy from taxing the territories they were "managing".

A UN report acknowledges they used to have from $70 to 100 million a year from these kinds of taxes! They even managed to racket the pirates that were getting funds from kidnapping and hijacking! What an intriguing eco-system!

The Shebab might seem on the decline nowadays, with tighter finances and some internal fights on whether to continue with Al Qaeda or rather join ISIS. They however know how to surf on Somali nationalism feeling and this is probably what provides them with some local strength. Despite the announcements of various military failures they have had, and the killing of more than 150 of their fighters in American drone and air force attacks, one cannot forget the massacres they have perpetrated in Nairobi at the Westgate shopping mall in 2013 killing 67 people at once or the later Garissa university attack leading to 148 casualties. These terrorists are unfortunately still very active and, they will continue to thrive in an area where central government is weak and the whole population held as a hostage…

Different geographies, same stories as we can see with AQIM, Boko Haram or ISIS.

DAESH OR ISIS

Let us focus now on the latest rising star of terror! Thank God, they are on the decline… Daesh or the Islamic State in Iraq and Syria. We need to make it clear first. The media should stop calling them a State. They do not have a single attribute of a State. Still, on most western media, we keep hearing this name! You began to know them, not because of the thousand or tens or may be hundreds of thousands of people they have killed or raped. No, you know them especially because of the 4 or 5 Americans, British or French they have beheaded, in atrocious scenes they have publicized. These shocking images and videos have not only circulated on social media but they have been shown, in one way or the other, by all world media and managed to put ISIS on the spot!

The origins of Daesh come from Al Qaeda in Iraq. They were part of the insurgency in Iraq following its invasion in 2003. It seems that the Camp Bucca prison offered them a great gathering and networking place. Many of the happy guests of Camp Bucca were snatched by US soldiers in various parts of Iraq and flown to this infamous place, the local, US-run, desert version of Guantanamo. Several young prisoners were exposed for the first time to Abu Bakr Al Baghdadi, the Emir of ISIS and probably one of the most dangerous and bloodthirsty terrorists. The conditions they had, and the abuses that happened, thanks to US soldiers, in the Abu Ghraib prison, cemented the links between the Bucca alumni and produced enough jihadists to make ISIS successfully combat Iraq's national army.

Do you feel you have any responsibility for this? Really, by destroying the State in Iraq, you opened the ground, a fertile ground, to such terrorist organizations to thrive. They grew stronger as they could control portions of territories and have access to financing sources in the form of oil fields. These people are guilty of major ethnic and religious cleansing on a large scale. Being extremist Sunnites, they have been killing Shiites and Christians equally. Both can be found in Iraq and Syria.

At a point in time, they were also one of the richest, if not the richest, terrorist organizations in the word. According to the Guardian (it's not an American but a British newspaper, still a trustable one I believe), ISIS had assets in excess of $850 million before taking Mosul (that is a city, in Iraq). After that, they added another $1.5 billion, with money robbed from the banks and military weapons they looted. Yes, at its peak, this organization, which was a small start-up ten years ago, was sitting on over $2bn of resources. That is a serious budget! In October 2015, the Financial Times has published a paper on "ISIS Inc.: How oil fuels the Jihadi terrorists". It estimated production in ISIS-controlled oil fields at around 34 to 40 thousand barrels per day, which is earning them $1.5 million a day. The paper insisted that the organization has had a serious approach and strategy to oil from the onset. It has been making recruitments of Engineers and technicians. It was capable of operating refineries…but who was buying this cheap oil?

When the fight started against Al Assad in Syria, ISIS were among the nice crowd that gathered to take him down. You did not know that? Because you supported the actions against the Syrian ruler… Did you change your mind now? What is worst, the plague or the cholera? If I had to choose, I would respond very easily… I am not sure what your choice is right now, and that is putting my life in danger, not yours! Indeed, these people have been expanding. They have had a subsidiary in Sinai, in Egypt and quite large operations in eastern Libya as well. They controlled large territories in Iraq, they were active in all the regions mentioned, they had access to arms, to oil, to funds and to manpower… All the unemployed people that we have in our struggling countries were finding a Jihadist job with them. They were even enrolling some crazy young women for entertainment. Looks like a summer camp, where they take care of your transportation, your catering, your partying and they even guarantee you a spot in paradise! They have a powerful recruitment message "from the heavens", and they are good at macabre marketing.

These stupid people are not only attacking contemporary civilizations. They have also taken as theirs the mission of erasing all traces of previous civilizations, and unfortunately, they operate on fertile ground. The areas they used to control are rich of world heritage remains. They have scenarized the systematic annihilation and ransacking of statues and objects in the Mosul museum. They have videoed the bombing and bulldozing of the complete and well-preserved city of Nimrud, the capital of the Assyrian kingdom which flourished between 900 and 600 BC, a city dating back to over 3000 BC. Not to mention Khorsabad, Hatra, Jonah's tomb… As quoted by Sturt Manning of Cornell University in a CNN column, Confucius said "Study the past if you would define the future". As these people are destroying the past, their actual aim is to tell us "there is no future"!

I was getting sick to see almost every day on TV and social media their new inventions to destroy all that make us human, all that make our collective history, all that is a common and shared heritage. There is this very unpleasant feeling of watching this B-series horror movie without being able to even think of a reaction. They are raping us when they are raping Yazidi women, they are killing us when they are killing thousands, they are terrorizing us when they are filming their horrible murders, and they know it! When are we going to wake up and seriously fight back?

What is the world doing against this cancer? Do we understand all the ramifications? OK, thank you for the drones you sent to fight them. And yes, you did some air strikes too. I read somewhere that it cost some 50 thousand dollars of F16 and other air fighters missions to take down one Daesh four-wheeler… Well, we'll need millions more to start getting any kind of result there! If you look on a map, and see the expansion they have had on the ground and the area they used to control, you can only pray! At least, this is my case with the little means I have for such a fight.

Back in 2015, Daesh was almost becoming a fact of life. We were wondering: will they have their Caliphate next to Syria and Iraq? It would definitely keep the region under pressure, as Iran and Turkey would also have to take part of that stress. Fortunately, Iraqi and Syrian ground forces have made some progress in restricting their territory. Mosul was taken back in July 2017, soon followed by Raqqa in Syria. It was not before March 2019 that ISIS gave up its last controlled territories in Syria, while its self-proclaimed Calif got killed eventually in October 2019.

Besides all the money it had, another big danger of ISIS was its use of social media and the internet to recruit more and more people. ISIS was Al Qaeda 2.0. These people were playing the media game better than any other terror organization, scenarizing their murders in a terrible manner. On the organization side as well, they have managed to melt into the "cloud". They have pushed a lot of literature into the internet. You can have tutorials on making bombs, and beheading people…They call for action, but, except for the countries where they have installed their backbone, there is no central command which decides on which actions to do, but rather an organization that gives its blessing to the projects that people bring along from their local on-the-ground terror cell team…

Their model is decentralized and favors "personal initiative", very entrepreneurial indeed! The objective is clear, but the means are to be invented all the time. This makes it much more dangerous as it becomes more unpredictable.

TALIBAN

One cannot close this section on major terrorist organizations in the world without a special mention of the Taliban! This plague is devastating whole regions in Pakistan and especially Afghanistan. They got along very well with Al Qaeda for a long period of time, and Osama Bin Laden was Mollah Omar's (the head of Taliban) best friend... However, later on, with the fight for the driver's seat, and because ISIS had a hegemonious worldwide project, the Taliban and ISIS were fighting each other in Afghanistan, as reported by the BBC. The Taliban have created special forces in October 2015 specifically to fight ISIS, which was becoming a major threat to their very existence, after the creation in early 2015, of a Daesh offspring in the "Great Khorasan", a historical region that overlaps with Afghanistan, Pakistan, Iran and Central Asia.

The Taliban were also the first terror organization to launch the "trend" of historical monuments destruction. They have exploded the spectacular Buddha statues of Bamiyan in March 2001. They were listed as World Heritage sites by UNESCO and were the most prominent landmark of that region. The statues were dating back to the 6th century and were carved directly in the rock of a cliff. The destruction work took several weeks, but the Taliban eventually managed to accomplish this aggression against the Buddhist heritage of the valley that was part of the silk road, and also against world culture in general.

Where did these people come from and how did they manage to rule Afghanistan? The word itself, Taliban, is the Pashto version of the Arabic word "Talib", meaning student. Most of these people were "students" trained in the Pakistani "madrassas" that were established for Afghan refugees... Madrassa is the Arab word to say school, any school actually. However, in this particular context, we are more referring to religious schools. With the Soviet invasion of Afghanistan, many people fled the country to neighboring Pakistan. At the same time, Pakistan managed to secure the financial support of Saudi Arabia, of the US and the UK to train Afghan Mujahidin to combat the Red Army. It was claimed that some 20 billion dollars were used to train close to a hundred thousand Afghans and provide them with arms and ammunition...

After the fall of a soviet-backed government and the withdrawal of the Red Army, an Islamic State of Afghanistan was proclaimed in April 1992, but the country never became united under this umbrella and fell into civil war, with various provinces experiencing a different fate, being run by competing militias under the influence of various external parties. The Taliban started emerging as a strong politico-religious force in 1994 when they were able to take Kandahar with very little losses and they managed that same year to extend their hegemony over 12 of 34 provinces not under central government control. With the help of Pakistan intelligence services and army and Bin Laden's Al Qaeda, the Taliban entered Kabul in September 1996 and established the Islamic Emirate of Afghanistan.

The Taliban claimed they would be applying the Sharia, the Islamic rule. They were using a combination of Sharia and Pashtun (that is their dominant ethnic group) tribal codes in an anti-modern interpretation... and committed several atrocities in the name of Islam. They were involved in human trafficking, women oppression, and civilians' killings. They forbade women from being educated and forced them to wear that horrible Burqa. They had however some resistance within the country, mainly personified by Ahmad Shah Masoud, the "lion of Panjshir". This Tajik commander claimed "the Taliban have a very wrong perception of Islam" and he was able to forge a multi-ethnic alliance, with Pashtun commander Abdul Haq, and Hamid Karzai (later to become President), bringing Tajiks, Pashtuns, Hazaras and Uzbeks under the United Front command. Unfortunately, Masoud did not survive another assassination attempt to see the Taliban ousted from power and from all major Afghan cities with the help of an international coalition, after the 9/11 World Trade Center attacks...

Just like Al Qaeda, the Taliban are a creation of the 20th century. They have no deep historical roots. They seem to be another output of your secret service's unfortunate manipulations! You wanted the Soviets out. With some of your strong allies in the Arab and Islamic world, you financed and trained people to do this. There were good Mujahidins, and there were undesired babies that ended up "on the dark side of the force" as would Yoda say in "Star Wars". With the advent of ISIS at a later stage, and with all these evils fighting for the control of the brains of simple minded or desperate Muslims, some media started suggesting that Al Qaeda and the Taliban might be more acceptable than ISIS… Once again, we are faced with the choice between the plague and the cholera… we should refuse both.

One cannot forget all that the Taliban have done! Besides all the killings, women's oppression, historical monuments destruction, human rights slaughtering, drugs trafficking, one of their biggest sins is that they have brought to the world a hideous contribution to fashion: wild dirty-looking beards for men, and black burqa uniforms for women. Can you imagine living in such an environment for a week? You would lose any sense of aesthetics… and would be ready to commit suicide!

BLACKWATER

You might wonder what this has to do in the "terrorist section" of this book? Blackwater is nothing like Al Qaeda or Daesh or Shebab! This is partly true… Blackwater is an American company that provided mercenaries to the war in Iraq. The issue is that these supposedly freedom fighters behaved very badly, killing many innocent Iraqis… One of these freedom warriors was even quoted for willing to kill as many Arabs as he could, as a revenge for 11/9… as if we, Arabs, should all be held responsible for 9/11. This is as stupid as saying that all Germans were Nazis or all Italians were fascists or all Americans were behind the Ku Klux Clan or all white people are racist!

Shall we classify Blackwater as a terrorist organization for what they have done? True, they did not kill Americans, or Europeans, or their friends… and sorry, yes, you are the ones doing the classifications and telling us who is right and who is wrong! Who am I to even think that I could be suggesting this?

Well, you will find on the FBI website that "Four former Blackwater employees were found guilty of charges in fatal 2007 shootings at Nisur square in Iraq". Indeed, in September 2007, these paramilitary agents killed 14 unarmed civilians, and injured several others. According to US attorney Machen, "these Blackwater contractors unleashed powerful sniper fire, machine guns, and grenade launchers on innocent men, women, and children". They were posted in Nisur square, a busy traffic circle adjacent to the "Green Zone" in Bagdad. They simply and cold-bloodedly fired their weapons at Iraqi citizens, killing among others two children of 9 and 11 years, an aspiring doctor in his twenties with his mother, a businessman, a whole family, a truck driver… a similar scenario to what happened in 2015 in Sousse, Tunisia, where an Islamist terrorist killed over 30 tourists and later on in Paris, France, where again some other Islamist terrorists killed innocent people in the streets and cafes. These terrorists got shot by security forces, and that was right. In Iraq, nobody fired against the Blackwater terrorists because…they were the security forces!

I doubt they were Islamist terrorists, but no one really cares about their religion, right? The only one religion worth mentioning for terror acts is Islam. These guys were not Muslim and not Arabs. Not really interesting for the media. A somehow similar story to that of the German pilot that crashed his plane in France in this fantastic year of 2015 (again!). In the initial coverage of the event, we saw a famous French journalist, M. Elkabbach, asking an official representative, if they had names on the passenger list that could suggest a terrorist action! What does that mean M. Elkabbach? If there were names of Arab passengers, or may be anything similar from Chechnya or Turkey? This was a real racist and nonprofessional stand on a public media, and yet, this journalist did not have to face any sanctions or charges.

Eventually, the evidence was that the responsible for the crash was "simply" a German pilot suffering psychological disorders. With a name like Andreas Lubitz, cannot be more German. Maybe we should look if he didn't have some Arab origin after all? Don't call him a terrorist but rather insane, sick, fool… almost deserves sympathy for his depressive status. Of course, if the pilot's name were Ahmed, even if he were suffering from a similar psychological situation, I bet he would be a terrorist!

KALASHNIKOV

Mikhail Kalashnikov is far from being a terrorist. He is a Russian General who designed probably one of the most famous rifles of modern times, and a terrorists' and insurgents' favorite: the AK-47. Unlike what the General wanted for his arm, it is no more known as a weapon of defense, but rather, a weapon of offense. Indeed, the Kalashnikov has become the rifle of choice that gets mentioned almost on a daily basis in the media, and Kalashnikov has surpassed Vodka as a Russian icon!

The weapon made a difference in Vietnam. Used by Vietcong guerillas and North Vietnamese army, it worked almost flawlessly in the harsh environment of the jungle, while the M-16 used by American soldiers experienced jamming and corrosion. Experts believe that over 100 million AKs are being used today and over a million is manufactured yearly. The AK has made it to Hollywood, as Stallone was carrying one in Rambo movies. Other actors did as well... It has made it to video games as the famous "Grand Theft Auto" features several AKs. It was the weapon used to kill President Anouar Al Sadat in 1981 and it was Osama Bin Laden's favorite companion on his propaganda videos of Al Qaeda.

Kalashnikov was all over the place in 2015: in the Charlie Hebdo shootings, the Bardo shootings, the Sousse shootings, the Thalys aborted terror attack and the Paris shootings of the Bataclan and various cafes...

Mikhail Kalashnikov claimed he has made this weapon development to secure his mother country's borders, and that he made no money out of it... Indeed, if he lived in the capitalist part of this world, he would have been a billionaire. Anyhow, his grandson Igor has been able to commercially utilize the Kalashnikov brand name to sell vodka!

GUANTANAMO

Now that we have talked about the terrorists, let us talk about one destination they might be headed to…

This could be a fantastic "Club Med" destination. It is in a tropical island. The Latino name sounds like Salsa, Pina Cola and great fun… but I definitely pass my turn to go there! This is a big shame on you, the icon of democracy and human rights. How to qualify Guantanamo? What is it really? An unlawful big jail? A restricted military zone? A terrorist concentration camp? Years and years after its opening, after all the controversies, after all the promises to close it, Guantanamo stands there. It is not anymore on the media. We do not know the number of remaining VIP hosts you have there, nor the cost to the American taxpayer or who else is paying for it, nor the date when it will be dismantled.

The Guantanamo detention camp was established end of 2001 by the Bush administration within the American military base in the island of Cuba. It was claimed to be outside the US legal jurisdiction and was denied the application of the Geneva Conventions on the protection of detainees until the US supreme court made a conflicting ruling in 2004. It was clear that there was no intention of a fair treatment of prisoners, which number has peaked at over 750. There were reports of torture, of detention of minors under the age of 18, and of several deaths, "suicide" mostly as claimed by American authorities… I wonder why I do not really buy into the suicide story!

Did the people held there get any judgment? Is there any investigation under way? What if another country did a similar thing? Would they deserve to be condemned at the UN Security Council? What if Iran was operating

Guantanamo? After all, with the help you provided in the past to the Shah's Savak, they have the know-how… Hundreds of people that were held in the camp for years were eventually released without charge. Did they get your apologies? Will you be paying them any compensation for being arbitrarily held far from their homes and families? It does not seem like it, especially that there are tens of detainees that you decided to keep indefinitely, because you decided they were too dangerous to be transferred but you had insufficient evidence to try them!

May be some of the prisoners there really deserve to be detained, but, as a democratic nation, a nation pretending to tell the world how to do things, a nation pretending to tell the world what is right and what is wrong, you should lead by the example and manage this thing properly… before they all die! Remember, the suicide rate in Guantanamo seems to be rather high. These people have no sense of humor: they did not like "camp X-Ray" as you call it? Nor camp Delta, nor camp Echo, nor Camp No and its interrogation center? Yes, "interrogation", or shall we say torture? You do not like this word to describe what you have been doing to these people? I can understand. It is true that the American administration never admitted committing torture in Guantanamo. Just barely accepting some instances of "misconduct", not even raising to the level of "abuse"… but why did the Red Cross, Amnesty International, Human Rights Watch, the BBC, the Guardian, the New York Times, all of them say that you used torture in the Guantanamo camp? Don't they all like you? It is hard to learn that your soldiers have been using against the prisoners all kinds of refined techniques: beatings, sleep deprivation, sexual and cultural humiliation, uncomfortable positions, forced injections…

Should you normalize your relations with Cuba, they will be asking for Guantanamo back… indeed, it is on their island! Will you return it with these rather unusual tourists? Or will you hold it for a couple more decades, until they all retire or pass away?

INTELLIGENCE

CIA: these three letters stand for a brand probably as powerful as Coca Cola or Google around the world. They are one of the symbols of America, and its hegemony. Who does not know what the CIA is? We all have in mind a whole bunch of espionage movies where the extra-ordinary CIA agents protect us against all sorts of dangers, be they Soviets, Islamists or Aliens!

CIA agents are always depicted as the heroes that can take care of all the threats that we are exposed to, whether we are aware of them or not. It is unfortunate that such a terrible report was produced end of 2014 by the Senate Intelligence Committee, and got so much attention, on bad CIA behavior. Of the over 6000-pages report, only its 524-pages executive summary got declassified, but that was sufficient to earn the report extensive media coverage. The New York times talked about "a macabre accounting of some of the grisliest techniques that the CIA used to torture and imprison terrorism suspects". It talks about the famous "waterboarding" technique, as well as "rectal feeding" … It talks about detention centers in geographies as diverse as Thailand, Romania, Lithuania, or Guantanamo Bay. We were all thinking this was the perfect Agency, with properly recruited, well-educated and well-trained personnel, protecting the rule of law, conforming to strict guidelines from the Congress and the US Administration in general, and fully respecting human rights, democracy and high moral standards. We suddenly discover that "No", it is not "Alice in wonderland", and the CIA is not much better than the highly decried KGB, FSB, Stasi, Savak or any other secret service agency around the world. The CIA is not nice and gentle…

Honestly, were you really believing this fairytale? Did anyone think that an Agency of this kind would be acting all by the rule? We did not. Maybe you think that we are used to these non-democratic, non-human rights respectful behaviors…Maybe we are simply realistic about human nature, and the way things are. CIA agents are no angels. Don't fool yourselves and do not try again to fool the world. I am not asking that they change. I am asking you to simply recognize this fact. They are responsible of many unlawful wrong doings just like any other people operating in similar "firms". That is their way of "doing business". I am not sure how much of this can be regulated and monitored. There are so many ways to get around it anyway. For some of the most illegal or unacceptable actions, the CIA will have the option to subcontract. Many such agencies and services exist around the world. They will always have room for an extra well-paid service. If you do it once, you can do it ten times. Once you have left your consciousness behind, the number does not matter anymore. Some torture professionals might even enjoy it. They will tell you they are doing it for some kind of ideal!

The CIA is said to be behind the overthrowing of seven governments in foreign countries as reported by Foreign Policy Magazine. Some say it is much more... Not all of them were dictators that needed to be removed to install democracy. In some instances, it was just the opposite! We can make the series start with Iran's Mossadegh in 1953. Millions of dollars were funneled into Teheran to finance street protests and eventually take out democratically elected Mossadegh. He spent the rest of his life under house arrest. Not so long after, in 1954, it was the turn of Guatemala. President Jacobo Arbenz was making too many land reforms threatening the interests of US-corporation United Fruits Company. The CIA equipped rebels and paramilitary troops and the Navy blockaded the coast. Arbenz was eventually forced out. Then, Congo-Zaire, in 1960, the Dominican Republic in 1961, South Vietnam in 1963, Brazil in 1964 and Chile in 1973. This list is not including later "successes" of the Intelligence Agency. It is however showing that in most instances, these interventions were not in the name of democracy or the best interests of the nations and people that were targeted. Indeed, in the cases of Congo's Lumumba or Brazil's Goulart or Chile's Allende, it was about removing a leader that was leaning towards a socialist approach, and the outcome was always a fierce dictatorship, with its corollary of corruption, kleptocracy and nepotism.

As an African, I still remember Mobutu, who came to power in Zaire (and managed to stay long with your help!), with his landmark leopard-skin toque. His personal wealth ended up being as important as the country's debt, as he stole the proceeds of the rich soil of the Katanga. In Brazil, they ended up having military rule from 1964 till 1985. In Chile, the CIA helped with the propaganda campaigns of the General Pinochet who took the power from Allende. And what do we associate Pinochet with? Human right abuses? Killings of political opponents? Not the exact type of democrat you would want… William Blum, an American author and historian, has written a book on the CIA, that philosopher Noam Chomsky has considered to be "the best book on the topic". Blum's title is self-explanatory: "Killing hope: US military and CIA interventions since World War II". He is covering interventions in more than 50 countries, not only the seven mentioned above!

But the CIA is no more the only famous intelligence agency that you have. These days, the once shy and mysterious NSA is also making the news. It became notorious for its many surveillance programs of the digital and communications worlds. Prism is one of them. You should tell them; the presidential campaign was not "Yes we scan!"

For you, the preachers of freedom, Prism is a big and heavy scandal. What is astonishing is that it is more as such outside of the US, but inside, people seem to be ready to accept all excesses from the NSA, under the claim that you are fighting terror. What is it really about? Have you heard of it? I have… This is a major electronic surveillance program, and all your blue-chip internet-based businesses such as Google, Facebook, Microsoft & Apple to name a few are said to be involved. However, keep something in mind: "if you have two ears and no brains, then, there is no use in having four ears", to quote Alain Bauer, a security expert cited by French magazine "Le Nouvel Observateur"…

And by the way, it is very bad to spy on even your closest friends! Why did you have to listen to the mobile phones of Angela Merkel, the German chancellor and three successive French Presidents: Jacques Chirac, Nicolas Sarkozy and François Hollande. Do you actually trust your friends?

You have to thank George W. Bush for his "Protect America Act" of 2007. This has allowed such special operations… The scandal has been brought to surface by a former NSA consultant, Edward Snowden. The Guardian and the Washington Post have relayed the news and then, the world has been talking about it. Snowden became a pariah. The US wanted him arrested. He is considered to be a traitor and some major politicians and public figures proclaimed in the media that he needed to be sued by putting the lives of operative agents at risk. I saw his interview on the BBC. He looked calm and accepted his fate. He considered having done the right thing and was perfectly aware of the personal consequences he would endure.

As quoted by Indian novelist Arundhati Roy in the Guardian, the famous whistleblower said about surveillance: "if we do nothing, we sort of sleepwalk into a total surveillance state, where we have both a super-state that has unlimited capacity to apply force with an unlimited ability to know (about the people it is targeting) – and that's a very dangerous combination. That's the dark future. The fact that they know everything about us and we know nothing about them – because they are secret, they are privileged, and they are a separate class… the elite class, the political class, the resource class – we don't know where they live, we don't know what they do, we don't know who their friends are. They have the ability to know all that about us".

Interestingly, the European parliament has voted in October 2015, with a short majority, a resolution to abandon all criminal charges against Snowden, to recognize his status of international human rights defender, to grant him protection and prevent his extradition to the US where he is still facing charges. Exiled in Russia since 2014, Snowden's world should be significantly widening, and his diet would be able to expand beyond Vodka and caviar! The European parliament has urged for a higher degree of protection of the personal data being transferred to the US, to a level comparable to what is imposed in the European Union. Who are these friends that are letting you down? Don't they understand the cause?

Unfortunately, the vote of the European Parliament is not binding for any of the member States, and Snowden was denied asylum right in France once again in 2019. He will have to get used to the cold winters of Moscow…

Similar story for another big evil of the internet world that has seriously destabilized the well-established order maintained by your hegemonious agencies: Julian Assange. The editor in chief of the WikiLeaks website has been living in the Embassy of Ecuador in London since he sought refuge there in 2012. In 2019, newly elected Ecuador President Lenin Moreno decided to end his asylum. He got arrested by British authorities and sentenced to jail. The Australian hacker and journalist has been under US criminal investigation since the release of data that made WikiLeaks so notorious in 2010. He is under threat of a prosecution under the Espionage act of 1917 and might incur up to 175 years jail sentence!

How do I view this? me, the Arab… In fact, in the past dictatorial times, this was normal life for us! Everyone had to consider by default that he was spied upon in all his communications, be they by phone or mail or any other form. Can you imagine that during the darkest periods of dictatorship, when we were going to have a rather "touchy" conversation, people resolved to shut down completely their mobiles not to take any risk? Sometimes, they would go to the stage of taking out the batteries! There was indeed the well-spread idea that your phone, even idle, could be used to spy on you and activated at distance to forward what was being said in the room where you were. This is the level of fear that we had, especially after the "well documented event" that everyone could tell you in Tunis: a guy was stuck in a traffic jam caused by our dictator of that time. He complained about the matter to his wife, to whom he was talking on the phone. OK, it was a little more than a complaint; he might have insulted his highness or talked about him in a bad way! He got immediately (Maybe not quite immediately, but within hours) found by some special police forces that brutalized him.

Now, with the fresh air of freedom brought by the revolutions, we are still not sure that we can talk or e-mail freely. You know, it is difficult to get rid of reflexes you acquired over the years. May be the next generation… For us, this is normal life. If it were not the case, it would be a dream. It would be luxury beyond our craziest dreams. Therefore, we keep quiet, we cannot believe it is over, especially when we see that such a supposed model of democracy in this modern world is spying on its own citizens and on others… The very bad justification that was given was: American citizens should not be afraid as they were not the target of this program… Prism was mainly aiming at non-American citizens it was claimed. I doubt this. And I also find the explanation disrespectful of the basic freedoms of the citizens of the world. Maybe I am wrong, and you are right. The American citizen is not just like any other citizen of the world. He is a super-citizen of the world!

However, even in America, not all citizens are equal and not all of them get the same treatment, especially when it comes to security, to the police and to basic rights. Without going back to the whole civil rights not so old history, let me quote here Daniel Ellsberg, the guy who leaked Pentagon papers during the Vietnam War: "We are not in a police state now, not yet… White, middle-class, educated people like myself are not living in a police state… Black, poor people are living in a police state. The repression starts with the semi-white, the Middle Easterners, including anybody who is allied with them, and goes on from there… One more 9/11, and then I believe we will have hundreds of thousands of detentions. Middle Easterners and Muslims will be put in detention camps or deported. After 9/11, we had thousands of people arrested without charges…". I should add that, even with a black President at the head of the State, during Obama's Presidency, we have continued witnessing several police shootings against the black (and often poor) US population.

Going back to World War II history, this is exactly what happened to the Japanese people, or the US-citizens of Japanese descent, living in the US, after Pearl Harbor. President Franklin D. Roosevelt ordered the incarceration of some 110 000 to 120 000 people living mainly on the West Coast. 62% of them were US-citizens! People like Sanji Abe and Thomas Sakakihara, were among the detainees, despite the fact that they were elected Hawaii legislators! Abe was detained for nineteen months in sands island and then, in the famous Honouliuli internment camp. It was only under President Carter (1980) that an investigation was launched about the matter and only under President Reagan (1988) that the US Government admitted that this action was commanded by "racial prejudice, war hysteria and a failure of political leadership". The signed law apologized for the internment and authorized the payment of a compensation for the survivors… Don't we learn from history? Or maybe M. Trump ignores this chapter of American history, as this is what he is asking to do with Muslims!

And let us just not forget another venerable institution of the trio that looks after the wellbeing of the American citizen: the FBI. The Federal Bureau of Investigation, as its name might hint, is the principal domestic intelligence and investigation service of the United States. Its major current objectives include the protection of the US from terrorist attacks and to protect civil rights. A report published by Human Rights Watch in 2014 shows that it has been doing just the opposite with some Muslim Americans. Indeed, this report says that the FBI has "encouraged, pushed and sometimes even paid" Muslim Americans to incite them to commit terror acts they might have never envisaged, with the objective of increasing the number of arrests, and justify anti-terror law and surveillance programs that could limit civil rights. The study, performed by Human Rights Watch, with help from Columbia University, focuses on 27 specific cases out of 500 terrorism cases investigated by the American justice since 9/11. It shows that the infiltrated FBI agent has played an active role in 30% of the cases…

The theory behind these excesses is that these individuals were in any case "to be terrorists". If the FBI did not help them "come out", Al Qaida would have done it. This is quite scary! Just like what was hinted in the movie "Minority report", featuring Tom Cruise… People would be arrested before committing the crime they are going to, but, what if they were not actually going to do it? When I hear this, I really wonder about what happened to all the civil rights debate, about what makes a free nation, what is terrorism after all? And what fabricates terrorists?

I am a big fan of analogies and I am going to use one from the world of finance. You know, when I had the opportunity to meet George Soros after the Tunisian revolution, I googled him before the event and discovered he a was a big promoter of "Reflexivity" in economics. He claims that his grasp of the principle of reflexivity is what has given him his "edge", contributing to his successes as a trader. To make it simple, reflexivity refers to the self-reinforcing effect of market sentiment, whereby rising prices attract buyers whose actions drive prices higher. The same effect can be seen downwards.

The changes occur in a cycle when things become instable. This somehow means that "the situations that men define as true, become true for them". I later discovered that this was what the father of reflexivity has come up with in the 1920's. William Thomas was a sociologist. He explained how observations or actions of an observer in a social system affect the very situations he is observing. Sociologist Robert K Merton called it in the late 40's the "self-fulfilling prophecy", and this is exactly what it is now: an Arab and a Muslim is a terrorist: your intelligence services are making this statement true because they took it as a working assumption!

CORRUPTION

Corruption is seen as an illness of poor countries, developing countries… Arab countries fall under this category and are often considered to be very much corrupt. It is still a long way to reach good governance, transparency, accountability of the ruling class and parties… I agree to this and my frustration is to see that the current changes in the Arab world did not improve the situation. Getting rid of the dictators did not get rid of corruption. Not to mention the countries where no changes occurred and where you are still doing very good business…

In fact, there are two sides to the corruption coin. There is of course the benefactor from the act of corruption, the party that is getting an immediate unlawful advantage from being corrupt. There is however the second party that is often not publicized, the party that gets also unlawful advantages by corrupting the other party. This could mean getting a business or a contract under unfair competition protocols. This party is often you, your companies and your allies… shouldn't this be condemned at least as strongly as the corrupt side? Without corruptors, there will be no corrupts and no corruption! However, if you look at most of your laws and accounting practices and rules, they accommodate very well with corruption. Look at what newly elected President Trump did in less than a month in office, he repealed an Obama administration SEC regulation that forced companies to disclose payments to governments.

As reported by most media, and I can cite here Bloomberg in a February 14th 2017 paper, "President Donald Trump has overturned an Obama-era anti-corruption rule that would have forced oil, gas and mining companies to disclose payments to foreign governments, becoming the first president in 16 years to take advantage of a law that allows him to rescind a predecessor's regulation…Backers of the SEC regulation say forcing companies to disclose foreign payments would curb corruption in resource-rich countries, such as Nigeria. The oil industry says the rule would put U.S. companies at a competitive disadvantage"

The excuse is of course that, if you do not do it, others will… What about pollution? What about child labor? What about all the things that we should combat together to make this world a better place? If you don't, and you put a lot of pressure on those who do, and educate the world around some basic principles, then, of course, things will change. But if you continue to accept immoral business practices, that actually pervert the world, then it all goes on. It is common knowledge that major arms contracts, oil, real estate, infrastructure etc. are impregnated with corruption, and it is not going to change any near.

Maybe there is another "incentive" for it. Once you start doing illegal things, all rules can be disobeyed. Indeed, in many corruption schemes, there are "retro-commissions". This means that not all the money claimed to go to the corrupt party stays there. Some of it, sometimes a significant portion, flies back… This helps finance rogue politicians, or black boxes that can be used for various ultimate goals. It can also simply accelerate the enrichment of some middle-men or even high-ranking professionals in institutions involved in the deals. Money has no odor, nor color, especially when it has been laundered in such a nice fashion…

I would like to conclude this chapter by a quote of Ayn Rand, the Russian-born American novelist and philosopher, who was saying already in 1928: "When you see that trading is done, not by consent, but by compulsion - when you see that in order to produce, you need to obtain permission from men who produce nothing - when you see that money is flowing to those who deal, not in goods, but in favors - when you see that men get richer by graft and by pull than by work, and your laws don't protect you against them, but protect them against you - when you see corruption being rewarded and honesty becoming a self-sacrifice - you may know that your society is doomed".

OIL

This is the curse of the Arabs… you know this joke the French have on their neighbors from Belgium? God made a competition to choose between French fries and oil, and the Belgians chose first. I wonder today if they were not right in doing so. A country that can afford to spend over a year without any government deserves respect! This is for the Guinness Book of records! Well, the Belgians did it, and they are doing rather fine… But look at the oil rich Arab countries. Look at Libya and Iraq after you "freed" them from their dictators. Look at all the others…

Let us be serious! This is normally a very serious topic, "Oil". It is at the center of many controversies. It is one major source of carbon emissions and a cause of global warming… It is a natural resource that is so precious that is has already caused many wars and will probably continue to do so in the future. Who is going to dominate the oil producing nations? Historically, you have. Your various private companies do the exploration and the drilling and the production. Sometimes, when things go a bit wrong, the army is here to serve, and the politicians will always find a way of legitimizing the action!

There is a fantastic book on this topic, which I have read long ago but from which I have kept a lot of information in mind. It is called the "Le Défi Mondial – the World Challenge" and dates back to 1980. There was in one chapter a discussion on what the US would do in case its oil-related interests were threatened. The author, the famous French journalist Jean-Jacques Servant-Schreiber, talks about one young hawk at the Pentagon asking to consider the nuclear option in the gulf if US interests were under threat: that guy was Paul Wolfowitz! Is it worth reminding you of who he was and what responsibilities he has endorsed under M. Bush's rule? And later at the World Bank?

Iraq was definitely not the place for "weapons of mass destruction", but guess what? It is full of oil! Some talk about the second proven world reserve...Libya is another "free" nation now, and its oil will be easily flooding western economies with the so much needed fuel! It is also cited in Servant-Schreiber's book who gives Kaddafi the real paternity of the oil crisis of 1974, even if the King of Sauds managed to gain all the media benefit of this first attempt to get some balance between the oil-producing countries and the exploration and production Majors!

In Tunisia, there isn't much oil. There isn't much of anything else... Our oil is olive oil. We are amongst the top 5 world producers (This is probably one of the rare things where we can pretend to be in such a worldwide position!). However, most of that precious oil is exported bulk to Italy & Spain and it is then blended into some of the fine productions those countries export, getting at the same time most of the value.

But let us go back to the "real" oil, the one that shapes politics and wars and commands all geostrategic moves of all major nations. There has been something going on in recent years that is not easy to understand. Oil prices have been sky diving from over the $100 a barrel to less than $50 in a few months. Who is benefiting and who is losing from this? At first sight, when you see the ruble falling by more than 40% to the dollar, at a time where the US and Europe have been imposing sanctions on Russia, to punish it from what was happening in Ukraine and Crimea, one can think that this is a clear action against Russia, to make life harder for our friend Poutine who has been defying the West for too long. In this move, where Saudi Arabia has been instrumental in maintaining production quotas and pushing the oil price down, traditional alliances between the US and the Gulf Monarchies have been at work as usual, and this is targeted against Russia, and potentially as a collateral, Iran and Venezuela, two other countries that do not like the US (which does not like them either!).

There is however another important collateral effect, which is probably not desired in the US, but might be sought by Saudi Arabia, and this is where the interests of these two parties are diverging, and where some people are explaining that the US are not necessarily behind this sharp fall of oil prices. Indeed, this level of pricing has killed many developments in shale gas and oil, mainly in the US. The exploration boom has been fueled by venture capital and hedge funds. At over $100 the barrel, this was good risk and worth investing. Today, many firms operating in this field have collapsed, and we have seen an oil crash on the stock exchange, after the subprime crash and the internet crash... too much speculation and too much financial flows not always relying on tangible assets and value creation have made your economy rather fragile to such events. We have witnessed in 2020, for a few days, some oil prices getting negative!

Are the US and Saudi Arabia (KSA) collaborating together on the issue, aiming mainly at Russia, Iran and similar nations, and accepting the collateral effects on shale gas companies, which means that the movement is mainly piloted from the US, or, do we have one of the first acts of rebellion by which KSA is confronting the US, as the development of alternative oil resources and exploration is putting at risk its strong position and market share in the worldwide oil market. What will be the consequences on the longer run of such a move? KSA has always had a close tie with the US and its interests or, to be closer to the reality, the interests of its governing class, have always been intricately connected with those of the US. Such a noticeable change in attitude might be opening a whole new era of US-KSA relationships, which could mean a lot more riskier future for the oil-rich monarchy, which is certainly not the model democratic nation in the world or the Arab world, but which has always benefited of a friendly attitude of the big advocates of human rights, and democracy for all! Too much oil in the balance…

In May 2020, the Wall Street Journal has published a paper titled "Oil Becomes a Risky Game for Saudis". It says that the Saudi prince, Mohamed Ben Salman (MBS) in now tinkering with the US oil industry, its national security and Trump's re-election! The latter got personally involved to ask the Saudis and the Russians to lower their production, and we are now far from a time when Trump was fully supporting MBS as he did during the crisis with Qatar or the assassination of the journalist Khashoggi.

Another collateral effect, which is affecting KSA directly, is the imbalance it has caused in its budget and the staggering deficit this has led to. Oil revenues for Saudi have melted down to some 148 billion euros whereas spending has remained around 240 billion, leading to a deficit of more than 90 billion in 2015… the situation has not improved since. KSA is often referred to as the biggest oil exporter in the World. That is definitely true. But guess who was the first oil producer worldwide in 2019? the US, with over 15 billion barrels a day, against 12 for KSA.

The future of oil exporting nations is seen to be a little darker. Some of them have already been tapping into their reserves and sovereign wealth funds. Many of the Middle East and North Africa economies will be hurt. They will be prevented them from having the resources for much needed investments…The world can be happier for cheaper oil but not the so-called "Arab World"!

THE CAMEL

You might think: why am I talking here about that animal! It is so much tied to Arab culture, to the desert, that I had to touch on this iconic companion of the nomads! It is an animal that is exemplified for its patience… it can resist harsh dry Sahara weather. It provides milk, meat, and warm clothes for the freezing winter desert nights.

Though, some people down-under are talking about a massive massacre of camels in the Australian desert. Not because they have gone wild! Not because they can contaminate you with rabies or any other lethal disease! No, the reason is that they are seen to be one major contributor to the global warming. The stupid animal's flatulencies are high on methane! These camels gone back to the wild do not have natural predators, and they are farting big time… the sentence is to kill them. Some people are even thinking of setting companies for that. They will be able to trade carbon credits from the elimination of camels! They will turn a camel fart into dollars! What a crazy world we live in.

This news has really annoyed me, not that I live with camels all day long. Some "civilized" people still probably believe that our streets are covered with dust and crossed by convoys of camels. The old caravan concept! Imagine those magnificent lines of camels in the dunes of "Lawrence of Arabia". Fabulous sceneries… you cannot think of all the carbon emissions!

But guess where does the camel come from? Not from Arabia, or Africa or Asia…in fact, according to the newest findings on the topic by researcher Natalia Rybczynski, camels were thriving in the Arctic in ancient times, and they are of American origin! The animal was a boreal forest specialist before crossing the Bering strait from North America to Eurasia, and then to the

Arabian Peninsula and North Africa... The camel got his fat-filled hump to survive in the chilly polar forest rather than the harsh dry desert. What an adaptation! This animal is really a champion of acclimation to the environment...

I hereby launch an official request to save the camels. Despite all the impolite behavior they might be having, I am convinced that this is not the major issue facing our civilization. In any case, anyone ever talked about slaughtering all the caws, all the sheep? Anyone talked about turning down all air-conditioning in the planet? What is contributing most to the global warming? A camel's fart or all the electricity being consumed just for comfort purposes... farting for the Camel is vital, it is not just a matter of convenience. Think about it! I am sure from now on you will not be looking at camels the same way. Have to find one though! Not a common animal in your neighborhood! To be honest, not very common in the cities I live in either. No camels cross the streets of Tunis, Cairo or Dubai...

THE KYOTO PROTOCOL

First of all, Kyoto is a Japanese city, and we are talking about an agreement that was signed in Japan. The Kyoto protocol is not about sushi eating or Geisha's hospitality... no, it has to do with the environment, especially environmental protection and lowering carbon emissions.

On paper, it is a great achievement that humans have managed to agree on something to protect their planet and preserve it for future generations, something that does not suit necessarily the immediate benefits and greed of some big and influential businesses. However, there is a major issue: who is the big Nation that refused to sign this Kyoto protocol, despite all what its intellectuals and scientists are telling us about the necessity of environmental protection and the danger of global warming? You bet! This Nation is the US... Why?

Well, because it is the US, and nobody will be able to impose anything on the US! Imagine if it were Iran? There would have been more sanctions (I wonder if that is still possible!). They would have been depicted as more evil and more destructive to the entire human race! There would have been some UN resolutions condemning them one more time... but it is the US! Why is this a major issue? Well, let us make another guess: who is the Nation with the heaviest carbon emissions?

I once red that, besides being the largest energy consumer in the world, the US were definitely not the most efficient in using energy. Indeed, the cost of fossil fuels, be they oil or coal, is so cheap in the US that people are not necessarily incentivized to save on it. The paper said that if the US used energy as efficiently as Europe, its consumption would drop 25% and if it used it as efficiently as Japan, the saving would be 50%... I have no means to verify these figures or statistics, especially today. I don't even know which level of confidence we should give them. However, I truly believe that the US still has a long way to go when it comes to environmental protection, to carbon emissions reductions, and overall, to lessons it can be giving to the rest of the world!

According to the US energy information administration (at least, they are not shy of communicating these figures!), coal was the premiere source for electricity generation in 2014, at a percentage of 39% (down from well over 50% in the nineties), far ahead of gas, oil, nuclear and of course, renewables! I thought coal was the worst in pollution and carbon emissions… According to a group calling themselves "Union of Concerned Scientists", coal is the single biggest polluter in the US. Not only that, coal pollutes when it is mined, transported, stored, and burned. It generates several wastes such as ashes, sludge, toxic chemicals, smog, and acid rain. It pollutes land, water, and air! Honestly, I do believe them as it doesn't seem to be rocket science to reach these findings.

But wait a minute, the coal lobby has found a very serious argument to maintain coal against renewables and especially, wind energy: in an incredible advertisement, it was warning that wind farms could just blow the Earth off orbit! This is a more serious danger than just warming up a few degrees every decade. Frightening indeed... OK, this is not true! It was a funny satire video released by "the Onion", an american digital media. In any case, the clout of the coal lobby, and especially its money, is a game changer at the Congress, and it has prevented any serious climate-change law to be enacted. That way, we'll all keep on the right orbit and be happy!

Moving from the stratosphere into the atmosphere, 2019 has witnessed the arrival of no less than 1500 private jets to Davos, the Swiss jet set skiing village… to discuss global warming. You know, Davos is pretty cool, from a weather prospective. It is not necessarily very cool when all politicians and money-makers meet to discuss what is good for the planet, their planet to be frank! To go to Davos (to the Davos Economic Forum I mean!) as pointed out in some newspaper, you have to pay a serious membership and some fees to get close to the world rulers. This is a $60k ticket a year at least. Nothing compared to the operating costs of your private jet of course. So, imagine 1500 such jets arriving in a very short time span to this village in the Alps. Enough heat and carbon to melt the snow? Fortunately not, may be enough to make the Swiss air a little less pure, still pristine by Shanghai or Cairo standards… What is confusing to me is the message that this is sending: yes, we are discussing global warming. No, we are not giving up our comfort or lowering our consumption. We will tell you how to do better for the sake of the planet, but WE are above these rules…

Since Kyoto, there have been several other meetings including Doha (that is in Qatar), Copenhagen (Denmark), Paris (France), Marrakesh (Morocco)… At the COP21 meeting in Paris, global leaders were expected to conclude negotiations for a new agreement to tackle climate change and address its impacts. Paris was more successful than the preceding meetings, and the final declaration looked at maintaining global warming underneath the 2 degrees above pre-industrial levels in 2100. There was also a promise to reach zero net emissions between 2050 and 2100. Will we have the will and the finances to enforce it in the future? The text relative to ratcheting up climate finance to $100 billion a year starting 2020 is a non-legally binding commitment, and this is seen as a concession to the US, which knew it would not be able to pass such a text through the Republican-led senate.

As a matter of fact, the US Supreme Court has put President's Obama "America's clean power plan" to a stall on February 9th, 2016… This plan, which is an integral part of the US commitment to the COP21 agreement, was aiming at reducing carbon emissions from power plants by 32% in 2030 compared to 2005 levels. The Court was seized by 27 States, mainly republican, and several industries…Major figures of this "guerilla" against cleaner energy were West Virginia's attorney general and Kentucky's senator McConnell, who was heading the republican majority at the Senate. Two of the three "coal" States of the US against the rest of the Planet! Once again, the World's plans for a better future were being ruined by one single superpower, the only one that really matters… Indeed, if the US do nothing against global warming, the combined contributions of many other nations would mean absolutely nothing! And with the election of Donald Trump as President, the final stab into the Paris agreements just happened on June 2nd 2017: as promised during his campaign, the US pulled out from these accords, the Planet can wait… keeping your campaign promises is more important than keeping an agreement that was signed with 195 countries!

There is a real urgency, figures are frightening: the year 2016 ranked as the warmest in recent history (2019 is only a fraction behind) and the 10 warmest years on a 134-year record have all occurred since 2000. Sea level has been rising at over 3 millimeters per year since 1993. Antarctica and Greenland combined have been losing over 400 billion metric tons of ice per year. This means that a lot of coastal areas in the world are exposed to being submerged in some future which is not that remote, and this will affect substantial numbers of the world's population.

I have just been a witness of a very funny situation between two friends debating the subject recently. One of them was claiming that water will be seriously threatening constructions built too close to the sea in a very nice suburb of Tunis called "La Marsa". The other friend had his house just on the second row from the sea in that location. We therefore told him jokingly that he had better sell it now, before people start knowing about the sea level rising. And then, we even came with a better idea. No, he should keep it for now and sell it only when the house between him and the sea gets submerged: he would sell a direct view on the Mediterranean, which would add considerable value to his house!

Do I feel concerned as an Arab? Of course, I am… You know, the country I live in and the whole Arab region is exposed to a severe hydric stress. A warmer climate will mean less water resources in an already thirsty environment. It will mean less land in those coastal areas where most of the population is prospering. Eventually, this would certainly mean more conflicts because of another resource becoming scarce: water, the source of all life…

THE ARAB SPRING

This is what most newspapers have written about the revolutions taking place in several Arab countries since end of 2010. The initial spark came from Tunisia, it was soon followed by Egypt… Libya was more complicated, Yemen too and Syria is a never-ending story, or rather a nightmare with a huge daily life toll.

In Tunisia, some people talked about the "Jasmine Revolution". Jasmine is this gentle white and very nice smelling flower of ours! It is a real symbol of Tunisia, of its hospitality, of its cozy summer atmosphere. However, commenting two or three sit-ins in front of "la Kasbah", the place of Government, one journalist claimed that it smelled all but jasmine!

Can we really talk about spring, now with a few years of "democratic" process going on? Isn't it rather an autumn? What did we see in Tunisia & Egypt? The elections led to Islamist governments or Islamist-led coalitions. You might wonder why this result from free democratic elections? The population rejected the "past". It rejected all that was close to the corrupt leaders they had, but also tried to stick to the strongest figures of opposition they had in mind, and those were the Islamists. This is also a model that appeals to them as it has much more cultural roots than communist parties.

The phrase we kept hearing on and on in Tunisia and Egypt is "Democratic Transition". I would almost say that we are lost in transition now! This is all but a seamless process. When people threw out dictators, they initially thought they have made it! They thought they moved to democracy, at last, after years of tyranny, of excessive use of force, of denial of freedom of speech… It was a dream. They started discovering that they were now free to talk, but nobody really listened to them! Yes, you do not get jailed for what you say, which is in itself a major improvement over the past, but this is not exactly what you have been dreaming of. When you say something, especially when you are not really happy, when your life depends on it, when you are looking for a job, for dignity, for your own security, you want someone to listen! Instead, we started having some "political leaders" questioning our identity, questioning all that has been built over years by the nation as a whole, and trying to divert the people from what they really made these revolutions for. It was quite astonishing to hear in Tunisia a debate on polygamy, or young girls' excision from imported preachers! We do not want to transit to the middle ages. That is not the reference period for democracy! We do not want to transit to a period where women, which make up half of the society (at least, this is what simple demographic statistics say!) are marginalized and cornered. We do not want to see three-years old babies veiled!

The whole process does not seem right! People have been fighting for democracy. They have elected an assembly which in Tunisia was supposed to draft a new constitution during a short transitional period. Instead, they were getting an Assembly that was taking time to discuss many other issues than the constitution and was in no hurry to take decisions. Indeed, we could often see that over half of the elected people representatives seemed to have other occupations than going to the assembly and doing what they have been elected for and what they were being paid for!

We are now several years down the track. Tunisia and Egypt have taken different routes, but in both cases the Islamists are not leading the country anymore. They do remain a major part of the political scene in Tunisia. After the Spring, we had the heat, and the cold, and no real improvement from the economy point of view! We have more unemployment and higher inflation. We have less "FDI", meaning "Foreign Direct Investment". Our tourism, which accounted for a significant portion of the GDP is ruined. Are we happier? Are we more stressed? Are we optimistic? Difficult to say, especially that this famous Arab Spring is heading to so many different directions depending on the country you are looking at. The only common denominator I would see is tougher life conditions for all, higher insecurity, more violence.

Yes, I forgot, I am being too negative and forgot about the real asset we got: freedom of speech. It does not make a living, but it is probably one of the rare positive outcomes. We are free to say we don't like our rulers, and free to talk about just anything and we have no more internet filters to prevent us from wandering in all remote areas of the World Wide Web, even in its darkest faces of cyber-terrorism and bomb making toolkits.

With this great new freedom, we have also discovered something called Unions. And, as people refrained for over twenty years, they seem to be willing to do all the strikes they missed for such a long period of time. We are enjoying strikes and demonstrations on a daily basis. It is affecting education, public health, transportation, telecom operators, phosphates production, airports, ports logistics, even the customs… While we need more hard work and greater wealth creation to cope with all the problems our economies have endured, we have less productivity. The workers that have been oppressed and exploited by the "ugly" capitalists are asking for their "legitimate" rights. This is the souped up message now served by the unions that have been nurtured by these revolutions.

What they forget to say is: who is the most suffering from all these strikes and public service disturbances. Who is using public transportation and public hospitals? Not the wealthiest, you bet! What we started seeing post revolution is somehow confusion between the exercise of freedom, and the temptation of anarchy and chaos. In their move to breaking the rules, the old coercive rules, many people went totally wild. Why stop at red lights and obey basic traffic rules? Why put garbage in the bins? Why respect my boss? Why be productive at work?

Right after revolutions, we suffered from an acute "degagite". You know, the famous saying that started in Tunisia was the French word "Degage!", meaning "go away". And this was used even in non-French-speaking Egypt. After the dictators went away, people started applying "Degage" to just about anything they did not like! Did they "degage" their soul? After "degage", what is needed now is the "engage", to engage in building a better future and there are no short cuts. You do not create wealth out of the blue. The only way is to engage in producing something valuable that some other people or nations will buy from you!

A TALE OF TWO DOGS

Before the revolution in Tunisia, we had several jokes on the political situation and the lack of freedom. One of them was very symptomatic of the lack of freedom of speech: it is about two dogs which meet at the border between Tunisia and Algeria. Each one wants to cross to the other side. The Tunisian one asks the Algerian one: why do you want to cross? What are you looking for in Tunisia? And the answer was very clear: I want to enjoy life, I want to go clubbing in Hammamet, I want to go to the beach, spend time in nice hotels… but you are the crazy one, why do you want to cross to Algeria? And the poor Tunisian dog answers: I simply want to bark!

Since the revolution, we have had a lot of barking… of biting too. All of it for nothing! A popular saying around here says: "a dog barking after a plane"… you can imagine how useful that is, and how the plane will be affected. Clearly, this is the situation in the Arab world now, after the revolutions. A lot of barking, all the accumulated will for barking during over twenty years has led to a major explosion. But we see no real effect. At least, no positive one! What a dog's life… Now Tunisians do not need to cross the border to enjoy barking. They practice at home, still needs some adjustments of course, but doing this, no one is listening to the other. Too much frustration to be externalized. The focus is on your own barking, not on listening to what the neighbor is saying, especially if he is on a different tone! The risk is, if you focus too much on this, that you would even loose what made the Algerian dog cross the border… in fact, he was not the only one that enjoyed Hammamet, and tourism is a big business for the country. If we lose it, then the whole economy is at risk, and all the barking will fade away.

FEMEN

This is a new feminist group that has emerged in Ukraine in the early 21st century and where the activists were young women that were demonstrating with nude breasts, which is not necessarily the worst spectacle you can have, but which in many countries can be seen as contrary to the law. Is it the case in the US? I am not sure… I do not believe that it is permitted for women to expose their boobs in public. This is of course more shocking in certain cultures, in certain regions, while it is definitely not an issue in certain tribes still existing today in parts of the world that you can watch on National Geographic Channel. Clearly, I can hardly imagine a Femen demonstration in a Taliban-led country. They would probably be immediately caught in 70% of the countries around the world.

We started having a lot of buzz about Femen in Tunisia, in the first quarter of 2013. A young Tunisian girl, Amina, went crazy and claimed she was a Femen while she exhibited her breasts. You can imagine that this not a common move in and Arab and Muslim country. We already had a whole debate with the Harlem Shake thing, which was much lower in the scale of public opinion provocation. Here, a new limit was crossed. The family of the young girl cried of shame, another violent debate erupted between the so-called laics and the heavily bearded pretending to be the guardians of morale and Islam. Do I approve of this? As an average citizen in a rather conservative country, and especially in the current situation, I do not. This was not needed, and it only helped feeding a wrong and useless debate. It especially triggered a very bad handling of the situation from the authorities, which found themselves engaged in an increasing escalation after arresting the poor girl and handing her over to the courts…

We had a group of German and French Femen coming over showing their breasts in front of the court building in Tunis where Amina was supposed to be judged. They got arrested and even got sentenced in first instance for four months, with no execution suspension at all… while the Salafis that have attacked the US Embassy in Tunis months before got this favor and were not taken immediately to jail. This double standard treatment was heavily criticized and commented. It also led to further escalation as we had Femen activists showing up at various Tunisian officials' visits abroad. One former Prime Minister of the Islamist party could closely admire the boobs of a Canadian Femen at a meeting where he was speaking in Montreal. His successor did not have as much chance in Berlin as the Femen demonstrated in front of Angela Merkel one day before he arrived for an official visit, asking the Tunisian authorities to free the other Femen…

We also had a group of French activists mocking a Muslim prayer, breasts at the open air, in front of the Tunisian Embassy in Paris. This is one demonstration I really did not like, even if I claim to be rather open and progressive. This is too aggressive to the people that are keen on religion, without being fundamentalists. Such provocations have the opposite effect of making even the rather moderate people go to the extremes.

To conclude on the whole story of Femen and the Islamists, I believe that very poor handling of the matter from the roots amplified the phenomenon and concentrated the debate on something very anecdotic. It is true that it also highlighted that we had double standard in handling various manifestations of freedom of speech: while Femen were excluded and condemned, middle-eastern preachers were allowed to fly to Tunisia, to conduct major gatherings and deliver dogmatic speeches where they called for excision and Jihad!

Interestingly, Amina, the only Tunisian Femen we know of, has made it to the 2015-BBC's 100 Women list! She is mentioned among those that the BBC has identified as the most inspirational women of the year. The list includes young Muzzon El-Mellehan, the "Malala of Syria", a 16-year refugee urging fellow refugee girls in Jordan to study and go to school.

HARLEM SHAKE

I have never heard of this before it got such a buzz in post-revolution Tunisia as a major form of resistance against the Islamist-Nahdha-led government. You can tell I am getting old. I would probably know much more if I were eighteen… but do you know yourself what it is? It is from your world: Harlem is in New York, isn't it?

I went searching the web, and found two potential explanations: one that says this is a song released in 2012 by American DJ and producer Bauer… the second, which fits better what happened in Tunisia and I will come back to it, is that the "Harlem Shake is a dance, that originally began in Harlem, New York" (not in Venice, LA, that's clear!) in 1981! Since its beginnings, it has spread to other urban areas and became popular in music videos. The self-purported inventor of the dance was "Al B", a Harlem resident. Al B is quoted saying that the dance is "a drunken shake anyway, it's an alcoholic shake, but it's fantastic, everybody appreciates it." He said it comes from the ancient Egyptians and describes it as what the mummies used to do. Because they were all wrapped up, they couldn't really move, all they could do was shake!

You can imagine how this fits nicely with a resistance movement against an islamist-led government. It has roots in the region thanks to the Egyptian mummies and it is an "alcoholic" shake! I am not sure that all the Harlem Shakers we had in all the schools of Tunisia knew about this. All they knew was that several government officials have tried to ban this dance and proclaimed it was decadent and unacceptable, and that was just enough to have all these youths willing to dance it… the spread of the movement showed the level of decline of Nahdha popularity, amongst students and younger people.

Now that we are getting back to some "normality", the Harlem shake craze has faded away… It was really a youths' reaction that showed the political leaders in the country how to adapt to the Tunisian way: the approach to Islam is much softer and is probably more of a culture than a religious dogma. This certainly contributed to having our Islamist party mature in the right direction! At least, in appearance…

WELD EL QUINZE

After the Arab spring, we started discovering the whole underground arts scene that we had in the various countries where freedom of speech was prohibited. This young rap singer became famous because of the prosecution he experienced during the short-lived rule of the Ennahdha Islamist party in Tunisia after the first democratically held elections. One of his songs is particularly aggressive towards the police. Titled "Boulicia Kleb", which means policemen are dogs, which has a strong negative meaning in Tunisian dialect: it would mean someone you cannot trust, someone who will hurt you, someone really mean, with no morals or ethics… This should clearly be an oxymoron with what the definition of a cop is.

Weld El Quinze and friends are using a very crude language, a disturbing language. I personally do not like it and do not agree to it. It is very harsh to listen to, but it is the simple translation of the rhetoric that is found in English or French rap. Maybe the fact of hearing it in Arabic is more disturbing to us. Maybe we find those bad words even worse when they are pronounced in Arabic…

Together with Femen and the Harlem Shake, Rap songs and artists seemed to be another form of expression by which youngsters were fighting for the newly acquired freedom of speech against the looming Dogma of religious beliefs. Indeed, they did not want another form of dictatorship to prevail, a form that would have everyone self-censor his behavior because of an even stronger force than oppression, a force that will be in his own mind.

Weld El Quinze got sentenced for two years in jail in absentia in 2013. He was found guilty of "insulting civil servants," "undermining public decency," and defamation. After being on the run for a while, he decided to turn himself to court in Hammamet (a Beach resort in Tunisia) and saw eventually the sentence reduced to four months. Human Rights Watch reported the case and said it was in violation of international standards. Ole Reitov, founder of Freemuse, an international organization defending freedom of speech of musicians and composers, condemned the sentence as well. Meanwhile, various unions of Police forces complained against a verdict that seemed too clement.

A few years down the track, another rap artist got similar issues with the police and the justice, Klay BBJ… This time, it was not anymore Ennahdha ruling the country. Freedom of speech seems to be always at risk, whatever the rulers are! Our democracy is still so fragile…

CHOKRI BELAID

For many Tunisians, he is one of the icons of this post-revolution Tunisia. His death - he was murdered on the 6th of February 2013 - was mourned by millions in the country. Hundreds of thousands of them went to bury him, and the UN Secretary General, the US President, the French President, and many of the World's leaders sent their regrets…

This sounds surprising when you know that the guy was a leftist, I would even say a leftist of the extreme. He would not have survived McCarthyism. Chokri was only a few months older than me. He was excellent on TV shows, he was a strong defender of liberties, and was dedicated to the poor. He had strong views on society, and expressed them clearly in all instances, being a lawyer by training. I do not share all his views, certainly not on the prominent role of the state in the economy, but I fully join him on many issues related to the secularity of the state, the role of women in the society, the necessary separation of religion from government. Chokri was the first victim of a political assassination in the Arab world since the revolutions. He was coldly shot four times while he was leaving his home to work. Several hardline Salafists were arrested in connection to his murder. President Essebsi, the first democratically elected President in Tunisian history has promised during his campaign to shed all lights on this ignominious crime.

Unfortunately, years after the event, no findings have been revealed. Only speculations, accusations and shouting in the media. Clearly, the murderers were close to the Salafi Ansar Al Chariaa movement. Some claim that the links go further to "softer" Islamist movements. Some others link the assassination to the Libyan Islamist movement. Some ask to change the investigators because they did not seem to be very diligent in their searches…

A few months after Chokri's assassination, we had another similar sad event in the killing of Mohamed Brahmi. Ten years older than Belaid, Brahmi came from the town of Sidi Bouzid, where the spark of the Arab Spring ignited. They both share socialist ideals and were members of the same left-wing coalition. The motives for the assassinations looked similar and the act was once again blamed on the Salafis.

Why do I mention Chokri here? Because he will probably be one of those people that history will raise above the average level. I especially wanted to insist that his story, his existence does show to the world that an Arab is not necessarily an Islamist, that this model does not fit many of our countries and that the vision that a majority of us have of Islam is much more progressive than what you might think!

GEORGE SOROS

The man who made billions attacking the Pound! The man who crashed Britain's Central Bank, he has nothing to do with Brexit though… This man of legend came to Tunisia post-revolution! I had a chance to be amongst a few businesspeople having lunch with him, and I remember quite well several interesting moments spent with him. We talked about the Euro as it was floundering because of the Greek crisis, we talked about Africa and we talked about Tunisia.

I have asked the question of where his next investments will be and if he was willing to do something in Tunisia, and he was very clear: for Tunisia, do not expect anyone to come in the next coming one or two years. The instability, the image, the politics, all of that is not yet attractive to investors and you have to sort out your mess on your own (this is in my own words, not his…). Help yourselves first… Soros will get involved through some organizations he is funding that help countries in transitions go along the difficult route of democracy and build the right governance and empower civil society… But this is no investment, not the kind we were discussing.

As far as where he was going to put money, for him, in Africa, the Eldorado destination is Nigeria! And I thought he is right: high risk, high reward. If you think about it, even with all the security issues we might have after revolution, I believe that Tunisia or Egypt are much safer destinations than Nigeria, South Africa or Brazil… this is my perception. But from the eye of a foreign investor based in Europe, Asia or America, he will not see it that way. The insecurity and uncertainty perception in our region is for sure amplified, and clearly at a much higher level than mine.

In relative terms to the other destinations I mentioned, the bias is even bigger, and the opportunity that is seen in those other destinations, because of the size of the population, because of the market growth, because they are somehow "stabilized", even if their "nominal" status is different than the one we experience, that opportunity is seen to be much higher... We need to engage into a virtuous circle, which will repair the image and eventually bring back investors, thus fueling growth, wealth, and stability. This requires decisive political actors that are not thinking of the next election, just like Francois Mitterrand said: "to govern is not to please".

Georges Soros's interest in Tunisia was therefore only from the philanthropic point of view. He was not here to make money. He came back another time and announced the installation of a Tunisian office of his Open Society Organization, which is meant to support developing democracies. Many critics voiced that this organization and its funds acted as covert operations for intelligence agencies and served dubious objectives. Some other critics questioned the source of Soros's wealth and the honesty of his goals... Clearly, a lot of controversy is surrounding him. Some see him as an icon, some see him as an opportunist who has no morals. Honestly, having read about his personal history, and also his thoughts on economy and politics, I must admit that I am quite appreciative of the guy. His focus on reflexivity, a theory his mentor, Karl Popper, has taken up in science, and which he used in finance and politics shows a highly sophisticated thinking.

He applied reflexivity even in analyzing anti-Semitism. Born in Hungary in a Jewish family, he had the courage in 2003, at a Jewish forum in New York city to say: "There is a resurgence of anti-Semitism in Europe. The policies of the Bush administration and the Sharon administration contribute to that. It's not specifically anti-Semitism, but it does manifest itself in anti-Semitism as well. I'm critical of those policies... If we change that direction, then anti-Semitism also will diminish. I can't see how one could confront it directly... I'm also very concerned about my own role because the new anti-Semitism holds that the Jews rule the world... As an unintended consequence of my actions... I also contribute to that image".

Back to the economy and politics, it is interesting to see that, despite the fact of having benefited from speculation in the markets, Soros advocates that speculation undermines the proper development of many countries and he takes position against what he calls, together with Economics Nobel Prize winner, Joseph Stiglitz, market fundamentalism. That is the blind belief that the "Laissez faire" free-market approach will eventually solve all economic and social problems. As one can see, fundamentalism is always bad, be it in economy or in religion!

MUHAMMED YOUNUS

What an inspiring chap! Don't let his name mislead you. Yes, he is Muslim, but he is not an Arab. He is from Bangladesh… know where that is? In Asia, close to India and Pakistan, one of the poorest countries in the world, and that is what made Pr. Younus so well known. He got a Peace Nobel Prize for it. He really deserves it. He has dedicated his life to the fight against poverty, in a very smart way, inventing what is now called Micro-finance… He said: "In my experience, poor people are the world's greatest entrepreneurs. Every day, they must innovate in order to survive. They remain poor because they do not have the opportunities to turn their creativity into sustainable income."

In 1983, against advice from bankers and officials, Pr Younus decided to become "the banker of the poor" and established Grameen Bank, providing very small credits to the poorest people in Bangladesh. Today, Grameen is providing over 2.5 billion dollars of loans in the country, and Younus has inspired thousands of institutions around the globe that do just that: lend to the poor. Interestingly, micro-credit institutions are biased towards women, and their clients have shown fantastic creditworthiness, much better than in "traditional" banking, with repayment rates approaching 100%.

He has become a big advocate for social business worldwide. I wanted to talk about him because I had the wonderful opportunity to meet him in Tunis. That is one of the marvelous outcomes of our revolution. It helped put the country on the world's map, and it opened the door for extra-ordinary men and women to come and visit and freely talk to the people. We also opened the door to some fanatic preachers, but that is another story…

Professor Younus is the kind of person that makes you feel comfortable at first sight. A smiling and welcoming face, a humble look that was not changed or disturbed by his Nobel Prize award, a traditional outfit that tells you where he comes from and where his cultural roots are. I saw him speak to a crowd of students, packed in their Carthage-based university near Tunis, and then I had the chance to meet him in a closer circle of ten people. He wants to empower everyone, to let them take care of themselves and not expect that help will come from a defective State or unwilling institutions.

He is for the poor to take care of their destiny and to change their world. He has the message for that, and he has shown that it can work, with very little financial means. I am sure that if he could dispose of 1% of the US military budget, he would wipe up poverty from this world. This is what the so-called Arab spring came for: giving people the dignity to earn a living, to depend on themselves, to be proud of their achievements and to contribute to the community welfare not to be a burden on it. As Pr. Younus puts it, "Poverty is the absence of all human rights. The frustrations, hostility and anger generated by abject poverty cannot sustain peace in any society. For building stable peace, we must find ways to provide opportunities for people to live decent lives". This is what we had: poverty leading to revolutions! This world would be better with 10 Muhammed Younus, with a 100, with a 1000. He is trying his best and preaching. He is not preaching dogma; he is preaching for some light and some hope for those who feel completely left behind. This is the real war that we should all embrace, fund, and join as soldiers.

NELSON MANDELA

No doubt one of the personalities of the Century. I like him because he is not the typical hero that Hollywood movies often show us. He is not WASP; he is not from the West; he is not rich; he is not from a Marvel Comics book. No! and yet, he has inspired the World. This man has fought a bulldozer machine called Apartheid. What is Apartheid? It is the South-African version of racial segregation. It is a form of racism, of abject racism based on the color of the skin. It is similar to what the Jim Crow laws have led to in the southern states of the US between 1876 and 1965, not so long ago! Apartheid is based on the concept of white supremacy. It is in continuation of slavery practices. The system was officially in place in South Africa from 1948 till 1994.

It started earlier, in 1913, with the controversial Land Act, forcing black Africans to live in reserves and giving birth to what has become later the ANC, the African National Congress, the party that Mandela became the leader of, which was considered to be a terrorist organization by the regime in place. Apartheid is about separating races and their access to various public services, including education, transportation, health, clearly providing the whites with superior treatment. It is also about preventing races to mix, forbidding therefore interracial marriages. You can imagine the level of hate and resentment this has triggered into the populations deprived from their rights…

Hollywood paid tribute to Mandela by making him the hero of at least two excellent movies; "Invictus" and "A long walk to Freedom". Invictus is a Latin word meaning invincible. It is also the title of the favorite poem of Nelson Mandela, written by William Henley in 1875. The movie, featuring Morgan Freeman in the role of Mandela, was directed in 2009 by Clint

Eastwood. It is about how Mandela, which became President of South Africa, used a rugby sports event organized by the Rainbow Nation to unite the country behind the national team, the Springboks, which were the symbol in the past of white domination… It was a risky political and human bet that Mandela won. "One team, one country" was the motto! "A long walk to freedom" is based on the autobiography of Nelson Mandela, where he tells the story of his extraordinary life. From the upbringing of Rolihlahla, as was his name at birth, to college and law studies, to the start of the first Black Lawyers practice with Oliver Tambo, to joining the ANC in 1950, to the long tenure in prison, for some 27 years and eventually to negotiations and to becoming President in 1994!

Musicians paid tribute to Mandela as well. Who did not hear about Johnny Clegg, the white Zulu and his "Asimbonanga" song, meaning "we have not seen him" talking about Mandela being held prisoner at Robben Island? Elvis Costello recorded "Free Nelson Mandela" from "the Special AKA", and Stevie Wonder got his songs banned by the South African Broadcasting Corporation for dedicating his Oscar for "I just called to say I love you" to Mandela.

Adopting initially the Gandhi "non-violent" approach in 1944, Mandela eventually decided to shift to armed struggle to resist Apartheid. He founded in 1961 a military offshoot of the ANC and started the first guerilla and sabotage actions. He got arrested and sentenced several times. In 1964, he escaped the death penalty and got sentenced for life imprisonment. For his defense, he gave probably one of his best speeches, from which this famous quote: "I have cherished the ideal of a democratic and free society in which all persons will live together in harmony and with equal opportunities. It is an ideal which I hope to live for and to see realized. But if it needs be, it is an ideal for which I am prepared to die".

He spent 18 of his 27 years of prison in the infamous Robben Island jail. Early 1990's, Mandela and fellow political prisoners from the ANC started having talks with the de Klerk administration, and this led eventually to their release and the end of Apartheid, hence his famous saying "If you want to make peace with your enemy, you have to work with your enemy. Then he becomes your partner".

In 1994, Mandela was elected as the first black President of South Africa. He won worldwide recognition for reconciling between whites and blacks, despite all that he personally endured. He had no hate and looked for no revenge. He brilliantly managed to ensure a smooth transition of the country from a minority and apartheid rule to the majority rule with respect of the minorities. He did not run for a second mandate and preferred to dedicate the rest of his life to continuing the pursuit of his ideals of poverty relieve, equality and democracy promotion at global scale. He even convened a group including Desmond Tutu, Jimmy Carter, Mohamed Younus to name a few, which were called "the Elders" to support the same ideas.

The legacy of Madiba, as he is affectuously called, is huge. It is full of key learnings for those willing to learn, both at the personal and the much larger world level. It shows that justice will ultimately win. It shows that the worst enemies can reconcile and build something new together. It shows that segregation can never last as we are all human and alike. It brings hope no matter the difficulties and the atrocities that we might witness. It gives the strength to endure and the will to pursue the journey for a better world.

MUHAMMAD-ALI CLAY

Some say simply Ali… Hollywood has celebrated him under this name, Ali. This was the movie title. The guy is American. To be precise, he is Afro-American, and he is one of the most famous names in boxing. Born Cassius Marcellus Clay Jr. in Louisville, Kentucky, he converted to Islam and decided to change his name to Muhammed Ali, claiming that Cassius Clay was a slave's name he did not chose. He said: "I am America. I am the part you won't recognize. But get used to me. Black, confident, cocky; my name, not yours; my religion, not yours; my goals, my own; get used to me."…

I wanted to mention him here as I regarded him long ago as one of my heroes. I wander why now? May be because he was a winning emblem of communities that were often on the losing side: Black, Muslim… He was restoring some dignity for all of us who felt ignored or sidelined. With the current Muslim-bashing in all the media around the planet, it is kind of fulfilling to see all those same media praising Ali, the Muslim that claims his faith so strongly. He was kind, he was inspiring, he was caring, he was giving, he was fighting for so many causes… and he was Muslim! This implicitly means that we are not all mean, jihadists and terrorists. Thank you Ali!

I thought he really deserved to be mentioned as an icon, just in the quest of getting you closer to understand the kind of values I cherish. I hope at least that you know now who Muhammed-Ali was and what he stood for. With the Islamophobic stand taken by Donald Trump during his presidential campaign, Muhammad-Ali has appeared in a video next to Will Smith (you know, the famous actor of the Man in Black and also of the movie on Muhamad-Ali…) and he simply said:" I'm a Muslim. I've been a Muslim for 20 years. I'm against killing and violence, and all Muslims are against it. People should know the truth about Islam. You know me. I'm a boxer. I've been called the greatest of all times. People recognize me for being a boxer and a man of truth. I wouldn't be here representing Islam if it was really like terrorists make it look. I think all people should know the truth, come to recognize the truth, because Islam is peace. I'm against killing and the terrorists, and the people doing that in the name of Islam, are wrong, and if I had a chance, I would do something about it"

Ali was a great boxer that managed to conquer the heavyweight title three times. He self-proclaimed to be "the Greatest". After taking the title from Sonny Liston in 1964, he managed to win it again in 1974 and 1979. The 1974 fight was probably one of the most famous in boxing history. "the Rumble in the Jungle" against George Foreman took place in Kinshasa, Zaire, now renamed Congo. Ali adopted an unconventional strategy, the famous "rope-a-dope", whereby he stuck to the rope and let Foreman punch him…until he got tired, allowing Ali to knock him down at the 8th round. Another famous bout Ali fought was "a thrilla in Manilla" against Joe Frazier, the same he won earlier in 1974 but to whom he lost the "fight of the century" in 1971…It was only until the 15th round that Frazier's manager did not let him answer the bell. Despite his victory, Ali said that the fight was the closest you can get to dying! One of his best quotes is: "do not count the days, make the days count"!

Ali was not only a great boxer. He also fought for his ideals and paid an expensive price for that! Indeed, having refused to be inducted in the US military on the ground of religious beliefs and opposition to the Vietnam war, Ali got arrested and stripped of his boxing title in 1967. He was banned from boxing for a period of nearly four years, until a Supreme Court decision. Probably the best years where he could have made a career…Getting back to his fight with Sony Liston in 1964, the fight was initially scheduled for February 25th in Miami, Florida. However, the fight almost got cancelled by its promoters on the news that Ali had joined "Nation of Islam" and was becoming a Civil Rights activist!

Ali has his star in the Hollywood walk of fame. Of the 2500 five-pointed brass stars that lay on the ground of Hollywood Boulevard, Ali's star is the unique one that is on a wall. His request was clear "I bear the name of our beloved prophet Muhammed, and it is impossible that I allow people to trample over his name"… this was long before the famous "Muhammed cartoons", and no one really complained about it!

Muhammed Ali's early Parkinson disease did not stop him from doing his best to pursue his ideals. He wanted the world to be a better place. He served as a UN Messenger of Peace in places like Afghanistan. He managed to free

American hostages from Saddam Hussein's Iraq. He campaigned to reduce third-world debt. He supported Palestinians to liberate their homeland and participated in a Chicago rally during the first Intifada. He participated in the Longest Walk, a protest march in support of Native American rights. He tried to raise awareness about famine in Sudan, and helped various charities… As his wife Lonnie mentioned in her eulogy at his death, he would often say: "I just want to get to heaven, and I've got to do a lot of good deeds to get there"… We need more people that want to go to heaven!

POPE FRANCIS

I know! You are probably thinking that I am not the best qualified person to speak about the Pope, the highest authority for the Catholic Church, the Bishop of Rome and the Head of State of the City of the Vatican. After all, I am Muslim, and I am Arab. Even Christian Arabs belong to the Orthodox Church rather than the Roman Church… I wanted to talk about Pope Francis as he is today the leader of a faith that is embraced by over 1.5 billion people on this planet, a faith that I see comparable to mine, and especially, in the way he is advocating for it.

Indeed, this Pope is a revolutionary… He has been modernizing the church in many instances and taking new open positions towards many issues facing our societies. What I really like about him is his profound humility, his great tolerance and his continuous pursuit of peace with love and compassion. He is a real model leader, and no matter for me that he is the symbol of "another" faith… My perception is that he is making religion smarter and closer to modern needs, and this is what people are looking for in the 21st century, in this material world!

In an interview to French magazine "Paris Match", Pope Francis had a very strong statement on capitalism and the quest for profit, which became not a means but an objective in its own right. He condemned the hypocrisy of the Powerful on this planet, who talk about peace and sell the arms at the same time. He clearly referred to what was going on in Syria… At the 2016 celebration of World Youth Day in Krakow, Poland, one day following the horrific killing of Reverend Hamel in France, Pope Francis said "The World is at war, but it is not a religious conflict". He said he was once again referring to "wars of interest, and domination of people"… Earlier on in that same year, he has taken back to Rome 12 refugees families from the Greek island of Lesbos, in a highly symbolic move meant to show Europe the way for solidarity. They were all Muslim… It should be pointed out that, while in Argentina before becoming Pope, he had close ties with the Jewish community as well and was involved in joint Jewish-Catholic programs aiding the poor. He can definitely be seen as a champion of interfaith dialogue, and he has also shown a strong commitment to ecumenism with other Christians. This has translated in having Patriarch Bartholomew 1 of Constantinople attend his installation, a premiere since the great schism of 1054. Talk about tolerance, compassion, and simply put, humanity!

Jorge Mario Bergoglio was born in 1936 near Buenos Aires, Argentina. He was elected pope in early 2013, and he chose his papal name after St Francis of Assisi, in a clear message showing his caring of the poor. As he once mentioned, "St Francis brought to Christianity an idea of poverty against luxury, pride, vanity of the civil and ecclesiastical powers of the time. He changed history". Pope Francis is also changing history with his progressive and liberal views. He is changing the church's approach towards contraception, abortion, gay-marriage, divorce, and so many societal issues. He played a key role in helping restore the relationship between the US and Cuba (during Obama's time!). He got the Vatican to recognize the State of Palestine and urged for resuming peace talks between Israel and Palestine. He did not hide his thoughts on Donald Trump either: "A person who thinks only about building walls, wherever they may be, and not building bridges, is not Christian". And you can follow him on Instagram now… A Pope that rocks!

MALALA YOUSAFZAI

One CNN headline was depicting her as the "Bravest girl in the World". In Time magazine, she was selected as the no2 person of the year in 2012, second only to US-President Obama… This young Pakistani activist is a true symbol, a symbol for women, a symbol for youth, a symbol for courage, a symbol for what education can do in combatting terrorism and darkness. Her story is absolutely fantastic: Malala has stood against the Taliban, and they have tried to silence her by shooting her in the head in October 2012, in the school bus taking her back home… Two years later, Malala became the youngest recipient of the Nobel peace prize at the age of 17.

Born in 1997, in Mingora, Swat Valley, Pakistan, Malala was named after a Pashtun heroin who resisted British rule. Her father was an education activist. Ziauddin Yousafzai has been publicly defying the Taliban in his hometown, where he had founded the Khushal Khattak school for girls. By the way, he, and his daughter, are Muslim, and his name, Ziauddin, literally means "the light of religion" in Arabic. They have been fighting fundamentalism and obscurantism in a much better way than those using drones and armed forces. They have been resisting the darkness messages, they have shown tremendous courage, putting their lives in the balance and they have been advocating and acting for education, and gender equality, the only real long lasting arms to keep the true light of religion shining.

Malala is certainly a name to remember. She is still young. She is just starting! Her miraculous recovery from coma after being shot at point-blank range has opened the way to a fantastic journey. From the young 11-year old BBC-blogger in Urdu that she was, fighting Taliban rule in the Swat valley in 2007, she has become an international icon winning worldwide recognition and meeting the most powerful on earth. She gave speeches at UN assemblies and she talked to people like Queen Elisabeth II and President Obama. She told him that drone attacks were counter-productive, feeding in terrorism rather than abating it. Now, you can watch her story in the excellent documentary by Davis Guggenheim: "He named me Malala" or you can read her own biography co-written with Christina Lamb, the famous British foreign correspondent journalist and author: "I am Malala". For the 2015 person of the year poll of Time Magazine, a year after getting her Nobel Prize, she was still second, ahead of no less famous people such as Pope Francis…

Being action oriented, Malala has set up a fund, whose objective, as stated in its website, "is to enable girls to complete 12 years of safe, quality education so that they can achieve their potential and be positive change-makers in their families and communities". At the age of 18, she has set up a school in Lebanon for young female refugees from neighboring Syria. Being outspoken as she has always been, Malala told UN members: "Your dreams were too small. Your achievements are too small. Now it is time that you dream bigger!"

What else?

AUNG SAN SUU KYI

This is another Asian Peace Nobel Prize winner. She got the title in 1991, and she is another symbol of resistance against oppression. Aung San Suu Kyi was on house arrest for years under the ruling Junta of Myanmar… The younger daughter of Aung San, known as the Father of the Nation, having negotiated Burma's independence from Great Britain, was born in 1945 in Rangoon. Her father got killed when she was 2 years old. She lived in India and the UK before moving to the US, working for the UN. She married a British historian, had two sons, and eventually got arrested a year after returning to Burma in 1988, trying to foster change towards a more democratic political scene. She was an adept of Gandhi's non-violence philosophy, and she devoted herself to studying Buddhism while under house arrest. Over the 21-year period ranging from 1989 to 2010, she spent 15 years arrested. She got eventually released in 2010, was elected to parliament in 2012 and became State Counselor, a position created for her, after the 2015 general election, cumulating this with the role of foreign affairs minister amongst other ministerial positions.

Mrs. Kyi, "the Lady" as she is often called and as picked by Luc Besson for the title of the movie he made on her story, has deserved and obtained a lot of international support for her cause. She has also received several international distinctions, the Nobel Prize being probably the most notorious one. It is however disappointing to see her position towards Rohingyas, the Muslim minority (4% of the population) in that country which has been facing serious discrimination and prosecution. In an interview for the BBC, with journalist Mishal Husain, Aung San Suu Kyi not only did not want to condemn the discrimination faced by the Rohingyas, preferring to blame the whole situation of Myanmar on the ruling Junta, but she even seems to have concluded with "Nobody told me that I would be interviewed by a Muslim"!

As reported by the Guardian, the British newspaper, in June 2016, Mrs. Kyi, acting as Foreign Affairs Minister, "has told the UN even the term "Rohingya" will be avoided. The statement came as the top UN human rights official issued a report saying the Rohingya had been deprived of nationality and undergone systematic discrimination and severe restrictions on movements. They had also suffered executions and torture that together may amount to crimes against humanity, the report said. Members of the group of about 1.1 million people, who identify themselves by the term Rohingya, are seen by many Myanmar Buddhists as illegal immigrants from Bangladesh".

For a Nobel Prize winner and a State Counselor and Foreign affairs minister of her country, a country neighboring a major Muslim country (Bangladesh), this is rather disappointing to say the least. I was looking very highly to this thin and elegant lady that was another symbol of a country's fight for freedom of speech and democracy. I am now wondering if she still deserves her Nobel prize! Will Myanmar be a real democracy for all its citizens, or will it continue to be hell for this Muslim minority, just because they are Muslim? Oh, I forgot, the Rohingyas are not given the Burmese nationality, they are denied the right to vote, and the problem will soon be over as they are being seriously ethnically cleansed… Once there will be no Rohingyas, there will be no discrimination, and Aung San Suu Kyi will not have to worry about the issue anymore. Of course, if she decides to go outside Myanmar, which is something she will probably need to do as Foreign Affairs Minister, she might unfortunately run into Muslims, as even the BBC does not seem to be immune!

JIMMY CARTER

Do you remember this former US President? I am not sure how you would evaluate his performance for America and its economy. It will certainly depend on whether you are a democrat or a republican! In my view, he is one of the greatest Presidents in recent history, just because of his quest for peace… He is a man who made the impossible possible. He managed to get Israel and Egypt agree on something and sign a peace treaty. Those were the Camp David accords, a major achievement for American diplomacy, and Carter was the architect.

Years later, he founded with his wife Rosalynn the Carter Center, a nonprofit organization that prevents and resolves conflicts. It is also very much present to survey elections in potentially still unstable or "newly converted to democracy" countries.

In a coherent and continuing effort towards peace in the Middle East, M. Carter committed a book in 2006 called "Palestine, peace not Apartheid". A book, the least we can say, that was not acclaimed in the US. Why? Why did most media and people react so badly to a piece of courage, from a former US President striving for peace? Is it because he is blaming Israel for not willing peace, for harassing the Palestinians and treating them in a segregationist way, just like the whites did to the blacks in Afrikaners-led South Africa (by the way, that is what Apartheid is)?

I read the book. Did you? Many people rejected it without reading, simply because it had "Palestine" in the title, and those people have the same Palestine-phobia as the Israel-phobia I used to have when I was a kid. You know, I have grown up and matured… Do we want peace in the Middle East or not? If we do, if we sincerely do, then, everyone should be ready for some concessions.

Carter knows probably better than anyone the intricacies of the subject. He has simple and convincing proposals: back to the 1969 borders, dismantling of the colonies, a way of "sharing" Jerusalem as a Capital… This is based on UN Resolutions, nothing extra-ordinary. Just a matter of each one conforming to commitments already made.

ANOUAR AL SADAT

I still remember, and I was very young at that time, a day of November 1977 when stunning news hit all the media. We did not have satellite TV nor the internet, but that was the News all the world heard about and saw on their screens: Anouar Al Sadat, the President of the Republic of Egypt, was paying a State visit to Israel! He gave a speech at the Knesset…

The son of peasants, that became an army officer close to Gamal Abdel Nasser had radical views on the British occupation that he fought and on the West as a whole. He was part of the several wars against Israel, and notably that of October 6th, 1973, when he was already President, as the successor of Nasser. And now, he is visiting Israel. The first and unique visit of an Arab leader at such level to the Jewish State.

The news came initially as a shock and the complete plan, which included giving back the Sinai to Egypt and also some autonomy to the Palestinians never got fully achieved, despite all that was in the Camp David accords, which Jimmy Carter helped negotiate and to which Menahem Begin was the other party. Instead of reinforcing the position of Egypt and its President as a leader in the Arab world, this unachieved peace process isolated him from the other Arab leaders. The Head Quarters of the Arab League were moved from Cairo to Tunis.

The last years of Sadat in power were troubled and he eventually got assassinated by an Islamic commando during a military procession commemorating the 1973 war. His funeral was held in the presence of massive western delegations but total absence from the Arab world.

Sadat was awarded the Nobel Peace Prize in 1978 and has made it in many ways into modern history. What will the world remember of him? I would like to retain the idea that he had the courage and the intelligence to make the move he made towards Israel. He spared his country more wars and fights and military spending. Maybe he was not fully successful… At least he opened the way. Unfortunately, not many others were ready to carry on the same path, on both sides of this everlasting Middle East conflict.

MENAHEM BEGIN

One cannot mention Carter, Sadat and forget about Begin. He was the other party to the Camp David accords and the other winner of the 1978 Nobel Peace Prize... Surprisingly also, Begin was the founder of the Likud, a right wing party, and a partisan of the "Great Israel". He started his career on an even more extremist tone. He was part of the Irgun. People are shy today to call it a terrorist organization, but that is clearly what it was. At the time, the British and US governments, as well as the UN, recognized it as such! Irgun was responsible of several explosive attacks, the most notable being probably that of King David hotel in 1946, the headquarters of the British administration in Palestine, causing over 90 deaths. In 1948, a terrorist attack conducted against the Palestinian village of Deir Yassine caused over 250 casualties, mainly civilians, and accelerated the exodus of Arab populations.

This extremely aggressive organization caused David Ben Gurion to take action against it, in May 1948, when he ordered to fire against a ship bringing arms to Irgun. The relationship he held with Begin remained very tense for years. Begin was in the opposition and kept a hard Zionist line. He was an advocate for more colonies in the occupied territories and the annexation of the Syrian Golan heights. His party won the elections in 1977 at the first real transition of power in Israel and it was soon after that he hosted Sadat as a visitor. Both men, looking at their history, do not necessarily seem to be the best candidates for a peace treaty, but that was exactly what they have done. The moral one can get from this, from real history, is that a solution always exists and with the right people, with a genuine will to find solutions, nothing is impossible, even to the worst enemies. Both Begin and Sadat can be blamed on some parts of their history, but well, one can only be admirative of the achievement they have secured for the good of their people. Why did it stop there?

BOURGUIBA

He is my idol. A great man like you only get a few in a century… He is our George Washington, our Abraham Lincoln, our John Kennedy, and our Martin Luther King all in one! Like many fellow Tunisians, I will tell you I am one of Bourguiba's children. He had the courage right after Tunisia's independence to abolish polygamy by law in 1957. That is a unique case in the Arab and Muslim world. He had the courage to start an ambitious birth control program and to dedicate at the same time over one third of the country's modest budget to education!

Bourguiba built modern Tunisia on three pillars: Education, Healthcare and Women rights. He has profoundly reformed society and was using a well-balanced step approach. His great saying is that one should prefer a small change that will allow immediately another change to an impossible reform.

There is so much to be said about Bourguiba that it would deserve not a single book, but a whole encyclopedia. He was ahead of his time and changed so many things in his home country Tunisia. My dream would be to make a movie, a Hollywood super-production, on Bourguiba's life and combat, an epic that would be directed by someone like Spielberg or Scorsese, not less! A movie in the shape of Mandela's "long walk to freedom" as I strongly believe that Bourguiba is the other African leader that truly deserves this. The movie could be called "The seeds of the Arab Spring". Indeed, it is all that Bourguiba has done for women and education that helped build a strong civil society in Tunisia, a civil society that eventually rejected dictatorship and managed the transition period that followed in a peaceful way.

He has managed to get Tunisia's independence from France, but intelligently maintained very good relations with the former colonizer. French is until today the second language in Tunisia. It is often the language of business and is widely used, including in official documents. France remains the major economic partner of Tunisia. Bourguiba has had the intelligence to urge Tunisians to support the allies against the Nazis during World War II, even though the direct "enemy" for Tunisians was the French colonizer… He had the right vision for the future and knew how to convey it to the population.

In the sixties, Bourguiba told the Palestinians in Jericho that they had to accept the UN split of the territory with Israel. He did not get any applause for it. He got tomatoes and eggs… The Egyptian leader Gamal Abdel Nasser is said to have told him in private that he supported his view but would never announce it in public. As the figure of Arab Nationalism, Nasser was asking what all Arabs were vainly requesting: Israel to disappear and the land to be given back to the Palestinians. We all know how history has evolved…

Bourguiba had a lot of charisma. He was building a modern society, too modern for many of the Gulf Monarchies that saw him as a non-Muslim. Imagine a President drinking a glass of water during fasting time in the holy month of Ramadan on national television! It was a message he conveyed to the population during an awfully hot summer day. He was fighting the dogma. He was telling people that religion is all about your wellbeing and that god (Allah if you prefer) did not want people to suffer needlessly.

After the Tunisian revolution, Bourguiba was back under the limelight! Several political parties or personalities were looking for popular support by saying they were adopting his ideas and political views, except may be for democracy. Still in the 21st century, being a modernist in Tunisia is being a Bourguiba's follower, 60 years after the independence!

THE TUNISIA-LIBYA UNION

This union lasted one day! Is it serious for two sovereign countries to make such a major announcement and eventually cancel it the next day? It actually happened in 1974 – the union was announced in the Island of Djerba, in the southern part of Tunisia, where Kaddafi and Bourguiba, united for the event by Mohamed Masmoudi, brilliant Foreign Affairs Minister at that time, signed the agreement. The problem was that Prime Minister Nouira was not in the country, and he was not even informed of this major event!

The deal was cancelled, Bourguiba sacrificed his Minister as a scape goat and Tunisia and Libya went back to their separate lives: Tunisia with not many resources, but rather good governance and a lot of focus on education and health; Libya sinking in oil, getting a lot of money out of it, and spending on all but infrastructure or well-being of its people! Kaddafi bought a lot of arms, played several games in neighboring countries such as Chad, but never structured a Nation! Instead, he has destroyed all its institutions, making it the reign of anarchy, and incidentally that of his clan or close family and friends. He even thought he was clever enough to share his great experience by publishing the "green book", just like Mao's "Little red book"!

We will not change the course of history, and the trajectories of both Libya and Tunisia, as different as they are, both led to simultaneous revolutions! Sure, the outcome after revolution is different. It has to do with what Bourguiba and Kaddafi once discussed: Kaddafi did not understand all the effort Bourguiba was making on education "better keep them ignorant and stupid, easier to govern he said". Bourguiba answered that, if things go wrong, it is better to have to deal with educated people… Anyway, we will not change the course of history, but I would like to make some politics-fiction: What if? What if this union lasted? What if Tunisia and Libya really united their destinies back in 1974? What would have happened? Tunisia had institutions that worked. It had a leader who was a visionary, and accepted as such by the Libyan leader, who was still very young at that time. Libya had huge oil reserves and production, a wealth that could have fueled an immense common growth. Would the pair Bourguiba/Kaddafi have worked? Or would Kaddafi have made another coup, depositing Bourguiba, and getting hold of a bigger territory and population in no time?

It was a period when Kaddafi was still new to politics and power, and I tend to believe that the genuine admiration he had for Bourguiba, the Intellectual, the Statesman, the Modernist, that admiration would have led to the right balance of powers that could have made that union a real success. With the right policies in place for education, healthcare and infrastructure building, with the right resources in place from oil-rich Libya, that union could have transformed the history of North-Africa, and could have made an earlier success story in the model of Dubai! Yes, I know, another option could have been that Kaddafi manages to kill Bourguiba to retain the power for himself, and this would have been a major disaster for the region and a much bigger source of instability.

After the union was cancelled, Kaddafi felt humiliated and rejected, and like in a classical Hollywood scenario, he turned to Evil! He had the money, he had a nation, he had some ambition, and he was turned down by this "small" neighbor. This has led to a great frustration and he fell gradually into the role where, to exist and be respected, he had to do more and more exactions, and become more and more eccentric. This has led to the Kaddafi we all know. Some say he was crazy; some say he was on drugs… What is obvious though is that he was ugly, incontrollable, unpredictable, and this is particularly dangerous when you are a head of State, a State with no institutions, meaning that the head of State concentrates 100% of the power!

OBAMA

When President Obama got elected, he garnered a lot of sympathy from around the world. Non-Americans would have voted for Obama as well. Not exactly the same story for Donald Trump, as one could see from a Davos Forum video that circulated on social media, showing an overwhelming Clinton vote in various countries as diverse as Saudi Arabia, India or Germany… Obama has therefore united America and the world!

Being the first African American President of the United States was also a fantastic achievement, and he managed to stay in office for the second term! Somehow, many people in the rest of the World liked him because he was not the incarnation of the WASP Establishment. He was from a minority and he had some origins from Kenya. This made him closer to us in this other part of the world! His opponents claimed he was a Muslim, which of course was meant to make him repellant in the US, but which made him closer to the hearts of so many people in our region.

With the election of his successor, social media were flooded with images rivalling to show the nice President he was, the caring father and loving husband that had such a brilliant wife, Michelle… Many photos of him are becoming iconic. His humor is simply fantastic…

However, looking at his legacy after 8 years in power, I am not sure that he was so successful in all endeavors. He was full of energy and will when he came to power but was not able to deliver to the expectations he raised, and this is probably showing the limits of any President of the United States. He is simply not as powerful as your local Banana Republic dictator doing what he wants when he deems useful! A good point for the American democracy would you think? May be… May be also a disturbing fact about the power of the Establishment, the Establishment being not only the Congress and its legislative power... The Establishment encompassing all the lobbying forces that are so active in Washington DC!

At the start of his presidency, Obama made a memorable address in Cairo. "A new beginning" he claimed on the 4th of June 2009 from the major reception hall of the Cairo University... The speech was intended to mend American-Muslim World relationships which were "severely damaged" during George W. Bush time according to Ross Colvin of Reuters. It touched upon several topics, including nuclear weapons, democracy and economic development, but the most memorable part of it, the one that drove most reactions from all over the world was probably the one about the Israeli-Palestinian dispute. Obama's call for a two-state solution earned him a great positive feedback all around the Arab World, and even Israeli Prime Minister Netanyahu seemed to endorse for the first time the possibility for a Palestinian State to exist...

This speech drove a lot of hope for a negotiated peace in the Middle East at last, as everyone in the region is convinced that such a peace is really suspended to the will of the US. If they decided to make it happen, it will happen because of the intimate relationship they have with Israel. It raised expectations in the Arab street... but Obama and his administration failed to deliver for two terms of Presidency!

If we look at other topics in international relations and foreign policy, how would one qualify what happened, or continued to happen, in Afghanistan, in Iraq, in Syria, in Guantanamo! The one subject that we could consider close to completion is about bringing back Iran into the international community. The same also happened with Cuba... The situation had evolved for the better, until it was reversed by Donald Trump. However, in the overall balance, American hegemony failed in making the world a better place during Obama's time!

IBN KHALDUN

When you are asked to pick a scientist name associated with physics, chances are that you would say Albert Einstein. If someone told you who would be the father of psychology, you would probably respond Sigmund Freud. Well, Ibn Khaldun is the name that would be associated in a similar manner with sociology. He invented it in the fourteenth century. He was also a politician, a historian, a geographer, and a precursor in economics.

President Reagan, the one who used to be a Hollywood actor, the 40th President of the United States, quoted him in the early eighties on the benefit of lowering tax rates. He thought he was Egyptian, which is not right. It is true that he died in Egypt, but Ibn Khaldun was born in Tunisia in 1332. His family is of Andalusian origin, he traveled to Bejaia in Algeria, to Fez in Morocco where he was jailed for a couple of years before going to exile in Granada in Andalusia. He then went into retreat in Bejaia, where he wrote most of his Muqaddimah and he spent the last part of his life in Cairo, where he eventually died and got buried, in a Sufi cemetery.

In 2015, another big fan of Ibn Khaldun was recommending reading his famous Muqaddimah: Marc Zuckerberg, the founder of Facebook. "It's a history of the world written by an intellectual who lived in the 1300s. It focuses on how society and culture flow, including the creation of cities, politics, commerce and science" he said on a Facebook post. In 2019, Boris Johnson, the British PM, explained in an interview with the Telegraph : "Ibn Khaldun observed that if you cut taxes on the olive harvest, or whatever it was in 14th century Tunisia, that actually people grew more olives, and tax yields went up". Not only has Ibn Khaldun been called the greatest Arab intellectual ever but many believe the historian and sociologist was hugely influential in shaping economics and free marketeers some 600 years later.

Abd Ar-Rahman Ibn Khaldun was born in Tunis in 1332. His family was of Yemenite origin, thus from the Arabian Peninsula, and has been established for a long while in Muslim Andalusia, before settling in Tunisia, after the fall of Seville. In Tunisia, they were close to the ruling Hafside dynasty. The period was a turbulent one in the Maghreb. The economy was at a stall and the conflicts were numerous for the power. This has allowed young Abd Ar-Rahman to witness many of the intrigues. It has also raised his curiosity and led him to travel extensively. Eventually, he decided to abandon his rich political life to dedicate himself to write about universal history, starting with the Maghreb.

I wanted to talk about Ibn Khaldun, not only because he was born in Tunisia, but mainly because of his intellectual legacy. He theorized one very important aspect of the history of humankind, the rise and fall of empires, of civilizations. His major contribution lies in philosophy of history and sociology. Indeed, before writing about history itself, he felt there was a missing link, a missing science, and he decided to put some foundations to it. He did not want to simply describe events. He wanted to understand the forces that are behind them. He wanted to extract some patterns that are inherent to human civilizations and to human societies. He tried to explain the need for the emergence of a central power in organized societies, as this is not a "natural" status for humans but rather a necessity. He looked at various stages of power consolidation and also of power loss and decay. He compared urban and rural societies and talked about social cohesion and social capital.

We have seen in the recent past several political and intellectual figures from the West quoting Ibn Khaldun and referring to his work. I would say that this is mostly needed in his own land, in the Arab World, in the Maghreb. Our politicians should all read "Al Muqaddimah". They should all understand sociology. They should all care about what their fellow citizens are expecting from them. Quoting Ibn Khaldun would help them enforce the long-needed reforms and revive some pride in their populations.

KAFKA

You might wonder: what does Kafka have to do here? He is a Bohemian born in Prague at the end of the 19th century and who died from tuberculosis at the beginning of the 20th… His literary work often described a world that is gloomy, bizarre, illogic, surreal… a world where a ruthless bureaucracy makes people feel totally helpless, and uncomfortable with no recourse and no escape! Hence the adjectives that have become so common nowadays to describe such absurd situations: Kafkaesque or Kafkian.

And that is exactly the link with Kafka that I am making. He might have never lived in the Arab World, but his "world" is exactly what most of us are experiencing: we drift from one Kafkaesque situation to another, with no clear route to escape. We are trapped in a labyrinth of rules and procedures that no one is really sure of, no one is really able to describe, and no one is interpreting in the same way… This administration that is overpowering people in so many Arab countries is creating even more frustration and revolt against the established order, which is felt to be corrupt and unfair.

A situation like the one from "The Trial" looks so familiar in the many countries of this world where the rule of law is not applied: a person gets arrested by unidentified agents for an unspecified crime. Many characters interfere with the trial while the rules are not clear, the court is not apparent and the bureaucracy behind seems tentacular and dark. The person gets eventually executed "like a dog" in a totally absurd situation. How many of us live with the fear of being arrested while boarding a plane or while going to work or simply at an ID control at a traffic light? You might be doing everything scrupulously right, but for some reason that is beyond your reach, you could be caught and jailed and harassed with no hope of escaping… I must confess: this is probably not valid in Arab countries alone. So many parts of the world, in Africa, in Latin America or in Asia experience this. It is probably less of a concern in Scandinavian countries...

Another unfinished philosophical novel from Kafka talks about bureaucracy in its most pejorative meanings. "The Castle" is about a person arriving in a village governed by mysterious people living in a nearby Castle. The official rules developed by the Castle are not written and the villagers have all their own interpretations. The situation that is described is clearly about operating in an environment with no clearly defined rules, non-transparent to the people while the "authorities" that have developed the rules claim to have a perfect and flawless model. This major discrepancy or mismatch is what we experience on a daily basis in the so-called Arab World. If there is something that is uniting it, it is clearly its Kafkaesqueness!

Kafka, as you can see, is not about having fun... His world is dark and gloomy. I enjoyed reading his absurd novels early in my life, and I believe that you can still have some fun with him: have you ever tried the game of reading a few pages of a Kafka novel and then getting a group of people to each elaborate for 2 minutes on the story, making it more and more absurd? This is a great experience that I recommend for creativity. In the Arab World, we will beat you at this exercise, not because we are more creative, but because we just need to pick examples from our daily life!

EDUCATION

Education is the key, the key for the future of mankind, the key that provides the basics for democracy and tolerance. All success stories that we see in this world are built on education and on educated people. Quoting Nelson Mandela, "Education is the most powerful weapon which you can use to change the world". Some countries have the actual brains and count on their own citizens. Some others bring the bright brains needed from where they are available to set the pace. America does both and hovers all that sparks around the planet! The search of excellence is the engine of success, and this quest needs some tools.

When I say education, I do not mean only Maths and Physics or know-how. I mean social intelligence, I mean high moral standards, I mean civism, I mean arts…

Too many countries in this world do not provide access to education to the masses. Many of those who claim to do so offer a failed educative system that only puts more burdens on their national budgets but adds no value to their populations. Meanwhile, because of their embracing of a "modern life", more urban populations in the so-called developing countries lose that important educative link that was provided by the family or the tribe. They lose high moral standards that often characterize small communities where people know each other and where preserving your reputation is the most important thing for you as it is your most precious asset.

It becomes harder for children left on their own, either in the slums or in beautiful houses, to develop the right moral standards in the absence of a caring family or educator at school. There is no new system to take over from the traditional one, and those youngsters find themselves trapped in an educative desert. As economist, writer and public speaker Kjell Nordstrom puts it, in modern urban areas, we are now "together alone"! Yes, you are surrounded by people, but you hardly know them and you cannot depend on them: you are alone…

The paradox is that, as we concentrate more people, more different people, in denser urban areas, where nobody knows nobody, we need higher and higher standards for intrapersonal interactions. We need people that respect the rules of proper interaction so that everyone's rights and liberties can be respected. For that, we need rules, and we need people to know the rules!

You might have noticed for yourself, in many parts of the "developing" world, people do not care for traffic lights, at least not always! This is very indicative of the prevailing state of mind. Is there a rule? Even so, do I have to respect it? Even if I sneak in and do not get caught?

Take that into the business world, and you get informal economy, a plague that is destroying the sound transparent operators. Take that into the public service, and you get corruption. If not that bad, you get at least inefficient administrations, not caring at all for the wellbeing of the population. Take that into politics, and you get dictators and rogue politicians…

Education is the key, but it has to be reinvented. I loved the book from Salman Khan. He is American… of Indian and Pakistani origin. I know, that is America! That is its strength. It attracts the brightest minds… In this specific case, he was born there and did not contribute to the brain-drain. But yes, this is a real issue that my part of the world suffers from, not only the Arab world. Many people that get their way in the education system, and then go to the West for more learning end up staying there! The poorer country gets the cost of raising that person and providing it already with a certain level of education, and the richer country gets the benefits of his/her thinking! For highly educated people, the frontiers often disappear, and immigration is less of an issue. They are welcome in the modern world. Remember my metaphor on "reverse osmosis"? Wealth and intelligence will be more concentrated where they are already abundant. Ignorance and poverty will do exactly the same! It's a catch 22. Where should we start the virtuous loop?

Going back to Khan's views on education and the necessity of reinventing it, I think he is right in saying that technology is now enabling us to see education differently. We should no more stick to the linear model where you get hours of learning and then an exam and then continue building on the previously learned concepts, whether you have assimilated them or not. His point is to say that, with an online lesson that one can watch any number of times he wants, every person will be able to master any concept, provided he or she takes all the required time to learn. The older model might let people think that they are not good enough for some concepts of Maths or Physics, but the problem is not them, it is the teaching methodology…

One funny way he uses to describe this is by making an analogy with a building that you have to make: you have 15 days for the basement. On the 15th day, an inspector comes and monitors progress. OK, only 75% is achieved. That is fine, we need to move to the first floor. Same story, you've got 15 days and at the end, only 60% are achieved. Move on to the second floor and so on. Eventually, the building collapses! So why do we continue moving children and students along the "linear" teaching model, building on concepts we know they do not master because we have tested them on and they did not get a 100%?

Another important aspect that is not helping the education systems, especially in developing countries, is related to the educators themselves. We need to educate the educators. In fact, we need our best people to educate our children, but this is not what is happening. Education jobs are not the best paid, far from that… They are no more well regarded either. No one wants his children to become teachers. That is not a career! The best students go to finance jobs, to engineering, to medicine… The less successful go to teaching the youngsters. That is not the best model to take care of the youth.

At the same time, a parallel system is developing to the public education. Private schools, which used to be the solution for failing students have become the ones for the elite, the lucky ones who have the money to afford this better education. In developing countries, public education is failing more and more, leaving more room for private education. This is blocking the social elevator as the poor only get what they can afford, not always the best while money can buy you a much better education. What would be the long-term results for this? I am not saying that private schools are a bad thing. Today, they are part of the solution, when the State is failing to offer a proper public service. However, we need to think of equal opportunity and how to provide it in all remote areas and for the least favored people, and that is not so simple…

It is not simple, but it is the key. It is the key for a more harmonious world and I would like to conclude on education with this quote of Malala Yousafzai: "with weapons, you can kill the terrorists; with education, you can kill terrorism"…

EMPLOYMENT AND JOB CREATION

One of the big diseases of our modern world is unemployment. It is a problem that many economic theories deem necessary. There is nothing we can do, and it will always be there. The smartest rulers will be able to minimize it and the worst ones will have it explode, leading to severe unrest and potential revolutions! This is what has happened in the Arab Spring countries. Uneven wealth distribution, unemployment and no freedom of speech have made an explosive cocktail... the problem is that, a few years after the dictators were ousted and "democratically elected" governments were in place, nothing has changed on the most important front. The fight against unemployment has failed. Worse, it has not even started. Worse, bad policies and decisions have provided a fertile ground for further job destructions!

I have no miracle solutions and I do not pretend to propose any immediate one to this crucial problem. However, in my opinion, I would rather diagnose a political problem than an economical one! To create jobs, you need growth and the engine for growth is investment and work. How can you have investment if you have no visibility, no political stability, the fear of insecurity, no real incentive for investors to see the potential of returns they can get?

Creating real jobs is not adding another 20 or 30 thousand extra-jobs in the already crowded public administration. This is actually long-term job destruction with all the new inefficiencies it creates in the system. Such a measure will only increase the public deficit, for bad reasons. Indeed, the good reason (if that exists!) of more public deficit is to have healthy public investment. That is what most stimulus packages have included in countries that wanted to overcome the effects of the 2008 financial crisis. In our case, public deficit was taken to new heights by increasing the number of public servants and increasing the pay of the existing ones. There is clearly no economic benefit to that, but there is certainly one political benefit to it and that is probably what our new rulers have calculated! That buys loyalty within the administration, an administration that was reluctant to accept some of them. During a visit to Tunisia in 2015, the IMF Chief, Christine Lagarde, has warned about the hypertrophy of our administration and the cost of public servants wages being in excess of 12% of the GDP (yes, of the GDP, not of the state budget…), which is probably one the highest levels in the world!

Quoting François Mitterrand (the first socialist French President in the history of the fifth republic as they call it in France) "To Govern is not to Please". I doubt that the transitional rulers we have had in the Arab Spring countries agree with this statement. If they did, they would rather slim down the public administration by several hundred thousand people to ensure its sustainability. As a minimum requirement, they should not increase the gap by hiring more people. I would not even comment on the qualifications of the people being hired…

If I get back to the fundamental problem, job creation, and its engine, investment, how to move on? There is a major issue to be solved: trust. There is no trust left among the various political parties, there is no trust among social partners, ie, employee and employers unions, workers and business owners, there is no trust between government and the masses… Trust has been broken by those who are willing to impose dogmas, by those who are importing ideologies that have no room for dialogue. Trust suffers from the lack of application of the rule of law. Trust suffers from a logic of power game, it suffers from a lost system of values, replaced by some kind of a survival mode spirit that perverts mentalities…

Trust suffers from a problem of perception, of communication may be. What society model do we want? What economical model do we want? What system of values do we cherish? When the politicians send mixed messages, the people get disoriented and the situation worsens.

If I go back once again to the name of the game, which is the economy, and how to make it work efficiently, I would like to cite an interview of the former German Chancellor Helmut Schmidt who has expressed his doubts and pessimism regarding the future of Europe, saying it was no more governed by economists! This is certainly worth thinking about for all of us, even outside Europe…

EUROPEAN NEIGHBORHOOD POLICY

Tunisia is in North Africa, but that does not make it closer to South Africa than it is to Europe, and especially Italy or France! It is more Mediterranean than African if you really think about it. This does not mean at all that I am rejecting this other part of me: I perfectly live with the fact that I am Arab, Muslim and African! I know, you are thinking: the poor guy... But here, I wanted to focus more on the geographical closeness that Tunisia has with Europe, and this has led also to a historical closeness. Carthage and Rome have fought in ancient times; under the Byzantine Empire, Tunisia has given to Christianity a Saint, Saint Augustin; all of that before being conquered by the Arabs and becoming later part of the Ottoman Empire. The more recent history of Tunisia just before independence in the 20th Century ties it with France, which has colonized it for over half a century... All these facts make it easier to understand how close Tunisia is to Europe. There is no such common history with African nations beyond the Sahara... this was my point here.

Tunisia was one of the first nations outside the European Union to sign a free-trade agreement with the European Union. This was quite an achievement... After the revolution, the European partners were talking of a further "status upgrade"! of course, not an admission into the Union, don't forget: Tunisia is not in Europe, and it is somehow Arab and in majority Muslim, not the kind of members you want to have. Turkey has failed for less than that! Anyway, Europe is talking about granting Tunisia a "privileged partner" status which is far better than the current status limited to free trade. I was invited to some official debates on the matter. I must admit that I still do not exactly understand what this means. And if I do not, you can imagine what the majority of my fellow citizens think! Not that I am smarter, but I am probably better informed at this stage, and I still have lots of problems to figure out how this would make the lives of Tunisians better. Will they be able to travel to Europe with no visa?... No! Will they get the visas in an easier way?... No. Will they be able to sell their goods in Europe with no custom duties?... But they already are! What is new? A privileged partner status! Well, I must admit that this sounds great, but it is raising the level of frustration, and some fears too. Some Tunisians figure out that this is a new form of colonization! They are very jealous of their independence...

Sometimes, I wonder if independence was the best option for the ancient colonies, worldwide! Indeed, the discrimination that people belonging to those old colonies are now facing would not be possible if those countries had stayed under the rule of their former "colonizer"! Not convinced? I know, this is not an easy one. Let me give an example. Let us look at the situation in Algeria: today, Algerians have to get visas to fly to France, and they reciprocate the matter to the French. Their oil reserves give them the luxury to do so. This is not the case for Tunisia... If they stayed under French rule, and they were at that time a "département", not a remote territory, they would freely come and go from Algeria to France, from France to the rest of Europe. They would enjoy the situation of being part of the European Union. They would not be in need of any "privileged partner" status. They would in fact be at the heart of Europe! Surprising isn't it... Who is mainly regretting what happened today? The Algerians or the French? What would be the weight of the extreme-right political party of Mrs. Le Pen in France? Would there be an Algerian/Arab-friendly party as a counterweight to them? Remember, over forty million French would be of Algerian origin, that would be more than one third of the population... If you look at it from an economical point of view, with the technology and know-how the French have, with the oil and gas resources the Algerians have, wouldn't it be better on both sides of the Mediterranean? What would then be the relation with Morocco and Tunisia? Could this have achieved the born-dead dream of M. Sarkozy of an "Union for the Mediterranean"?

Focusing more on the southern part of this Mediterranean, there seem to be now two models of society that are fighting each other: one, rather open, rather pro-western, rather looking for modernity and progress, and the opposite one, rather based on a wrong understanding of Arab-Muslim identity, rejecting the differences, rejecting modernity because it is from the west, rejecting culture, music, joy of life and willing to impose this on you and me... That is their understanding of democracy! What model would have won if things were a bit different, if we had stayed closer between the two banks of the Mediterranean, if wealth were better shared?

THE ARAB JEW

I know, this is a new concept. So, let's go slowly because this is important. We have already talked about Arab Christians, yes? Those people exist in Lebanon, Syria, Palestine, Egypt… there are many of them. Hundreds of thousands, millions actually… but Arab Jews?

If we go back in history, to the pre-Islamic era in the Arab peninsula, there existed a kingdom, called Himyar, located in the current state of Yemen and parts of KSA, where the indigenous Arab population converted to Judaism in the fourth century. This Jewish kingdom of Arabia was known for its strict observation of religion and for persecution of its Christian minorities. It was the massacre of the Christians of the town of Najran which ignited the war that the Ethiopian Empire of Aksum conducted against Himyar. The ruler of Aksum, the Negus Kaleb claimed he killed the king of Himyar and destroyed the palace of Saba, and installed the last Christian king of Arabia, Abraha…This has put an end to what we could call Arab Jews of that time…

Arab Jews today? In fact, it was my friend Marco who told me this one day. He said this is the way I define myself. And it is so true: he is Jewish by religion and Arab by culture. He speaks Arabic, we share the same food, the same music, the same family-oriented mentality, the same taste for mint-tea and baklava…

I loved what he said, and I also loved the guy. No, no, do not worry, I am not gay. That would certainly be too much for people like our friend Donald: Arab, Muslim, and gay! Anyway, I really love him and all his family. It is funny how you might get along with some people like that. I later on met his wife, sisters, his dad, his mum… It was just like I knew them forever. I was so happy when, at a Sabbath lunch at his parents' house, his father told my wife:

I have two sons: one living in Geneva and that is Marco and the second in Tunis and that is Slim! One of Marco's saying which I find very true was that his mum told him one day: for the Israeli-Palestinian problem, if they had left it to us, Tunisians, we would have solved it long ago…

And it is true that the only Arab leader who told the Palestinians to accept the UN- map for Israel-Palestine borders in the 60's was our late President and modern-Tunisia founder, Bourguiba. He got enough tomatoes and eggs to make a gigantic omelet! Yes, it was not popular for an Arab leader at that time to say that. Gamal Abdel Nasser, the Egyptian "Rais" told him in private that he agreed, but never supported publicly the idea. The outcome, we all know: years of war and hate and killings, and yet no vision for a solution to this never-ending conflict.

Marco called me one day. He said: I am with a Palestinian entrepreneur in the West Bank. He is looking for a business connection. I'll hand him over to you. He is Christian! What came up to my mind immediately was a wonderful image: "Marco, that's so nice. You have managed to put the three monotheist religions together over a phone call!"

I had the opportunity to meet another Arab Jew. He is a New York Jew and I would say Arab by adoption, or by action! He might not see himself that way, but I believe he is doing more good for the Arabs than many Arabs themselves! Ron has made his fortune in real estate, and after the 9/11 events, which were very much traumatic to him as his eldest daughter worked close to the World Trade Center, he had the idea to put $10M of his own money at work to help educate and employ the youth in the Arab World. He created an NGO called Education for Employment (EFE), which he started in Palestine and Jordan. He expanded it to Yemen, Egypt, Tunisia, and Morocco, and still has projects to get it operate in KSA and Algeria among others. EFE is doing a fantastic job, training young unemployed people to make them employable. The dedication of the staff, and the soundness of its business model had enabled it to place thousands of young people and to get fantastic retention rates.

I still remember the story of Mohamed Sakr, a young street worker from Egypt, a guy who did not get his chance in the schooling system. He came before a big audience to testify in English, and with a great deal of emotion, about his experience. He was living on less than $4 a day in the streets of Cairo when he heard of EFE, and first did not believe that there could exist such an institution that would give him a chance and teach him for free. He applied and started thinking "this could be true" after he had a twenty-minute phone interview. To be able to get the training and continue to have some food while not earning his $4 a day, he asked his parents for some support and his mother had to sell a piece of land she owned, probably all her fortune! That gave him the opportunity to spend time on the courses that EFE was offering, which eventually led him to work for an e-commerce start-up and become fluent in English. "It changed my life": this is the one phrase from his very emotional and moving speech that I would quote.

This is why I thought that the man behind this fabulous initiative, who happens to be Jew, deserved to be called an Arab Jew, for all the good he is doing in the Arab World. In the association of the two identities, Arab and Jew, some people might see an oxymoron. I see a powerful call for tolerance, and a sign of intelligence. Arab Jews of all kinds are a bridge between cultures and religions. I wish there were more of them and I wish I could qualify to be one, at least, by adoption!

However, life is very tough for the Arab-Jew. He gets schizophrenic. On the one hand, he has sympathy for those so many Jews living in Israel. On the other hand, he also feels for those with whom he spent his youth at school, in the streets of Djerba or Essaouira, and who do not really share his thoughts of Israel! My friend Marco found a way around it. His great contribution was "Face-to-Face", a fabulous Art project he conducted with Ted-prize winning photographer JR.

ARTOCRACY

When I called Marco at the wake of the Tunisian Revolution, I was dreaming of initiating a Tunisian « Face to Face ». I have loved the work he has done with JR between Israel & Palestine. I still remember the first day I met Marco. He was coming to Tunisia for a YPO (Young Presidents Organization) meeting. That was long before Face2Face. I did not know him before. A common friend had introduced us through the e-mail, and we got along quite well…Many thoughts brought us together, thoughts, ideas, ideals, I cannot say… but there are encounters in one's life, encounters that really move you, and this was one of them… We went to a party together, with my wife, some other friends, and I discovered that one of my best friends, who was with us that night, was the son of one of Marco's father best friends… Tunis is a village, and for sure, Marco was part of it. He loved this country as much as I did. Then, there was an incident, one of our YPO friends got bothered by one « little nephew » of Ben Ali, the dismantled dictator…. A fight on the dance floor… the whole positive impression on the country that we spent the day building torn apart in seconds.

When Marco did Face2Face with JR, he told me about it. First by mail, then live in Tunis. That was fabulous! It was provocative, it was risky, but they did it. What Face2Face shows is that Jews and Arabs are the same, they are cousins, they are Semites. Tolerance, friendship, love, that's all much stronger than politics. At that time, I have flooded my address book with Face2Face news. It provoked several nice reactions, debates, discussions. Wonderful! I kept great memories of it, and Marco was always reminding me of this great adventure. He told me that, while they were doing "Face2Face", he entered one day a barber's shop in Ramallah or Nablus and told the guys in Arabic, in his Tunisian Jewish accent: "I am Jew!". He almost got kicked out, but that was not knowing Marco. He discussed, argued, joked and it ended up with hugs and kisses with people from the Hamas!

Tunisian Revolution… I call Marco, he had also thought about it. He will speak with JR… He calls me back : we'll do better, we'll do Artocracy, it will be a mosaic of Tunisian portraits. Mosaic really speaks about Tunisia. We have a fantastic roman mosaics collection, one of the best in the World, at the Bardo Museum. This will be the start of JR's Inside Out project, for his TED Prize will. Announcement will be made early march (2011) in L.A. It will be Art by Tunisians, for Tunisians, for Tunisia, as there will be a lot of buzz, and the subject is Tunisia ! It made my day, couldn't be happier…For the date, we need to be live on the 20th of March, Independence day (the Tunisian one, our 4th of July if you wish) and also the 21st, the youth celebration. It is short, very short, but doable if we start quickly…

We need authorizations. Who's gonna give us anything in this very complicated period, right after a Revolution ? The Minister of Culture ? How to reach him ? His colleague, in charge of transportation, is the friend that introduced Marco to me. I call him, got my meeting ! One hour meeting, the Minister loves the project. A very cultured man. He worked for years at UNESCO, in world heritage conservation. He is very cooperative, tells me that I do not need any other authorizations since the revolution. You can feel that censorship is no more what it used to be. Later on, getting the actual documents was a bit tedious. The administration was resilient, but not always up to speed, but at least, we had the authorizations

The making off team is here now. They invite me for some shots down town and in front of the RCD's headquarters, the former ruling party bunker in Tunis. We do not have all authorizations yet. With some ghosts form the past in my head, I am not very comfortable yet, but with this new wind of freedom blowing, who can resist? Let's go. I step in… the team is a great one, nice people. I speak almost too much. We get all the shots early morning. I have never been downtown this early. I had no objective reason of doing it in the past and I always feared traffic jams. In front of the RCD headquarters, the army is still here…

First day of pasting. I was not able to make it. My frustration is big. I have a meeting with all managers from our foreign subsidiaries. Why did it all have to be on the same time? I follow up the events on the phone and things are going wrong. We have to stop pasting at la Goulette. I am on the phone with Franck, Rachid, Joelle, Marco's father… No way to go on. The team is demotivated. I am surprised, disappointed, very sad actually. This is not Tunisia as we dream it! Why don't they understand? Why this?

As revenge to this first episode, the "pasters" decide to give it another shot at night. 2 a.m. at the Porte de France in Tunis. I decide to be there, with Amina, my wife and accomplice. We have a great time, meet a whole bunch of people. We talk and paste. A police car stops, ask what we do, a bit suspicious…I explain. They like what we do. "There are no policemen in the portraits you are pasting, we also belong to the people" they say! "don't worry, we are here to protect you! And by the way, your people have nothing to drink. Here is some coke. It's our contribution!" This is the Tunisia I like…

It was 6 a.m. when we went back home. Almost no time to go to sleep. Around 10, Franck calls. They are tearing all down! Oh no! 10:30, nothing's left. Our work at Porte de France did not last long. Our heads are full of images but on site, no traces left of our "pasting night". Too bad, it was really beautiful! At least, JR took some very nice shots of it.

I go pick up Marco at the airport. He's here at last, and we are all invited for dinner at his father's friends place. Mylene and Nathalie are here. I discover charming people. We are immediately comfortable. We share the bread and the salt, and a fabulous dinner. We discuss, shout, laugh… And else, there is Marco's father. I did not know him before, and he impressed me with his knowledge of Tunisia, of Tunisians, of people, of regions, of all! He's older than my father, but we really became friends. I was very happy later on that, every time he came back to Tunis, he would give me a call and we'll have dinner together.

Next day, it's Sfax, the second biggest town in the country. Most of the team is already there. Others have left in the morning. I arrived early afternoon, just on time to see a fantastic work on one of the oldest buildings downtown. Watch out, there is a laics demonstration which is planned. A counter demonstration from the Islamists… It's gonna be hot ! I am a bit worried for the kids who are with me! Eventually, all goes well. Now, the team wants to paste on the Head Quarters of the RCD, the party of the fleeing President. A real symbol, and it works! People like it. For the dinner, we have fish. It is the specialty in the region.

And now, here we are Sidi Bouzid! It was the epicenter of the revolution. As for the RCD HQ, I am a bit worried. But we have a great guide: Olfa… She'e been there several times. She knows that people are not looking for charity. They want dignity. And she is right… The shots we get are fabulous. We pasted on burnt police cars stacked in a wasteland.

Back to Tunis, a metro station, the RCD HQ in le Kram, the north suburb of Tunis! Franck calls me all excited. He got arrested by the police, and he's very anxious! No worries, I go there immediately... By the time I reached them, they were already out. The traffic jam we cause is huge. Everyone is stopping to see. Some people from the car windows shout at me: what are these photos? They smile, get fun, make big signs with their hands and eventually go away, happy...

For the last night, dinner at Rachid's place... Most of the team is here. A great atmosphere! All of us do not yet accept that it is over tomorrow. There is joy, there are photos, we do not want to part away... a true family...

ANTI-SEMITISM

If you look at the definition on Wikipedia, you will find that this is "prejudice, discrimination against or hatred of Jews as national, ethnic, religious or racial group. It is generally considered a form of racism" … can an Arab be anti-Semite? With regards to this definition, this is perfectly possible! But I thought that Arabic and Hebrew together with several of the languages spoken in Ethiopia are Semitic. According to the Encyclopedia Britannica, the most important Semitic language in terms of number of speakers in the 21st century is… Arabic!

For an Arab, therefore, being anti-Semite is rather schizophrenic, isn't it? By definition, it is not possible for an Arab to be anti-Semite! The definition should equally include Jews and Arabs as being together the victims of this form of racism… I have grown with the idea that Jews and Arabs were "cousins", and this is dating back to the old times of the prophet Abraham… He had one son called Isaac and one other called Ismael.

To further think about anti-Semitism, I find it interesting to simply cite the table of content of "Britannica on-line" on the matter: the origins of Christian anti-Semitism, anti-Semitism in Medieval Europe, anti-Semitism in Modern Europe, Nazi anti-Semitism and the Holocaust, anti-Semitism since the Holocaust and outside Europe.

Well, it seems that it was not the Arabs who were the champions of anti-Semitism. I would rather understand that it was born and nurtured in Europe. All major persecutions of Jews took place in Europe. The Spanish Reconquista and the inquisition that followed are one of the early examples that are often forgotten or hidden by the horrors of what Nazism did in the 20th century. Those Jews that were leaving in peace under Muslim Arab rule in Andalusia suffered terribly from Isabella de Castile and her followers. You can find many interesting details of this in the excellent book of Jacques Attali, the French economist and former adviser to President Mitterrand, "1492".

In fact, my reading of history is that the current hate that exists between some Jews and some Arabs, dates back to the events that gave birth to the State of Israel in the early 20th century, and it was the direct consequence of what the European colonial powers did to the Middle East. The resentments started between Zionist Jew zealots and the Arabs that had their land taken… these groups had the solidarity of the larger groups to which they belong, and people were dragged into a more generalized conflict by supporting the ethnic or religious group to which they belong. Of course, in the simple minds of many non-educated people in the Arab world, there is a major confusion between Zionist, Jew, Israeli…

Not only in those simple minds it seems. At a dinner in 2016 of the CRIF, the "Representative Council of French Jewish Institutions", Manuel Valls, the French Prime Minister, has associated antisemitism and antizionism as reported by the French newspaper "Le Monde". Whose interests does that serve? Being anti-Semite is clearly being a racist and that is not acceptable. Being antizionist is expressing a political opinion and that is quite different. Where is freedom of speech in the country of human rights? Is M. Valls banning it, at least when it comes to expressing a position towards Israel and its current rightist rulers? As commented in another French newspaper, "l'Humanité" by Sophie Bessis, Alice Cherki and co-authors, M. Valls is simply rallying Netanyahu in his rhetoric to justify more colonies in occupied Palestinian territories, deeming anyone criticizing it as being anti-Semite. As they mentioned, "there is actually a strong Jewish antizionist movement that marked the history of European Judaism in the 20th century. These declarations from a French Premier come as a stab in the back of anti-colonial Israeli people who are facing more and more difficult conditions to resist Netanyahu's government expansionist colonialism. Confusing antizionism with antisemitism leads to criminalizing political positions".

And it seems that M. Valls is not alone in doing so. As reported by the New York Time, the University of California almost adopted a resolution condemning anti-Zionism… the final text reads "Anti-Semitism, anti-Semitic forms of anti-Zionism and other forms of discrimination have no place at the University of California" … There are clear attempts to make any political speech criticizing Israel or advocating for Palestine anti-Semitic! On the other hand, it is true that opposition to Zionism can sometimes not be limited to disagreement over politics but might end up in showing intolerance towards

Jewish people.

And confusing Zionism with Judaism can lead to great misunderstanding: I was surprised the other day by the reaction of my 14-years old son on a discussion we were having with a French friend "How can you like Jews while you are defending Palestinian rights? Aren't they responsible for taking their land?". I was surprised, annoyed and ashamed to hear this, from my son! I was not expecting such a reaction from someone I am supposed to have a great influence on. It was probably the outcome of what he sees in the media, despite the fact that we watch not only local TVs but also CNN, the BBC, Euronews, France 24…and also the influence of what he discusses in school, inside and outside the classroom, knowing that he is going to a French school and getting that prospective on World War II and the Middle East recompositing. I had to go through a long explanation about what has happened in that part of the World, and about the fact that today, many Jews and many Israelis defend the rights of Palestinians better than many Arabs. I insisted that the best solution for the conflict was probably the two states solution that was sketched by the UN resolutions of 1967. He insisted "You know, I am not a racist! I don't want to bother you, but I want to understand…" Unfortunately, many people do not want to understand, and they simply get dogmatic about things.

RACISM

Racism is of course the extended version of Anti-Semitism and it should not be accepted as a fatality. Quoting Nelson Mandela, "No one is born hating another person because of the color of his skin, or his background, or his religion. People must learn to hate, and if they can learn to hate, they can be taught to love, for love comes more naturally to the human heart than its opposite". Racism can take various forms and target different groups! We have already talked about Anti-Semitism. Another prominent form of racism is the one against "colored" people and especially blacks, or shall I say African Americans…

Racism is the ideology that humans may be divided into biological "races" that will differ not only in physical traits but also in intellect and behavior. This leads to the idea that some "races" are innately superior to others. The advances in science, especially in biology and human genome sequencing has given the material proof that this is all wrong. Genetic differences within a so-called race may be greater than those between races. Science is profoundly anti-racist!

In history, "scientific racism" has been instrumental in justifying mistreatments of "inferior races" and slavery. Several pseudo-scientists in Europe developed a polygenist view, advocating that the different "races" have been separately created, opening the way for white supremacy thinking. The "others" were ugly, immoral, and animal-like. It was comfortable to believe this when you are trading slaves, using them in your farm, abusing their women or even killing them. Colonizing new territories was not an issue either because the superior race was bringing development, civilization, religion, and humanity to the inferior ones. Some famous writers such as Rudyard Kipling or Thomas Kingsley considered that this was the duty of

Europeans, the "white man's burden". Thank you!

After slavery was abolished, several States in the United States of America continued having a racial segregation policy, just like apartheid in South Africa. Apartheid statistics are staggering. They show how racism as a public policy can lead to such unjust situations. In 1978, the black population of South Africa was 4 times that of the white one. However, it enjoyed only 13% of the land and 20% on the national income, with an infant mortality 10 times higher!

In the US, the Jim Crow laws put in place racial segregation right after slavery abolition, as early as 1877, and this situation lasted till the civil rights movements eventually led to the Civil Rights Act of 1964. That late! During all this period, segregation, which was mainly a feature of the southern states, was practiced even in the absence of Jim Crow law. It was the norm…in 1912, with the election of Woodrow Wilson, it even made its way to the White House with a President claiming that this was good for both whites and blacks.

Today, it is difficult to practice racism in the form of a State policy or to have it integrated in the law! This is no more accepted by the international community. However, this is not precluding several politicians to talk and act in a racist manner. It seems to be very trendy to win the votes that way! If we analyze all that was said during the US Presidency campaign in 2016, we will reach an alarming level of racism and bigotry. We heard that all Mexicans (and probably Latinos) are thieves and rapists; all Muslim are terrorists and should be banned from the US, at least put under strict surveillance, even if they are US citizens… Many anti-Semite statements were also issued during the campaign… The danger of all this, even if the eventually elected politicians do not behave in an outrageous racist manner is that this heated speech raises the level of hate among societies and stigmatizes those minorities that were pointed as the bad guys…

And the consequences are to end up with "I can't breathe". The last words of poor George Floyd, a black american that got killed by a white police officer in Minneapolis in 2020 have become known to the whole world. Racism is still alive and kicking. It is present in all societies, despite the laws, despite the common understanding that makes it a bad thing in this early 21st century. George Floyd's death sparked a protest in many countries against racism from the police, from the authorities… and I must admit here that you do not have the monopoly of this plague, of this devastating pandemic. Indeed, the media will often talk about racism in developed countries and, as an Arab, I find myself more often on the victim side, of white supremacists. However, I can see in the society where I live that there is some racism against other ethnicities or religions. The victim turning into a slaughter…

This makes me wonder how to best fight racism in our societies. It seems that laws are not sufficient. Education should be able to help. Mixing with other people as well. However, mass manipulations based on nationalism and on ethnicity do the opposite and unfortunately, we see too many politicians using these strings to appeal to fragile electors.

1492

This is the date when Christopher Columbus went on an expedition to discover a new route to the spices of India and ended up discovering the Americas… this is somehow the start of your modern history. It is also a date that has marked the decline of Native Americans as they began to be massacred by the Conquistadores or the various plagues they brought with them to the new continents. There was no confinement and lock-down at that time (and no Covid-19)!

Today, Columbus Day is being more and more decried in the US. Several States are refusing to celebrate it, notably Hawaii, Nevada, South Dakota, and Oregon. Some people are asking to rebrand it as the Native Americans day… The guy that history was initially depicting as an explorer and a brave soldier is more and more considered to be a brutal mass murderer, who has killed over 3 million native Americans in a very short time span, decimating the population of the Caribbean islands. He could also probably qualify for being the father of the slave trade…

For the Spanish, 1492 is also the date that has marked the "Reconquista". This is how they refer to the fact that Isabel the Castilian and her troops were able to eventually vanquish the ailing Muslim emirates based in Andalucía, and managed to push all those people down the Gibraltar Detroit to North Africa and any other destinations outside a Christian Spain that was being cleaned of any Muslim or Jew remains!

For me, as an Arab of Andalusian origin, this is a date where a disaster has hit my ancestors. They ended up leaving the nation they have built in the southern part of Spain and starting new lives in North Africa. It is a date where the future of thousands of Muslims and Jews got sealed in a way where they had either to leave or to convert to Christianity (the latter was more the case for the Jews, some of whom ended up practicing their religion in secret).

"1492" is the name of a book by Jacques Attali. An excellent read by this author who has a great talent to talk about history and to make prospective projections by decrypting intricate signals. As he recalls, three Caravels meet a new continent, Muslims and Jews are chased out of Europe, Britany and Bourgogne merge into France and England opens up to the Atlantic and to the colonies and turns its back to the continent. Europe discovers tobacco, potatoes, and Syphilis! Venice fades away to the benefit of Antwerp which becomes the center of the economic world, showing that Europe is moving from its past turned toward the Orient and the Mediterranean to the West. As Attali points out, 1492 introduces a bifurcation in the course of history and contains all the seeds of the major changes to come.

"1492" is also the name of a movie directed by Ridley Scott, featuring French actor Depardieu as Columbus, and Sigourney Weaver as the Queen Isabelle of Castile. The Vangelis original soundtrack has been nominated for the Golden Globes.

Funny enough, this was the date of an ending prosperous and tolerant Muslim civilization of Arab origin in Southern Europe, a civilization that accommodated for the cohabitation of Judaism, Christianity and Islam under one roof, a rare example of tolerance in those ancient times. A fact that I am really proud of, that demonstrate that Arab does not mean barbarian and Muslim does not mean intolerant!

ALGEBRA

My major point in this chapter was to remind you that Algebra comes from Arabic, showing somehow that, once upon a time, the Arabs were leaders in Science and Technology, just as you are today! To be precise, the word Algebra comes from the title of the book, written in 830 AD, in Arabic, by Persian Muslim mathematician Muhamad Ibn Musa Al Khwarizmi, "Al Kitab al mukhtasar fi Hissab Al Jabr wal Muqabala": The Compendious Book on Calculation by Completion and Balancing, as translated in many sources. "Al Jabr" became "Algebra".

The common sense meaning of Algebra is to designate a branch of mathematics, in which arithmetical operations and formal manipulations are applied to abstract symbols rather than specific numbers. Algebra is therefore "similar" to Geometry or Arithmetic. It can be itself subdivided into linear Algebra, elementary Algebra or abstract Algebra. In mathematics, Algebra can also designate nowadays a specific mathematical structure...

Many references mention that Algebra started with the Babylonians and the Egyptians, as far as 1900 BC with the Rhind Papyrus around 1650 BC. Egyptians knew how to solve linear equations with one unknown but did not use symbols. In the Cairo Papyrus (300 BC), second degree equations were solved. Babylonians were more advanced. They knew how to solve quadratic equations and one of their famous clay tablets is there to testify! Some people allege that the Greeks had no Algebra, however, it is often considered that they had their specific approach to it, which was "geometric algebra" as can be found in the work of Euclid for instance. Actually, another Greek residing in Alexandria is sometimes cited as the father of Algebra, from those who want to take this paternity from the Arabs: Diophantus! Some others would rather give this paternity to François Viète, a French lawyer, mathematician, astronomer, and advisor to king Henry IV, who lived in the 16th Century.

A similar controversy exists as to the symbol "x". This is the letter used for the first unknown variable in any problem. In the French language, it is even used in legal cases when you are making a case against an unknown: "plainte contre x" and it is also used to solve some social issues with women abandoning their children at birth: "accouchement sous x". Anyhow, mathematics historians have been arguing whether we owe "x" to René Descartes in the 17th century, or to a Hispano-Arabic source...

Going back to the history of Algebra in the Islamic world, Al Khwarizmi was not the only contributor...at the same period of time, Abd Al Hamid Ibn Turk produced another manuscript. Later, in the 9th century, Egyptian mathematician Abu Kamil Shuja Ibn Aslam introduced irrational numbers. There were several other significant contributions from the 10th to the 13th century from people like Al Karaji on polynomials, Thabit ibn Al Qurra on amicable numbers, Abu Sahl Al Quhi on high degree equations, Omar Khayyam on algebraic geometry, Sharaf Al Din Al Tusi, Jamshid Al Kashi and Abu Bakr Al Hassar on the modern mathematical notation for fractions.

If we look at the numeral system, it is commonly admitted that the system used worldwide today is the Hindu-Arabic numeral system. The system was invented in India around 500 AD. A major contributor in its transmission to the whole world was the Arab mathematician Al Kindi who wrote several treatises on the use of Indian numerals in the 9th century. Syrian mathematician, Abul Hasan Al Uqlidisi introduced the notion of fractions in the 10th century and Sind Ibn Ali-Musa introduced the decimal point. The original Brahmi (Hindu) numerals split into three major typographical families: Arabic numerals, used in western Arab countries, Eastern Arabic numerals in the Middle East and Indian numerals in the Indian subcontinent. It was Leonardo Fibonacci, an Italian scholar, born in the republic of Pisa, who lived in the city of Bejaia, in Algeria, who brought the Arabic numerals to Europe through his book, "Liber Abaci".

An important number in the numerical system is zero! Did you know that this is also originally an Arab word? Indeed, Zero came to English from French Zero, itself from Zero in Venetian, originally Zefiro in Italian which was the "latinization" of Arabic "Sifr"!

As you can see, science is universal, and Arabs had their contribution. This is a glorious past I am very proud of. In other domains, such as medicine, one can think of Abu Sina, Avicenna... In astronomy, there were great contributions such as the Astrolabe. Of course, the Arabs built on existing knowledge. They could dig into Babylonian, Egyptian, Greek, and Hindu previous works. They have compiled and developed many of it and have transmitted a great deal of it to an emerging Europe through North Africa and especially, through Andalusia. This cross-fertilization and knowledge transmission was a complex story in those ancient times. Today, this is happening in a much more direct and immediate form. However, the knowledge divide seems to be increasing every single day! Another paradox that we have to live with?

ALCOHOL

Did you know that this word is also from Arabic? I know, as a Muslim, I am not entitled to drink it. However, one of the funny things happening in the Arab Spring countries under Islamist ruling is that beer consumption has been steadily on the raise! This is not necessarily compatible with the apparent islamisation of the political scene in these same countries. Is it a counter reaction? A rejection of the Islamist hard-liners? A way to escape the harsh reality? It is in any case a clear tendency that the official statistics were not able to erase…

On drinking and driving, there is a good joke by French humorist Coluche: Someone came saying: well, did you know that 35% of road accidents are caused by alcohol drinkers? And the guy at the bar answers: and the remaining 65% percent are caused by water drinkers, right?

Alcohol in Islam has been prohibited, just like any other substances that can lead people to lose control of themselves. This applies to all kinds of drugs, narcotics…and seems to be a respectable principle that all modern societies are applying in one form or another. It is admitted that narcotics are banned by law in all countries. No one is arguing against this. In most countries, including advanced occidental ones, liberal and democratic ones, it is not tolerated to drink and drive. It is therefore accepted that alcohol is prohibited for people on the go! Islam has gone one step further and prohibited it at once.

However, a Tunisian philosopher named Mohamed Talbi, made the news by claiming that alcohol was not explicitly prohibited in Islam. He defied anyone from citing any verses of the Quran that explicitly banned alcohol! No one really was able to cite those verses, implicitly confirming the thesis of Talbi. Instead, he suffered from a large campaign making him a senile old person and denying him any right to interpret the holy text! I am not sure if Talbi is right in his assessment of the story about Alcohol. What is more important is that this showed that, in the 21st century, many people were practicing "self-censorship". Too many Muslims are still not accepting any exegesis of Islam…

I will not pretend to be a theologist and tell you under which conditions alcohol could be or not tolerated in Islam. In any case, there are many Arabs, that are Muslims and have no problem to drink alcohol. There are also many westerners that will tell you that alcohol is harmful. According to "Drinkaware", a charity in the UK, The Chief Medical Officer (CMO) for England recommends against underage drinking stating an "alcohol-free childhood is the best option". The National Institute on Drug Abuse, a US federal scientific research institute under the National Institute of Health, U.S. Department of Health and Human Services, defines ethyl alcohol or ethanol as "an intoxicating ingredient found in beer, wine, and liquor. It is a central nervous system depressant that is rapidly absorbed from the stomach and small intestine into the bloodstream".

Maybe it is not a bad thing, as recommended by Islam, to stop drinking after all?

CARTHAGE

When you hear this word, do you go back in ancient history, into the antique world, and remember that this was the power that defied Rome at that time, and even held several wars against it before being defeated and destroyed? "Carthago Delenda Est" as claimed Cato the Elder in Rome... Or do you simply know that it is nowadays a nice and rich suburb of Tunis, Tunisia's capital, with some remaining roman ruins and a summer festival that is held in the roman theatre, capable of hosting some ten thousand people with fantastic natural acoustics? Or you might simply don't know!

Carthage does probably not sound Arabic. Carthage is part of mankind's history and mythology. Many famous names and stories are related to it: Elyssa, the queen that founded the city; Hannibal, the famous General who crossed the Alps with his elephants; Hamilcar, his father and also General who commanded the Carthage troops in Spain... Hamilcar and Hannibal were of the Barca family, a name in the Punic language which can be written "Baraq" as one can see from some online encyclopedia or even "Barak" (!), a word that remains in Arabic and Hebrew, with the same meaning: thunderbolt! Not to be confused with a certain President's first name...

Carthage is part of me as an Arab, as a Tunisian Arab. It unites two Arab countries through a firm historic tie, the second country being Lebanon. These are often seen as the two most open and liberal Arab countries, where women rights are the most advanced. The story or the Legend of Carthage starts from Tyr, in Phoenicia, the current Lebanon. It starts with a Princess that flew out of the country, from the harassments of her brother, Pygmalion, who killed her husband and uncle as soon as he sat on the throne of Tyr.

Elissa (or Dido as she is also known) ended up in Ifriqya, the name

Tunisia had at that time. She arrived to a place ruled by nomad Berber tribes, and she managed to peacefully get a sizeable piece of land. She asked for a land which borders could be limited by the skin of a cow. The Berbers accepted. She managed to cut that skin in such fine thongs that she was able to get a land big enough to found Carthage.

Carthage prospered and became the rival of the rising Rome in the Mediterranean basin. The world has always been the same. A few super-powers making the rules. At that time, the world was around the Mediterranean Sea, and the rulers were Rome and Carthage. Rome eventually won the game and Carthage was destroyed, and later rebuilt as a roman colony. It became the grain attic of Rome.

Much later on, in the early Middle Ages, and at the time of the Crusades, Carthage was also the place where Saint-Louis died, his army devastated by the plague, in the Punic port which you can still visit today… He was buried there, in a Basilica that dominates the bay, until when French President François Mitterrand asked for his relics to be transferred to the Pantheon, in Paris.

All of this is part of my history. That is in my genes. I wanted to tell you that I have deep roots. I wanted to tell you also that not all Arabs are the same. I am proud to be an Arab who has shared so much over the centuries with other cultures and populations around the Mediterranean. Carthage is part of my glorious past. I do not want to insist too much on this though. Many Arabs, feeling so miserable about their current status, live in some glorious past, the past when Bagdad or Damascus were ruling the world, the past when civilization prospered in what is called the Arab-Islamic world, while darkness prevailed in Europe and other parts of the world… This is another factor creating a lot of frustration, a frustration that is leading to violence, as a reaction of the hopeless, of those having nothing more to lose, and resolving to drag everyone down to their despair rather than keeping the light of hope of being once again under the limelight.

IDENTITY

I started my speech here telling you that I am an Arab and a Muslim… However, sometimes, quite often, I really wonder what I feel exactly about myself? An African? A Mediterranean? A Citizen of the World? Am I closer to a French or a Saudi or a Senegalese? If I look at my personal roots, I have a French grandmother, two other grandparents of farther Turkish origin, and the fourth one of an Andalusian origin, back in the fifteenth century. This indeed looks like a Mediterranean melting pot and that is where I feel I really belong. That is the historical and geographical space I am mostly connected to. It is a crossroad of cultures, of religions, of skin colors and of origins…I find myself getting schizophrenic, or even more. I do not have one identity, not even two… It is true, this is certainly not a feeling that all my fellow citizens would agree to, but this is the kind of feeling I would like to build on, and on which I need you to help me build on with a better understanding and more tolerance…

Do not reiterate what Isabel of Castile did to the Muslims and the Jews living in harmony in the ancient cities of Andalusia. Do not revive the Crusades wars… We are not trapped in the middle ages. At least, not all of us! The religious fundamentalists, whatever their religion, want to drag us back to the dark ages.

Talking about identity and being an Arab, I sometimes wonder if there exists anything that should be called the "Arab World". Such a designation hints to a certain unity, to something strong, coherent… Viewed from DC or Los Angeles, you probably believe that, yes, the Arab World exists. Viewed from Tunis, where I live, I can tell you that I have very serious doubts! Even if I look at a smaller sub-set of this, the "Maghreb" … Some definitions limit the Maghreb to Morocco, Algeria and Tunisia. Some others extend it to include Mauritania on the west and Libya on the East. Is the Maghreb something united? Something that has any other existence than what politicians will shout on their ritual and void speeches?

On the economical side, studies from the World Bank are telling us that the Maghreb is one of the least integrated regions in the World, if not the least integrated. What does that mean? A loss of 2% growth rate per annum for each of the countries of this happy group! Are we really in a position to afford this? With all the unemployed people, the ever-degrading environment, the ailing infrastructure and the overall low quality of life that we are trapped in?

On the political side, which is strongly impacting the economy of course, you have two of the major components of the Maghreb, namely Morocco and Algeria, that do not get along, at all! The borders are even closed for land traffic of goods. Can you imagine that for me to export goods from Tunisia to Morocco today, I have to ship them through Europe? Unfortunately, the two neighbors hate each other. There are regular posts on the newspapers of each party blaming the other. There are regular declarations showing that their hard feelings are far from an end… Why this? Who started? How long will it last? Very tough questions to answer… the conflict is so deeply rooted now that I am in despair of seeing anything evolve during my lifetime! Yes, we have witnessed the fall of the Soviet Union, of the Berlin Wall, of the Eastern Block, we have seen China change and awake to capitalism or some form of it, but well, they all are not Arab! Let's put it this way…

What we do have here in the "Maghreb" is not any better or worse than the "Mashrek" or the Middle East. There is no unity or solidarity among Arab States. There is a very unfortunate saying that we have in Arabic: "The Arabs agreed to never agree". I am not even speaking about the situation between the two parts: Maghreb and Mashrek. What about the people? The language? The traditions? There are so many differences in the dialects today that you will often see two Arab persons from different countries communicating in English or French for easier communication. Yes, normally, we should all know about classical Arabic. In practice, it is not as good as that. If you look at traditions, if you let alone what can be related to religion, many traditions will differ. For the food, there is no typical Arabic dish! There is the Berber couscous in the Maghreb. There are the vine leaves and falafel of Lebanon, Syria, Palestine, and Jordan. There is the "fool u taamia" of Egypt, and the "Kabsa" of the Arabic peninsula… In the Mediterranean part, you will also find the Ottoman Baklavas as pastry! If we look at mobility in this so called "Arab World", this is probably the worse story to tell… you can travel all over the place very easily with an American or French passport. However, with a "local" passport, you will need a visa for many of the other Arab countries. The Arab States do not trust each other, but guess what? They trust you!

Back to my identity speech, I was extremely surprised to see on social media the very rapid spread (among North African users) of a post, referring to a scientific study that was conducted in the early 21st century and which concluded that "genetically, Maghreb people were not Arabs". The paper said that, while a vast majority (98%) of Tunisians, Algerians and Moroccan culturally identified themselves as Arabs, the ethnological truth is that they were not. There is a very small genetical contribution of the Arabs in this Group. It is dominantly Berber, with some links to western Europe, especially Iberic haplogroups. The study says that someone from the Maghreb is at over 65% of Berber descent, compared with a mere 15% for Arab part from the paternal part. He (she) is at more than 50% of various origins on the mother side, which is a characteristic shared with Europeans.

With a reference to Ibn Khaldun and his Moqaddemah, he says that we are not Arabs but "Mostaaraboun", which means "made Arabs". It was therefore more in the minds, in the language and the culture than in the genes. What was interesting in the wide spread of this post, I thought, is not really the question it is raising, but rather the fact that so many people in the Maghreb were either asking themselves about this, or potentially showing that they liked the idea of not being Arabs. It is definitely showing an identity crisis!

An identity crisis that you are enforcing on us. Today, being an Arab is a bad thing! As reported by French Magazine Le Point in November 2015, Maher Khalil et Anas Ayyad, two American citizens of Arab origin as you can tell from the name, were prevented from getting on a Southwest Airlines flight because they were speaking Arabic! They were "interviewed" by security forces in the Chicago Midway Airport. It was another passenger who heard them speak and was afraid of travelling with them. Once aboard the following flight, Maher was forced to open the small white case he was carrying and "share his baklawa (that is an oriental pastry)" with the other passengers as he told local news TV channel, NBC5. And this is not an isolated case. Several Arab-origin passengers have been the target of such "preventive" actions from US police and security. Simply speaking Arabic is now suspect! You know, I found myself while travelling with my kids and wife to Europe last summer avoiding to speak Arabic! Indeed, we felt we had a different look from the crowd when they heard us use French…

People are therefore reacting in two very distinct ways to the racist message they are getting: some will be claiming that they do not belong to the group that is being targeted as "bad", and that is leading them to an identity crisis: they try to tell the world by all means that they are not Arabs, nor Muslims, nor both. To enforce the message, they will seek some historical evidence as exposed above, or they will start drinking alcohol or eating pork or doing whatever can deny their belonging to an Islamic culture. They would also try to hide their beliefs or disguise their identity fearing to be misjudged. I still remember this American-Pakistani gentleman working for an American company with whom I had dinner once in a very POSH French restaurant in Paris. We were with other American and French colleagues. When asked about the wine, he declined, claiming health reasons. I declined and claimed, on purpose, "because of my religion", and that made him eventually admit it was for the same reason! The others react violently by reversing the psychological pressure they are getting. OK, I'm bad, and I have nothing to lose now. I'll show you how bad I can be. You reject me, I will make your life harder... Did you watch the reactions you might get from your kids when you start blaming them for something? You can get very similar patterns. It is elementary psychology. It is now getting to a point where we will all need a psychiatrist!

CHARLIE HEBDO

You have probably never heard of "Charlie" before the month of January 2015. Now chances are that you will either say "Je suis Charlie" or "Je ne suis pas Charlie". It is better for you to claim the first statement. Indeed, in the name of freedom of expression, you are not really allowed to dislike "Charlie" or reject it. This is a small anecdote that happened in Tunisia, a Muslim and Arab country, at the French school where my children go. A young girl wrote a wall graffiti saying "Je suis Charlie", and a young boy added "ne - pas" making it "je ne suis pas Charlie". Guess who got punished for writing on the wall? Worse than that, in France, a young 8-years old boy had to stand before the police and get questioned for "apology of terrorism" as he claimed at school that he "was not Charlie" and that he was on the "terrorists" side. He didn't even know what terrorism was, but his teacher and his principal thought he should know or his parents should know at least, and they went telling the story to the Police, which did not hesitate to bring this dangerous and subversive agent to formally interrogate him. He could have been arrested for this. Can you believe this is happening in a western democracy, the hometown of human rights? Sure, you can be a criminal and a terrorist at 8…

First of all, in case you are not aware of what we are talking about, let us get the story right. Charlie Hebdo is a satiric weekly magazine published and distributed mainly in France. It boasts a great team of famous cartoonists and became really famous after it surfed on the wave of Muhammed's cartoons. You know, Muhammed is the Muslim's prophet and our tradition says that he cannot be pictured, good or bad. OK, the Charlie Hebdo guys felt that freedom of expression was in danger when a Danish magazine got a lot of negative and violent feedbacks on the publication of such cartoons, and they decided they will make their contribution to the debate by further picturing the Prophet. They got menaces and threats and the debate heated about this subject, not only in France…

In January 2015, two mad men irrupted into the magazine's headquarters. They killed twelve people with their military weapons and managed to escape. They made the killing shouting "Allahou Akbar". One of them forgot his ID card in the car. (I wonder why you should take your ID with you when you are on the verge of committing such a horrible action, just in case of a police control?) They eventually were found and got killed in a Paris suburb. End of story.

Is shouting "Allahou Akbar" making them Muslims? Shall we consider that this crime was committed in the name of Islam? Shall we ask all Muslims to claim their innocence and their rejection of this stupid and foolish act? As a Muslim, I feel offended and at the same time accused… I have nothing to do with these people. Islam has nothing to do with these people. These are criminals. These are killers. They are criminal in the right of the Charlie Hebdo's people as they took their lives. They are criminal in the right of Muslims making them in a position where many in the occidental world are associating them with such abominations!

In the light of what happened, I appreciated the position of Pope Francis and I would like to quote him here: "No one is allowed to kill in the name of any religion" and he also said "no one is allowed to insult the faith of others in the name of freedom of speech".

However, we had really stupid reactions from people like media Mogul Rupert Murdoch. He tweeted "Maybe most Moslems peaceful, but until they recognize and destroy their growing jihadist cancer, they must be held responsible"! and this guy is running a media empire? Maybe he can tell us, like Aziz Ansari so rightfully posted back to him, how he would see Aziz's 60-year old parents living in NYC act to destroy the Jihadist cancer? Indeed, we would welcome a guide, a methodology… We are afraid that M. Murdoch keeps holding us responsible for this because we are not intelligent or proactive enough to stop it. We agree on the diagnosis, yes, this is a cancer. All religions have their cancers. All ideologies too… Let us not dilute the topic by going back to examples incriminating specific groups of people, but can we try to understand what helped this cancer spread? The massive "radio therapy" that some US doctors tried to impose on Iraq and other places did not properly target the cancer. It missed the point and destroyed many of the protective cells that were containing this cancer. Yes, there were collateral damages, but are we happier now? With wrong wars, and wrong actions, and a lot of secret services behind the scenes dirty play, you helped fabricate this cancer! And once again, guess who is being contaminated first, on a daily basis? It is not you… you are in a remote location. We are sitting next to this cancer. So, as JK Rowling (the writer that had some success writing "Harry Potter"!) rightfully and sarcastically responded, taking responsibility and apologizing for the Spanish inquisition just for being a Christian, I will be apologizing for all that is happening, just for being a Muslim! Sorry M. Murdoch, I really do not have a clue to stop these people doing what they are doing. I do not see them being Muslims. Shall I remind them that Islam punishes the crimes they are committing? I am afraid I do not have an available media empire to reach them and send a clear message to them. These people are not acquaintances…maybe you can help?

On the same trend of Islamophobia, we have had another racist reaction from a so called "American Freedom Defense Initiative", a sister organization to something called "Stop Islamization of Nations" which has "subsidiaries" such as "Stop Islamization of America" and "Stop Islamization of Europe", all of which are labeled as hate groups by the UK Government and seen to be exhibiting anti-Muslim bigotry by the "Anti-Defamation League". In the name of freedom of speech, these organizations have paid advertising campaigns on San Francisco buses, as reported by newspapers such as "The Independent" in the UK, that were aimed at associating Islam and Nazism. With a base line such as "Islamic Jew-hatred: It's in the Quran", what can one say? Thanks to Pamela Keller, one of the founders of these organizations, we now have a new reading of the Quran! Maybe she will tell us many other wonders! Who knows…? She is probably fluent in Arabic and has a very creative mind to come up with such conclusions! I do not believe combating Jew-hatred by Muslim-hatred is the solution. These people are exacerbating hate and defiance between religious communities.

Two years before the "Charlie" tragedy, I have read an interesting view from a leftist French congressman, clearly rejecting the cartoons just published by Charlie Hebdo and stating that there was much better to do with the southern bank of the Mediterranean. His political analysis was that the magazine was engaging in a wrong battle, which was not helping all the turmoil that the region was already experiencing, with many countries engaged in post-revolutions construction of new States that were aspiring for democracy and a better living. Engaging the debate in the religious arena has the negative effect of sliding the gravity center of the public debate into an identity debate, and reviving the wounds of South versus North, not even a century after the end of colonization. We are already seeing in Europe a resurgence of heavy nationalism, pioneered by extremist right-wing parties. These cartoons can only push Muslims into a similar move of identity protection.

Charlie's DNA is provocation. However, was it right to continue on the line that can be seen as Islamophobia or Arab phobia? by picturing young Aylan, that 3-years old Syrian boy found dead on the beach of Bodrum, in Turkey, as a future sexual harasser were he to live, with the title: "what would have become young Aylan if he grew up?". The pictures of Aylan have moved the whole world. His angel face eating the sand has shown to the planet the horror of the Syrian refugees' situation and despair. Picturing a dead young boy, which carries the symbol of a whole nation and region, and their terrible fate, as a perverse and a criminal is outrageous. It is not humor. It is simply stupid…

What to say about their flashback on the Rwanda's genocide and civil war between Hutus and Tutsis? One other Charlie Hebdo's first pages was showing Belgian singer Stromae, with parts of the body of his late father, each responding "I am here"… this is referring of course to his hit song "Papa où t'es" (where are you, father?). The sad thing is that Stromae's father was killed in Rwanda during the genocide, and his body, cut in pieces.

Another useless provocation was made at the occasion of the Italian earthquake of 2016. 294 people were killed in this tragedy that hit the city of Amatrice in Italy. Charlie' cartoonist Felix has compared the victims to pasta plates with the blood being the tomato sauce. With strong negative reactions in Italy, relayed by major newspapers like The Corriere Del Sera which claimed that no one was Charlie anymore, the satiric journal reacted with another cartoon showing the quake's aftermath picturing torn down houses and claiming the houses were built by the Mafia and not Charlie… In this case however, there was less solidarity among French politicians to defend the newspaper's attitude in the name of freedom of speech.

Sorry folks, "je ne suis pas Charlie", even if I really do not care that they pictured Muhammed! I simply believe that emotional or relational intelligence is to try to understand how the others think and react to better interact with them. This means respecting their cultures and traditions. Freedom of speech does not mean freedom to insult. You do not engage a nice conversation with someone you just met in the street by saying "Hey stupid!" No one would like it… They would not want to talk to you, and yes, sometimes if they are already angry, if they are really stupid, they might badly react and punch you down. No excuse for that, but it can happen, and we all know it… I hope this does not make me a terrorist!

BARDO

Bardo got famous right after Charlie Hebdo for a similar reason: a terror attack. This was happening in Tunisia though, in an Arab and a Muslim country. It was targeting culture, as it was happening in the Bardo museum. It was targeting the Occident as the main victims were tourists. It was targeting the economy, as tourism is one of the country's major resources, and it was targeting the authority, as the Bardo museum is next to the General People's Assembly of Tunisia, a location that is supposed to be closely guarded and secured. Le Bardo is a suburb of Tunis, the capital. The location is home to a palace that was erected in the 14th century in the model of Andalusian architecture. It continued to evolve under the reigns of several monarchs to become a small royal city. Today, parts of the palaces became a museum, hosting a renowned roman mosaics collection. This is what it should be famous for, not the killings. Unfortunately, in 2015, the terror attack on the museum caused 24 persons to die and left 47 injured. Here again, and just like the Charlie Hebdo attack, the murderers claimed to act in the name of Allah. Interestingly, these attacks made France and Tunisia get closer. It spurred many reactions of sympathy on both sides of the Mediterranean, and it led to a march in Paris, which the Tunisian Prime minister attended and another one in Tunis, which the French President attended.

When I googled "Bardo", I found that it has also another very unexpected meaning: in the Buddhist tradition, bardo is a Tibetan word that means "in-between state", a state between death and rebirth. It is said that the "Bardo Thodol" is known in English as "The Tibetan book of the Dead"… I do not mean this was premonitory, as "our" Bardo comes from the Spanish "Prado" which is garden. What I hope is that we get the "rebirth", a rebirth that should propel us in the 21st century.

FACEBOOK

We all know this social network today. Of course, who does not? It is said that if Facebook were a country, it would be the third most populated in the world. Facebook is American, or may be, used to be! It is now a worldwide media. Many say it has significantly contributed to the so-called Arab spring. Many even call it a Facebook revolution: marches, riots, meetings were organized using this social media. Scoops and tons of information, right or wrong, were leaked using Facebook. When the other media were down, it was the only channel to give you some info.

The beauty of social networks, Facebook at their forefront, is that people take power and become actors. They become the purveyors of the information. I remember that immediately after the Tunisian revolution, during those days where the dust did not settle yet, we were chasing the news on Facebook: some guy was talking about army helicopters flying over a certain area and shooting, people in that neighborhood confirming the news; some other talking about a dignitary from the old regime having been captured; a third one about gun shots being heard close to his home… It was real-time news. People would be building on that primary info, adding precisions to it, or denying it was really taking place, and, depending on how well you knew the information providers, and the level of trust you had in either one, you would get a fair opinion of what was going on.

Facebook provided the thrill… It also made us feel together, united, sharing… while we were alone, at home, not taking the risk of going out, not even for a "baguette"! We ended up connecting to huge numbers of people, even people that we didn't know. In our quest for information, and our quest for solidarity in those very lonely moments, Facebook provided a caring shoulder on which to lean. The connection level of Tunisians and Egyptians rose to unimaginable heights.

At the same time, we could start testing the limits of the network, and the dangers of it, in terms of manipulation. As an example, I remember one day, after the Tunisian revolution, and before even the coalition forces led by France started hitting Libya, I decided to post that "Kaddafi has just been killed". It did not take long, just a few minutes, before I started getting reactions: some friends asking about the source of information, some others commenting this was meant to be and many simply sharing the news (as they trusted me!) and exponentially distributing my fake news! I was having a dinner party at my place, and was delighted to show all this hysteria to the friends that were present for dinner, giving them just another warning on how to use social media and what to trust or not. I wanted to make a point to those that come to you with some "absolute truth", and, when you start challenging them, their argument would be "I have seen it on Facebook".

It is important to mention that social media can be a very powerful manipulation means. We have seen the web become a recruitment tool for terrorist groups. We have seen it also become their propaganda tool through the horrible pictures or more shocking videos posted on YouTube! Cyber terrorism is now a reality, and we are faced with people that are technology aware. The hack of "TV5 Monde" TV station system in 2015 is frightening from that prospective. Not only were they able to disturb the web-presence of the company, but they have even interfered with its broadcasting platform. Once they have shown that this is possible, one can be afraid of simply imagining that they could do similar actions against major utilities. What if they started messing around with water and electricity distribution, traffic lights, airport systems? Are all these secure enough? Are we protected from such potential cyber-attacks?

Let alone cyber-attacks, we hear more and more about artificial intelligence and all the good it will bring to humanity. A.I. as it is lovingly called will make our lives easier. It will be embedded in most objects to make them smarter. It will enable machines to learn and to improve. We will have plenty of free time… to surf on social media! Some news that one can spot already on the web is that two separate artificial intelligences were able to communicate in a language that was not understandable to humans! Wahoo… were they gossiping on our back, us, humans? Or would this be too futile for them, superior intelligences? What if an artificial intelligence reaches some consciousness, the consciousness that its creator, the human, could unplug it any time? Would it develop a hostile behavior towards us? Some interesting movies have flourished in the years 2014 to 16 with these kinds of stories. Some are nice and gentle, like Chappie. Others are rather scary like Transcendence or Ex-Machina. Already, some scientists are warning that, with the ever-growing calculation power of computers, machines could rapidly outsmart teams of human engineers, and the phenomenon can only be exponential. The gap would widen rapidly, and the outcome is very unpredictable indeed!

CONSPIRACY THEORY

Following up from the previous chapter, and the fact that everyone has become a media himself, thanks to Facebook, Twitter, Instagram, Youtube and others, the most incredible stories and conspiracy theories are flourishing around the web!

Were you aware that Ben Laden did not die, and that he is having some good time in the Bahamas, well deserved vacations offered by the US taxpayer, all of this according to Snowden (the guy behind the NSA/Prism scandal)? Did you know that there were no planes involved in the 9/11 crashes and that there were no terrorists behind the attacks? You have certainly heard about all that the US-government is hiding from us regarding aliens, and which our great friend Poutine is about to tell us? Of course, a lot is going on in the famous Zone 51 in the Nevada desert, where a UFO crashed, and alien life is evidenced. A special mention of course to the Illuminati. They are the essence of a super conspiracy theory! They are the Masters of the World, the elite of the elite, the top of the pyramid… Their multi-century plan is designed for the World domination, and that is what they have managed to do since Babylon and Sumer for 5000 years! That's a performance!

All of these stories and much more can be found on some websites, tweets and Facebook posts… With the amplification effect of social media, and the credulity of so many people, not to say their stupidity, some very fantastic theses are well relayed and become almost the untold truth. With these new ways of communicating, anyone becomes an author, and the advocates of conspiracy theories have found new ways of reaching their fans. It becomes often difficult to tell what is true and what is wrong. What information to trust?

PROCRASTINATION

It is the "art" of doing nothing! And it seems that we are very fond of it in our part of the world. Nothing is really changing for the fundamentals. The issues are so horrendous that our rulers seem to surrender before even engaging the battle for modernizing the States, the administration, the governance, the society... Gandhi said: "You may never know what results come from your action, but if you do nothing, there will be no results". I believe he was wrong! If you do nothing, things get worse, and this is what we see in many countries of the Arab world. The situation is even more critical because of the very young population. You know, it is like the metabolism of your body. When you are young, your metabolism is very rapid. The older you get, the slower it gets, and this why some forms of cancer that can kill you at the age of twelve, will not degenerate rapidly when you are seventy... Here, we are dealing with a much younger population than that of developed countries. This population has more pressing needs: needs for education, for employment, for infrastructure, for housing... there is no possible containment. You have to cope with the continuous regular and expected flow of new demands on a yearly basis. If you do nothing, the situation deteriorates. The anger level rises to dangerous levels and the situation becomes more and more explosive!

Procrastination has never been the solution and will never be. Things are accelerating more and more today. With a world that is more connected, information flows instantly. Knowledge is being capitalized in a way that was not possible before the digital era. Progress is on an exponential mode, and the level of divide between those who are part of it and those who are left behind will simply be not bearable. If we do nothing, there will be no sustainable growth, for no-one, as the ever-increasing population of those who are left behind will reach a breaking point.

I HAVE A DREAM!

To paraphrase a famous American pastor, who was speaking for freedom, for human rights, for equal rights regardless of race, gender, or religion… These are really the words I would like to use for my conclusion: I have a dream, a dream of a world where people from the north or the south would have the same rights or at least, the same consideration, a world where equal opportunity will be for people from various nations and various backgrounds, a world where a Tunisian or an Egyptian passport will be worth as much as an American a British or a French one, a world where a Mossad agent and a Hamas guard will be working together, a world where the current budget of the military will be spent on fighting Aids, Malaria and Tuberculosis (and I should add Covid-19 for the incredible effect such a pandemic has had on the world), a world where I, as an Arab, will be looked at as who I really am, as a human being, not as what you think I might be because of my origin. Remember, history tells us that civilizations grow and decline, and the Arab of today could be the American of tomorrow, after the Chinese take their fame time!

I might be a simpler dreamer… but I believe in a better world. I want to be the winner as Mandela puts it "A winner is a dreamer that never gives up". I am not giving up. I will go on and on. I am not going to shut down and I will keep telling you these words until we unite and find a better way for humankind.

I Arab

237

ABOUT THE AUTHOR

The author is the CEO of an industrial company operating throughout the MENA region. He has studied in France and the US, where he got an engineering degree, a Master's and a Ph.D. He has travelled the world quite extensively for business and leisure. After the Tunisian Revolution, he was one of the founders of a new political party and of a new employers' union. He has made several TV and radio addresses, mainly related to economy and the local political situation. He managed to get street artist JR to start his "Inside out" project in Tunisia with an initiative called "Artocracy" which involved several local artists. He is a board member of one of the oldest business think tanks in the Arab World, and a board member of the Tunisian arm of an NGO helping youth employment. 55 years old, married and a father of two boys.